Sea Change

A MAN, A BOAT,
A JOURNEY HOME

Center Point
Large Print

**This Large Print Book carries the
Seal of Approval of N.A.V.H.**

Sea Change

A MAN, A BOAT,
A JOURNEY HOME

MAXWELL TAYLOR KENNEDY

CENTER POINT LARGE PRINT
THORNDIKE, MAINE

This Center Point Large Print edition
is published in the year 2019 by arrangement with
Islandport Press.

Cover image and interior images courtesy of
Maxwell Taylor Kennedy.

The text of this Large Print edition is unabridged.
In other aspects, this book may vary
from the original edition.
Printed in the United States of America
on permanent paper.
Set in 16-point Times New Roman type.

ISBN: 978-1-64358-355-6

The Library of Congress has cataloged this record under
Library of Congress Control Number: 2019944726

*This book is dedicated to my wife, Vicki,
with All My Love.*

Contents

Sea Change

A MAN, A BOAT,
A JOURNEY HOME

Valkyrien

Before the Mast

My wife Vicki gave me a print of a painting by Ed Ruscha and Nancy Reese for my fortieth birthday. The painting depicts a clipper ship tossed by a storm at sea, f'heeled over, decks awash, sails full and shining through the spray, scuttles pouring forth frothy ocean—making her way forward, courageous and defiant.

I love this painting with all my heart. I love it foremost, I think, because I love the sea. I am carried by the sea. The sea protects me from what is out there in the world that is dangerous. Sometimes I feel best aboard a ship at sea in a storm. I spend so much of my time each day worrying about things that will never happen, or chafing over the past. A storm requires all of my attention.

Above the ship, written diagonally from the upper left to the lower right on the painting, Ed Ruscha added to Reese's image the words:

BRAVE
    MEN
        RUN
           IN
              MY
                  FAMILY

With those six small words Ruscha transformed the painting from the kind of decorative art my parents collected into a pop-art commentary.

Yes, brave men run in my family. My ancestors and cousins fought in just about every war this country has ever waged. Brave men in my family also run for office. In my family, brave men also run away. My father disappeared when I was three-and-a-half years old. He had been shot and killed. I keenly felt his absence.

One of my favorite film characters is the minstrel in *Monty Python and the Holy Grail*. A minstrel's job is to tell the truth, but subtly. In the film, the brave man, Sir Robin, runs away from a battle. The minstrel sings:

> *When danger reared its ugly head,*
> *He bravely turned his tail and fled.*
> *Brave, brave, brave, brave Sir Robin.*

For me, it is much easier to brave the sea than to face the challenges of staying at home and living what Warren Zevon called "A Quiet Normal Life." For me, the truly brave thing is not holding the wheel of a schooner as she breaks up in a storm, but committing to the intimacy of marriage and being present in the lives of my children. My whole life I have sailed, but I had not, in the truest sense, recognized myself as a father and a husband. I had no idea at all how that was done. Vicki though, helped me figure it out.

I ran away on the schooner *Valkyrien*, for nearly a year. Sailed away, more accurately, though I was never actually gone for more than a few months at a time. I missed her too much.

Prologue

We have lingered in the chambers of the sea,
by sea-girls wreathed with seaweed
red and brown.
Till human voices wake us, and we drown.
—T. S. Eliot, *THE LOVE SONG OF*
J. ALFRED PRUFROCK

I had come to San Francisco searching for a wooden schooner.

Barack Obama had just been elected president, and for most of the past year, I'd volunteered for his campaign. That fall, I felt the world overflowing with the potential for progress and change, and understood for the first time why so many people remembered the election of 1960 and the extraordinary optimism of that earlier time. The transcendent importance of the election of the first black president did not mean the fight for equality was over, or won, but rather that it was more important than ever to educate people about our country's past, and particularly our treatment of people of color.

I wanted to illuminate a part of this past by creating a memorial to the extraordinary bravery of the men and women who took part in the largest slave break in American history. The story of the packet schooner *Pearl* was one that had shocked and angered but also fascinated me ever since my friend Bob Nixon had first told me about it several years earlier.

Nixon is a gifted filmmaker and dedicated environmentalist. We have been friends for more than thirty-five years. Bob was obsessed by the *Pearl*. In 1848, seventy-seven African-American men, women, and children had risked their lives aboard the *Pearl*, trying to escape slavery by sailing secretly along the Potomac and Delaware rivers toward the free state of New Jersey. Tragically, wind and tide slowed the *Pearl*. An armed posse of white vigilantes riding fast in a steamboat caught up with and captured the slaves. The idealistic whites who had aided in the daring escape were arrested and jailed, while the slaves were sold south to Black Belt plantations.

Bob Nixon has an extraordinary sense of what is right and good and just in the world. He convinced me to join him on the board of the nonprofit organization, The *Pearl* Coalition—a group of grassroots volunteers, many of whom live or work in some of Washington DC's toughest neighborhoods. The *Pearl* Coalition is dedicated to memorializing the heroes of the *Pearl* and to building a full-size replica of the schooner, to be berthed in Washington, DC. The new *Pearl* will serve as a hands-on museum and vividly convey not only the story of escape, but also the importance of schooners in American history.

Schooners built this country. The fish American colonists ate were caught from schooners. Tobacco, timber, rum, sugar, wool, and slaves were all shipped aboard packet schooners. Packet vessels of various sizes were used to ship mail, trade goods, and transport passengers among the colonies and between America and its European masters. American roads remained primitive up through the Civil War, and railroads did not have the capacity to ship sufficient goods, especially to towns isolated off the rail grid. Much of the shipping that is now done by trucks, rail, and aircraft was accomplished via the efficiently rigged packet schooners. A part of this maritime heritage is preserved even today. When we order goods from Amazon.com, we receive an email notice saying "Your package has been shipped," when of course they really mean "trucked."

The first Americans to defy the King of England were the captains of packet schooners. Dedicated to independence and fond of their coin, schooner captains avoided taxation by unloading their cargo on small piers along farmland and in rivers, away from the larger towns and out of reach of His Majesty's taxmen. They proved that colonists could disobey the King with impunity. Their defiance was one of the first great acts of American independence.

Although I had read about schooners in grade school, I did not truly understand in a visceral way how schooners shaped this country until the first time I stepped aboard one when I was nine years old. On a hot summer day, my uncle Ted had brought me and my brothers and sisters and cousins aboard an interactive museum-schooner in Boston Harbor.

Icons allow young people to gain a tactile sense of history. Stepping aboard this schooner, I heard the lap of the water on the sides of the boat and felt the gentle sway of the vessel in the harbor's soft currents along the wharf. I saw the huge interior jam-packed like some leviathan boxcar, full of goods for trade. I smelled the scent of hot pitch between the deck planks, mildew in the canvas, salt in the air. My arms felt the difficulty of raising the sails.

I was able to imagine a group of intrepid Americans cutting trees, sawing planks, wrapping rope, and building these boats, knowing that they could go anywhere in the world, free to trade and learn and experience. Once out of the harbor, no one could tell them what to do. How to live, where to sail, the risks to take. Each captain was as free and independent on the open sea as any king. The schooner represented that experience of freedom, absent in Europe and so new to America.

Boston, New York, Philadelphia and Baltimore

all have working packet schooners that teach this history to schoolchildren. But there is no schooner in Washington, DC, and no memorial to the heroism of the slaves aboard the *Pearl*. Our nation's capital needed a schooner, particularly one with such an important story to tell as the *Pearl's*. We had trouble raising sufficient funds to build a replica of the *Pearl*, so it was decided that we would find an old schooner on the cheap to serve as a temporary stand-in while we went about raising the money.

This proved more difficult than you might imagine. During the first half of the nineteenth century, schooners were the most common vessel on the coasts, but only a few hundred wooden schooners remain intact today. The rest burned or sank or were abandoned—left to rot as trains and trucks surpassed sailboats for transporting cargo on the seacoasts of the United States.

Wooden schooners in great sailing shape can cost over $1 million; our budget was $40,000. Essentially, we had to find a decrepit schooner about to be junked; then we had to buy her, repair her, and sail her to Washington, DC. We searched the internet and made phone calls to various marinas, captains, brokers, friends, and associates, up and down the East and West Coasts of the United States, trying to find an old schooner that looked and felt like the *Pearl*, and which we could purchase and sail to Washington.

Finally, searching on a site that specialized in "project boats," I came across an old schooner, built much like the *Pearl*, tied to a pier near San Francisco. Her name was *Valkyrien*. I knew it would be a long trip from San Francisco, through the Panama Canal, to Washington, DC. But I have sailed all my life, and this was a voyage I had always wanted to take.

My family moved to Hyannis Port on Cape Cod in Massachusetts in the 1920s. Hyannis Port is a summer town, so it may seem strange to say "I am from Cape Cod," having lived there for the most part only a few months each year, but I am more than anything a Cape Cod man. Hyannis Port is the one place in the world that every member of my large family (I have ten brothers and sisters) considers home.

Hyannis Port has always seemed to me to be the best possible place to be raised. Everyone in town sails. I lived regimented summers, almost like camp, but where the other playmates were virtually all family. We were awakened early in the morning and forced to jump in the ocean and swim laps back and forth as Sandy Eiler, the gigantic former Olympian, taught me how to improve my stroke. Ruby, our family cook, made breakfast with bacon and eggs and French toast, which was served after saying grace.

Then, we raced down to the pier where we took sailing lessons for an hour and a half, followed by tennis lessons. Each day, at precisely 12:30 p.m., we set sail with my mother aboard the *Resolute*, our Wianno Senior sloop. We sailed until 3:30 or 4:00 p.m., after which we played softball for an hour and a half before playing games like Chase One, Chase All, followed by a quick swim and then family dinner. After dinner we played various games like flashlight tag until 9:30 p.m., and then we'd read for an hour before bed.

The *Resolute* had been my father's boat. She was a 25-foot gaff-rigged sloop with a short keel and a centerboard, designed in 1913 specifically to race in Nantucket Sound. Because every Senior is virtually identical in dimensions of hull, mast and spars, and sails, winning races really comes down to who is the best sailor, with the best crew, and can tune their boat most successfully. We sailed the *Resolute* every day, no matter what the weather. My mother had once sailed with my father through a hurricane. No matter how windy or stormy the weather, she taught us always to sail. My uncle Ted used to say, "No one is interested in the storms you encountered, but whether you brought the boat home." I learned from my earliest memories to sail in every storm, and that the most important thing of all was to bring the boat safely into port.

I spent my first ten years or so of sailing often terrified. All wooden boats leak, and the *Resolute* was more or less in a constant state of sinking. We pumped her out each day before the afternoon sail. We often ran aground on the many shoals in Nantucket Sound. The *Resolute* could sail with the rails underwater, and even the seat coamings buried in the sea. Her sails made a terrible noise—so scary for me as a young boy, snapping back and forth—and every now and then the boom would crack or the mast would split, or the gaff would break in two. We learned to deal with these emergencies, and to take them on as our own challenges, without asking the boats around us for help. We brought the boat home each day on our own. The *Resolute* had no engine, but I learned to work on outboard motors, self-taught during long hours drifting around Nantucket Sound on a 13-foot Whaler with an old 35-horsepower Evinrude that refused to start.

When I turned about seven years old, I found my father's scuba gear on our front lawn where one of my brothers had left it. I dragged the tank down to the beach and figured out how to open the valve. Then I lay down, perhaps 18 inches under the water, breathing like Jacques Cousteau. I loved diving from that moment on, and ended up working with my friend, explorer Barry Clifford, on several scuba expeditions.

I used to sneak down to the Cape during college, on late fall weekends, with my girlfriend Vicki Strauss and take her sailing on the

Resolute. Sailing on the Cape became for me the most perfect way to spend a day—almost any day, whether sunny or rainy or even when it was snowing. One fairly rough afternoon, lightning struck the *Resolute* while my brother and I stood, furling her sail. We felt shock waves pass through our bodies, and St. Elmo's fire jumped along her stays and above her bulwarks.

My uncle Ted convinced me and my closest friend at the time to purchase a forty-year-old wooden Casey yawl, built in Fairhaven, Massachusetts. She had been sitting on a dock at the South Wharf yard in Padanaram for several years. That summer we sailed the *Glide* back to Hyannis Port and began restoring her. I spent more and more time in boat yards, and learned about diesel engines, and where fuel tanks should be placed, various types of varnish and bottom paint, the working of sea-cocks and a thousand other things—mostly by learning from experience how hardware works by seeing what happens when hardware fails. We sailed *Glide* virtually every day each summer, slowly learning how to maneuver under various conditions and also, how to take care of a boat.

Vicki and I got married, and had three children. Our daughter Noah, who was born at Cape Cod Hospital in Hyannis, began sailing on the *Glide* when she was only two days old.

To this day, I will sometimes see my wife

walking down to the pier, just after the sun sets, and shout out "Hey, Vicki!" My companions might say, "How did you know that was her?" I cannot explain how I know Vicki from so far off; I could tell you that I recognize her gait, or the way she holds her head on an evening stroll, or the lines of her sweatshirt—but these reasons are all misleading. They take me away from how I know my wife. The truth is, I just know her. I love Vicki, and I will recognize her always.

It is the same with the sea. I could tell you that I love the challenge of sailing, or the freedom of sailing. I love the sense of wind against my face, the salt against my skin, the sun glinting off the sea. I love the camaraderie of sharing a day sailing with friends, or the quiet isolation of a solo sail. Each of these reasons, and many others, are true enough. But the fact is that I love sailing in the same inescapable and intangible way I love my wife. Not just because she is smart, or funny, or skinny, or thoughtful, or kind and loving—Vicki is all of these things—but none of these reasons even begins to explain why I am in love with Vicki. In fact, defining these "reasons" limits any understanding of love.

It is the same with the sea. I simply love to sail.

Someone said that sailing is like war in that it is mostly long periods of boredom punctuated by moments of sheer terror. This is essentially true, and while many of the pages of this book are

24

dedicated to those brief moments of terror and action—these are not the times for which I sail. I sail because I love the long periods of boredom, when time creates an opportunity for intimacy among those aboard. Frankly, and perhaps oddly, those times are nonetheless probably just as boring to me as they are to everyone else aboard the boat. But when I take that moment and share some vulnerability—love, or fear, or mere delight—I feel most alive. Sailing calms the fire in my head. I am not one of those who stand grinning ear to ear all the while I'm at sea. In fact, most of the time, when I am at sea, all I can think about is getting off the boat. But after an hour or so onshore, I just want to get back in the boat.

When I was a college student at Harvard University, I walked to class each morning and passed by the Old Burying Ground by the Cambridge Commons and a stone sarcophagus in the shape of a Christian cross, bearing the name DANA in heavy block letters across the base. I always wondered who this person was. Later I learned that it was the grave of a former Harvard student who had dropped out to join as a crewman on a packet schooner. He wrote one of the most popular travelogues in American history, *Two Years Before the Mast*. Dana Point on the California coast is named for him.

Reading that book set off in my heart a fire

to sail the California coast. I eventually moved to California, and every time I turned onto the Pacific Coast Highway to pick up my children from school, I looked out at the ocean and imagined what it would be like to sail all the way down to Panama. I would think of Richard Henry Dana Jr. aboard a wooden schooner, and about that cold stone back at Harvard. I determined to make that sail before I grew too old.

My childhood summers, my love of the sea, my passion for sailing, the support of my wife and family, and my own curiosity and call for adventure led me to that moment on the pier in San Francisco, when I first saw the *Valkyrien*. And I knew in that moment that I would buy her.

Everyone said it could not be done. Any boat you could buy for that price would never make it all the way to the Panama Canal (much less to Washington, DC). But we figured it was worth a try.

This is the story of that journey.

1. *South*

*As for me, I am tormented with an everlasting
itch for things remote.
I love to sail forbidden seas, and land on
barbarous coasts.*
—HERMAN MELVILLE, *MOBY-DICK*

I arrived at the cement wharf in Port Richmond, California, by taxi, carrying a bag of tools by my side and a gargantuan 80-pound battery in the trunk. The sun, showing itself for the first time in a week, glinted off broken glass along the edge of the roadway. I stood at the entrance to the wharf staring up at the 8-foot-high chain-link fence. A bronze padlock held the gate shut.

I looked past the lock, down the walkway beyond a few decrepit boats tied up together, and across the narrow Santa Fe channel at an aging fuel storage facility—a dilapidated Superfund site, one of the most dangerously polluted parcels in America. Twenty-three million gallons of gasoline, diesel, and various other fuels waited to be conveyed to other storage tanks farther inland. In the distance, the green hills of San Francisco incongruously framed the shipping terminal and the aging industrial depots of Port Richmond.

For many, seeing Port Richmond for the first

time is a depressing experience. They might see evidence of poverty and crime and a village largely ignored by the thriving bankers and high-tech companies across the bay in San Francisco. But staring out there at the old lumberyard and fuel tanks, I thought of the men and women who built—and saved—America.

William Kaiser constructed more than 700 Liberty ships during the Second World War on these wharfs. Nelson Rockefeller built the refinery just across the channel from the marina. Some people go to cities to see the tallest buildings, or the most beautiful art. I love to visit old industrial sites and collapsing docks. Richmond was perfect for me. I had come to see a man about a boat.

I pushed my nose up against the chain-link fence and stared down to my right, toward the old gypsum loading dock. On the near side of the channel, tied up among steel barges and small rusted freighters, lay a group of old sailing vessels. I looked down the line of masts, wondering which was *Valkyrien*. My stomach ached a bit with the combination of excitement and anxiety I often feel in libraries—so many books I have not yet read. Here was a chance at great adventure, a glimpse of freedom, the possibility of honoring the *Pearl*—but it all depended on the condition of the boat.

The dockmaster tied all of the wooden boats to

the wharf like rafts, lashed side by side. *Valkyrien* had two boats secured to her port, and one on her starboard; each had tall wooden masts, clumped together so tight I could not at first discern one boat from another. The boats looked to me like a pack of homeless dogs left alone too long, lying entangled in a single desultory heap, hoping some passerby would drop them a scrap. I wanted to take them all home with me.

I was afraid *Valkyrien* had deteriorated so much that I could not buy her. At the same time I feared that *Valkyrien* would be just good enough to buy—then I would have to make the trip, an idea which both thrilled and scared me. I was very much looking forward to being at sea for a good long while. I planned to stay safe—I would rarely be out of sight of land, traveling south from San Francisco down the West Coast of the United States, Mexico, and Central America, until I hit the Panama Canal. Still, it was a lengthy trip along some dangerous coasts, and many things could potentially go wrong.

Despite these larger looming issues, my greatest immediate concern was rot.

Dry rot is a fungus that eats the parts of wood on a boat that keep the hull stiff and strong. Its effects are gradual and cumulative. In this, it is much like human illness. If left untreated, dry rot will spread and destroy a wooden boat, and it is not always immediately visible to the eye. Sometimes a boat can look sound from a distance, but underneath the surface it's turning to sawdust.

More than anything, I wished to jump the fence and race down to see *Valkyrien* up close, but I could feel the taxi driver's impatience. He did not want to hang around Port Richmond. I paid my fare and then, hefting the huge battery out of the trunk, I looked around for a rock, figuring that with a dozen boats on the wharf and no other way in or out save this padlocked gate, someone must have hidden a key. No luck.

Then I noticed that one of the vertical slats that held the sections of the fence to their poles had been loosened. A single nut and bolt held it in place—the telltale flaw. When I removed this lone nut, the fence opened as easily as any doorway.

I lifted the battery across the threshold, politely replacing the nut and bolt so as not to reveal to marina authorities the clever way around the lock that some forgetful sailor had left for himself (and now for me).

I am an experienced sailor, and a U.S.C.G. licensed Captain; I cannot recall a time before I knew how to sail. I have found that virtually every marina in the world is locked, whether in some filthy slum outside of Mumbai or with the air-conditioned guardhouses of Palm Beach, but sailors do not do well with locks. I slipped through the gap to get a closer look at the *Valkyrien*. She was a giant schooner with two masts made of solid trunks. Only a sailboat built before World War II would use tree trunks for masts. Wooden masts nowadays are hollow, made by gluing long planks with epoxy. This makes the masts stronger and lighter. *Valkyrien's* builders had simply stripped two trees of their branches and bark and stuck the masts into the centerline of the boat, the same method used on the *Pearl*. She amazed me.

I loved *Valkyrien* from the moment I saw her on that bright and cool fall day in Port Richmond. She sat decaying, untended, in one of the most polluted channels in America, yet she exuded undeniable majesty. There is something about a schooner rig with the aftermost mast taller than the mast in front, which seems to me uniquely American. Before the schooner, sailors always piled additional sails on the bowsprit to add three or four or five more triangular sails out in front. Some audacious fisherman in New England—not racing for a yachting prize, but rather to be the first to market with his catch, determined to build up the sails on the back of the boat. In nearly every painting of any American harbor before 1917, a schooner sits quietly, await.

This is how *Valkyrien* lay when I first saw her. She had not sailed in years. In fact, she had grown so accustomed to the channel that she appeared to be aground. *Valkyrien* did not move at all against the dock. It occurred to me as I approached her, walking down the gangway, that she looked like a boat buried to her waterline in a farmer's field. When I stepped aboard she did not react in any way. She remained as steady in the water as though I had simply stepped onto another pier. She was the most solid boat of her size that I have ever been aboard.

I became almost giddy as I walked along her deck for the first time and saw the Turk's head knots protecting blocks on the deck, the oak pin boards tied to the side stays, and the stained wooden balustrade encircling the cockpit where on a modern boat, mere safety lines would have been tied. I jumped down her companionway, barely glancing at the rotting cabin, and walked briskly through her entire insides, and out the teak and steel scuttle hatch at her bow. Then I climbed out to the end of the bowsprit and circled back to the foremast, climbing the ratlines fifteen feet up to the first spreaders.

I loved everything about her. And the historic beauty of her hull and hardware blinded me to the rot that had settled in. Pieces of the cabin top came loose in my hand, the wood disintegrating into broken particles and a fine dust. I noted but dismissed her flaws. She seemed seaworthy enough to make the voyage, and most of the defects could be taken care of along the way.

Much later during the trip, when the defects I so casually dismissed that first day challenged our survival, I recalled the look of real concern on the boat broker's face when he saw me climb the mast. He thought it might fall down. I should have known then that he knew more about the boat than he let on.

The original *Pearl* had been built to trade goods on the Eastern Seaboard—lamb's wool, iron, lumber, corn. *Valkyrien* had been built in New Zealand to trade similar goods among the harbors and islands of that nation. The two schooners were about the same length and breadth. They were likely similar in other ways, too—the types and cut of the sails, the size of the masts, the layout of the interior, the fittings used to hold the stays and the masts in place. The *Valkyrien* appeared to be the answer to our dreams.

Just then, I looked up and saw two black crows sitting on *Valkyrien's* spreaders, cawing. Another warning sign. It's an old sailor's superstition that a crow on a boat in port is a bad sign. I thought to myself, turn around right now. *Leave this boat.*

I was in a conundrum: My sailor's instincts told me to walk away from this great deal. But my gut told me this was going to be the only boat we could ever afford—that I had an obligation to The *Pearl* Coalition, and I would be a coward to not give this a try.

Instinct is discernibly different from gut. "Going with your gut" means responding to a test with emotion over instinct. For millennia humans have sensed that our emotions somehow reside in our guts. So different is instinct—a natural, intuitive power—some say it is our sixth sense, illuminated by a higher power. Instinct is an intuitive perception, based not on emotion at all— and not really on thought either— it is a talent that, when used often, becomes stronger. My instinct tells me when I meet someone, within just a few seconds, whether they are good or bad. It is nearly always correct.

That evening I called Vicki to tell her about the boat and my conundrum. My wife is extraordinary when it comes to making decisions, and she has honed her instincts to the level of pure genius. With just about every choice we've made in our thirty years together, Vicki's instincts have been right. But by then I was so excited about *Valkyrien* that I glossed over her many flaws and assured Vicki it would work out. We would deal with the details as I sailed south.

I did promise myself (and Vicki) that I would not buy the boat before making a thorough inspection. If the engine did not work, I would not even consider the purchase. So the first test was to get the engine started. The massive starter motor weighed 60 pounds and required a huge amount of battery power to turn over; that is how I found myself at the edge of a toxic Superfund site, pushing an 80-pound battery under a fence.

In the end, I went with my gut. I never mentioned the crows.

2. *Detroit Diesel*

A noble craft, but somehow a most melancholy!
All noble things are touched with that.
—HERMAN MELVILLE, *MOBY-DICK*

Once I got the battery aboard I began looking more carefully at *Valkyrien*. Paint on the mast peeled everywhere—leaving much of it bare— my first indication that the schooner was not in perfect shape. Still, she was absolutely massive, and steady on the dock, with remarkably dry bilges. And the price was right, at around $25,000.

A portable pump, permanently in the "on" position, sat in her bilge, attached to shore power by an extension cord that hung over her starboard rail. This was somewhat of a concern, as the broker had promised me the boat did not leak. The broker had also recommended a friend of his named Jerry, as a marine surveyor, so despite finding a huge pump plugged into a boat that "never leaks," I took the broker at his word and hired Jerry to professionally survey the boat so I could make a fully informed decision before the purchase. Jerry is also a carpenter, and, for a reasonable fee, could make repairs to any areas of *Valkyrien* that needed attention.

I don't know why I take people at their word, but I do it all the time. Sometimes I think I do it even when I know they are lying. Maybe it's because I don't want to live in a world that is filled with liars, thieves, and crooks. I don't really mind a thief in the night so much, nor someone who grabs the change out of my truck when I leave the doors unlocked. But liars I can't stand. Even the law seems to not want to confront liars. When I served as an assistant district attorney we prosecuted tens of thousands of men and women for a great variety of crimes; in fact, I think we charged people with every single offense in the criminal code, except perjury. It is just too hard to prove someone a liar.

Of course, that is no excuse for me being so often taken in by liars. But, the thought of confronting someone or calling them out frankly gives me a stomachache. It actually seems less unpleasant to let them get away with their lies. That doesn't really explain why I took the broker's recommendation of Jerry at face value. I probably should have been more skeptical. I feel better about the world when I give people the benefit of the doubt. Jerry told me that *Valkyrien* was one of the finest boats he had ever seen, and that she never took on any water. He assured me that the pump attached to the extension cord was there merely as a precautionary measure. She did not leak at all. Even in the heaviest San

Francisco rains, no water penetrated the deck.

I wanted to believe him and felt relief at his assurances. While *Valkyrien* appeared to be exactly what we were looking for, I really did not want to take on something that needed a huge amount of work. I was contemplating the long journey ahead and its many potential challenges. The last thing we needed was to begin with a leaking boat.

The first time Jerry met me at *Valkyrien*, he helped me carry the battery to the engine compartment to tie it into the 12-volt system. *Valkyrien* had sat at that dock for years—at least four, maybe as long as six. The engine hadn't run since then. We cranked the old Detroit Diesel for about 30 seconds and the engine caught, cranking on its own, and screaming, louder than any engine I had ever stood close to, seemingly in protest. I thought it might explode. But it ran on its own—never smoothly.

I should say a little bit about the engine—a Detroit Diesel 6V53, the same engine that powered the armored personnel carriers (APCs) used by the US Army in Vietnam. The 6V53 is known for its power and for leaking oil and running almost unbelievably loud. Vietcong fighters called the APC the "Green Dragon," after the piercing screech of its engine as it crashed through enemy positions in heavily forested jungle. Mechanics called the 6V the "Green

Screamer." They say you can tell if it's a 6V by looking for a pool of oil beneath the pan and earmuffs nearby. It is undoubtedly the loudest engine of its size ever built. I didn't know when I purchased it, but I found out quickly that even when working properly, the 6V burns oil nearly as quickly as it burns through diesel.

At the time I just wanted to make sure the engine would run and the transmission would shift before I put down a deposit. I pushed the lever into forward, and heard the dark clanging of gears soaked in heavy oil. The boat lurched ahead so hard I thought she might pull loose from the dock. I knew then she had a propeller bigger than anything I was used to.

Looking at *Valkyrien*, I thought about the young people living in the poorest neighborhoods of Washington, DC. Most schoolchildren there, indeed, most residents, are unaware that Washington was a port city. I imagined our Coalition members teaching history on board this boat to thousands of tourists in Washington each year. I also imagined teaching carpentry to DC school-children as they helped to fashion their own spars for *Valkyrien*.

I thought about sailing down the wild coast of California and Panama. Of taking schoolchildren from Washington, DC, through the Canal and stoking their curiosity about wooden boats and the sea. I thought, too, about my personal challenge. My responsibility would be to deliver *Valkyrien* and her crew safe and sound. I sent photographs of *Valkyrien* to the board members of The *Pearl* Coalition, and closed my report: "Enjoy these photos as you consider our dream of teaching young people across the District about our shared maritime heritage." The Coalition members loved the photos, but, knew little about boats.

I sent pictures to Vicki and my children, too. They know about boats . . . the pictures worried them.

"Dad, she doesn't look like anyone is taking care of her."

"Does she leak?"

"Dad, are you sure she can float?"

"Are you sure she won't sink?"

Vicki assured them I would be safe. She knew that even if the boat did not make it all the way to Panama, I would return. One of the things I have always loved about Vicki is her understanding that I cannot be separated from the sea. She has known this about me from the beginning.

When we first started dating, Vicki and I visited my mother often in Palm Beach. We would get up in the morning, walk down to the clear ocean beach and then swim out together, away from the long unbroken line of white sand, toward the darker water offshore. Vicki's long legs and lithe form glided beautifully through the water.

On one of our first swims, I challenged her to a race, and swam quickly past Vicki. She caught up with me after ten or fifteen seconds, and kept swimming. Three minutes later I had slowed considerably but, like a baby bluefish, Vicki continued outward, far outdistancing me.

We usually swam together, side by side. After an hour the two of us would stop and tread water and talk for a while, and then Vicki would swim back to shore and I would continue out toward the Gulf Stream. I swam until I couldn't see land, and I kept swimming until I couldn't see the tall buildings on Singer Island. I returned each day a little after lunchtime.

Vicki, her shining brown hair falling around her head, would be stretched on the lawn reading beneath a palm tree, gently holding a thick paperback with small print—James Agee, perhaps, or a collection of American short stories. My mother sometimes worried about these long swims, but not Vicki. Vicki knows that the ocean will not kill me.

And for this reason alone, she knew I would return.

The *Pearl* Coalition authorized the purchase. Before setting out, *Valkyrien* would need to be hauled, her bottom painted, and the rot on the deck repaired. I contracted Jerry to do all of this work.The wharf owners had given me a two-month grace period on rent, no doubt secretly happy at the prospect of our leaving soon afterward. (I realized later that they were deeply concerned that *Valkyrien* would be abandoned by the previous owners at their yard, or would sink on their wharf.) But after the first two months, Jerry had not yet finished, and we began paying a fortune to keep her docked in San Francisco Bay.

Each week, Jerry would send me an invoice. Without flying up to San Francisco from my home in LA to personally check on things, I waited patiently, thinking and trusting that the work progressed. Jerry had promised that *Valkyrien* would be ready to sail in November. But November passed, as did December and January, and he kept making excuses, ending with, "Well, you can't take the boat south until winter is past, in any case, so don't be in such a hurry."

When I realized Jerry was not caring for the boat properly, I hired two boat boys,[1] Bryan

---

1. Boat boy is a nautical term used in New England to describe the young men who work aboard a boat, usually for a set term. They are expected to deal with all matters above- and belowdecks. Most will be competent to navigate, handle lines, and steer the vessel in heavy weather, as well as service the engine, run the galley, cook, provide first aid, and care for the needs of passengers. Boat boy should not be confused with cabin boy, whose duties are to see to the needs of officers and guests in the cabin.

Idler and Steve Spring, to live aboard *Valkyrien* and take care of her while assisting Jerry in his carpentry. The two young men were twenty-somethings and appeared at *Valkyrien*, ready for hard work and an adventure. But they were not prepared to spend day after day in port, waiting for Jerry to complete repairs.

The boys spent nearly three months in port, holed up in *Valkyrien* during what was an unusually cold and rainy San Francisco winter. If that wasn't discouraging enough, *Valkyrien's* deck leaked like mad, despite what Jerry had said. Water seeped through, dripping maddeningly on them as they slept in their bunks whenever it rained—which seemed like every day.

Wet, cold, and with hopes of their tropical cruise fading, Bryan and Steve became increasingly frustrated and, in the end, they quit. In desperation, but still unable to fathom Jerry's lying, I flew back to San Francisco to give *Valkyrien* a surprise inspection. As I approached the *Valkyrien* I heard a terrible noise and nearly fell over when I saw Jerry with a gas-powered chain saw in his hand, cutting away at the stern of the boat. I shouted at him to stop immediately.

Jerry seemed as surprised to see me as I was to see him cutting up my boat with a chain saw. Wooden-boat shipwrights normally use carefully crafted and precisely applied hand tools—

chisels with wooden handles, carving gauges, and bevels. These artisans are often so fastidious and exacting that they insist on fashioning their own tools. One of my favorites is the *kugihiki*—a flexible Japanese saw with a flexible blade and more than twenty extremely sharp but tiny teeth every inch. This saw is used to make flush cuts, and allows a careful user to cut nothing beyond what needs to be removed.

Jerry's version of the *kugihiki* was a chain saw that screamed as it chopped roughly through *Valkyrien's* sides, tearing at her hull, shaking the boat and violently chipping away at everything near its line of cut. I should have fired him on the spot (I probably should have fired him many times before that), but it's tough to fire a ship's carpenter in the middle of an overhaul. I knew that if I did, it would take a new carpenter weeks just to figure out the layout of pipes and lines, and locations where deteriorated wood rotted out our boat. Jerry was the entire build team; he served as general contractor, advisor, designer, and purchaser and purveyor of hardware, and he did all of the physical labor himself.

It was imperative to get *Valkyrien* into good-enough shape to head south to Central America, where dockage fees might be cut by as much as 80 percent. Keeping Jerry on seemed the most efficient way to get *Valkyrien* moving. I did think of taking *Valkyrien* to a professional yard, but my budget was an issue: Boatyard shipwrights would charge more than three times what Jerry was billing us, and we were already burning through money merely by paying rent at the dock. And so, my relationship with Jerry continued, even though I knew he was lying to me.

The phone conversation recalled below is fairly typical of my talks with Jerry after I became aware that he had completed almost no work for months.

ME: "Jerry, you are the biggest liar I have ever dealt with in my entire life."

JERRY: "What's that, Max? I can't hear you—you're breaking up."

ME: "You, Jerry, are the biggest liar I have ever met. Please, just tell me the truth."

JERRY: "Max, I heard you say my name, but everything else came out garbled. The boat is nearly done, though, so that is great!"

ME: "Jerry, the boat is not done, and you know it. You're lying to me again, right now."

JERRY: "Max, I am in a place with really bad reception, I will call you later."

ME: "No, no, Jerry—wait! Wait—wait! Please . . . Can you hear me now?"

3. *Plotting*

Let us go then, you and I,
When the evening is spread out against the sky.
—T. S. Eliot, *THE LOVE SONG OF
J. ALFRED PRUFROCK*

In early February, I once again flew back to San Francisco, and boarded *Valkyrien* in a blinding rain, alone. Jerry had redeemed himself somewhat. He had finished her bottom paint to fend off the worms that eat through wood in the warmer waters, where we were heading. He had replaced some of the cables that hold the masts up, which made everything much more stable, and he had rebuilt the bowsprit and the boomkin using an awl and other antique tools. But each day of continued dockage in San Francisco cost us a fortune. I knew that if I didn't get her out of there before the end of the month, we would run through so much money that The *Pearl* Coalition board would give up and sell *Valkyrien*. I had to get her out of Dodge.

I spent day after day running around light industrial centers across San Francisco Bay, searching for various small parts—links of a certain gauge chain, or special putty that can be applied underwater. Each night I slept back aboard the *Valkyrien*, contemplating my journey ahead.

Back then, people would often ask me, "How big is your boat?" Boats, especially wooden boats, are extremely personal, and boaters tend to develop a relationship with their boat, which is, in some ways, quite intimate. So when you ask a captain how long his boat is, he may well take offense, finding it nearly akin to asking how long any thing he holds intimate might be. Most of the time landsmen are not really sure what they are asking when they say, "How big is your boat?," but essentially, they want to know how long the boat is. The proper way to ask this is to say: "How many does she sleep?"

Valkyrien had bunks for eleven people, more or less, but could be properly modified to sleep many more. She was a very large boat to sail with only three people on duty. Sailing her became much more difficult when one of the three was asleep. Her deck was nearly sixty feet long. Her total length was even greater, because she had a fifteen-foot bowsprit and a boomkin hanging ten or twelve feet off the stern. The total length of a boat is abbreviated "LOA," for "Length Overall." This is the total distance from the tip of the bowsprit to the end of the boomkin. *Valkyrien's* overall length was close to eighty feet; she was sixteen and a half feet wide; and the bottom of her keel sat eight feet below the waterline.

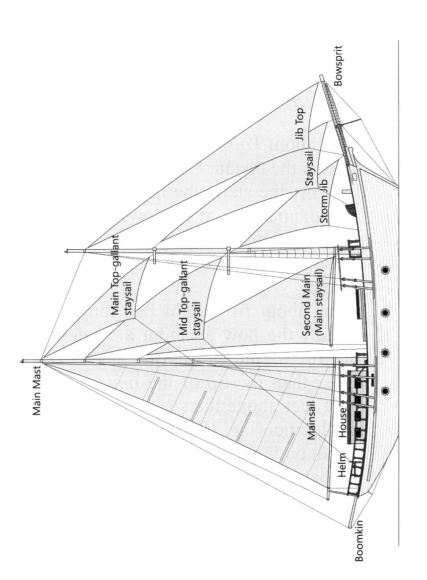

SCHOONER *VALKYRIEN*

Built: Charles Bailey & Sons, Auckland 1928

Bowsprit

Jib Top

Staysail

Storm Jib

Main Top-gallant staysail

Mid Top-gallant staysail

Second Main (Main staysail)

Main Mast

Mainsail

Helm

House

Boomkin

LOA: 77 feet, 6 inches (Length Overall)
LOD: 57 feet, 9 inches (Length On Deck)
Beam: 16 feet, 6 inches
Draft: 8 feet
Full keel with aperture and full rudder
Ballast: 18 tons lead
Scale weight: 40 tons

Most striking about *Valkyrien*, though, was her freeboard. This is the distance from the waterline up to her deck. At the stern she had about eight feet of freeboard, and even at the lowest point of the deck, near midships, she was still about six feet above the water. Lots of freeboard generally means a dry boat.

Her deck was about fifty-eight feet long. The bowsprit rose off the bow at about a 30-degree angle, so the tip of the bowsprit hung nearly four feet higher than the tip of the bow, putting it about twelve feet above the sea when the boat lay at rest on the mooring. (It proved to be great fun climbing out on the bowsprit and jumping off into the water before breakfast.)

Valkyrien did not have a boarding ladder—which could be an issue in a storm—but at the mooring, the portholes were so deeply set in the hull that they formed a sort of built-in ladder. And atop the portholes were all sorts of stays and balustrades that could be used to get a leg up.

In addition to questions about my boat, many

people wanted to know about the journey itself. Some of my friends in LA looked at me in near astonishment when I said I intended to sail to the Panama Canal. The first question asked was usually "How will you find it?"

For me, the coast—any coast, really—just appears as a line that connects every beach on the continent. I remember reading *Tarzan* by Edgar Rice Burroughs. When it was time for Tarzan to leave the jungle, he simply set out walking down the beach. Eventually he came to a village, and then a larger village, and finally, to a port where he jumped on a ship to another continent.

That's basically how I saw it. When they asked me how I would find the Panama Canal, I thought to myself, I will sail down along the coast until I see a whole bunch of tankers and container ships headed to the left, and then I will follow them into the Canal. It turns out this navigation method probably would have worked. I saw very few trade vessels until I got near the entrance to the Canal, where the sea was full of them.

Of course, with modern GPS systems, many boats will sail this route without the captain ever looking at paper charts. But I learned to navigate as a child using parallel rules, a chart, and a compass rose. So that is how I began thinking of this journey. The electronic navigation would make the trip a relatively simple matter, but I cannot resist a paper chart. I love the feel of the paper.

I love spreading out a chart and envisioning the coastline. Most good charts will give enough information for a navigator to imagine fairly accurately just about every beach along the route. The chart is marked to show cliffs and rocky beaches, and whether the bottom is filled with seaweed, or muddy, or only sand.

We often think of landmarks as historic buildings or monuments, but the term came into use on ships, and is still used today on charts. Nearly every large object that can be seen from the sea is marked onshore. The United States Department of Transportation maintains a list of special symbols for water towers, radar towers, steep cliffs, lighthouses, airport lights. Anything that might help you to place where you are in the world is marked on the charts.

No matter how lost, with a good chart, and if I can see the shore, I can nearly always figure out where I am. And for the vast majority of this trip, I would be near enough to see the shoreline, so, in reality, it would be very tough to miss the Panama Canal.

Charts outside of the United States are less accurate. Essentially, as a country becomes poorer, farther away, or less likely to be occupied by American forces, the information on the charts becomes increasingly sparse and speculative. To compensate for this, before the trip I read blogs written by other travelers, and spoke with every captain I could find who had navigated those waters. They provided the best information of what lay ahead, but I also read the cruising guides and various guidebooks for each of the countries in Central America. Perhaps more than anything I monitored various online weather sites.

The fact is, though, that even the best navigator will not be able to place you more accurately than a GPS, which even at night and in bad weather can locate you on an electronic chart—often within a few feet of your actual position.

I began plotting my trip by going to Google Earth and drawing a path down the coast from Port Richmond to the Panama Canal. Google Earth is beyond belief amazing when it comes to trip planning. According to Google, wending in and out of the larger bays, the voyage to the entrance of the Panama Canal would be at least 4,300 miles at sea.

Traveling 4,300 statute miles means about 3,700 nautical miles. *Valkyrien* cruised under power at about 7.3 knots. With a good wind she would make 8.7 knots. So, if you figure an average speed of 7 knots, to be generous, the trip would take 530 hours, or about 22 days. I intended to sail day and night, putting into port only to see something interesting or, occasionally, to fuel up. It seemed unlikely that the trip would take more than 90 days of sailing.

I planned to buy the boat, have some essential

work done in San Francisco to make sure she would make it safely to Panama, then, once in the tropics, take her to a local marina where artisans could re-create her to be as much like the *Pearl* as possible. Once she was finished, we would re-christen her *The Spirit of the Pearl* and bring down a corps of young people from Anacostia who would sail her up to Washington, DC, with me, where we would inaugurate the museum.

My grand plan was to sail the boat past Big Sur before Christmas, then spend Christmas with my family in the United States. Then, I would sail *Valkyrien* down to Cabo San Lucas where Vicki and our children would meet me for a long weekend, perhaps Dr. King's birthday, or, at worst, Presidents' Day in February. I'd

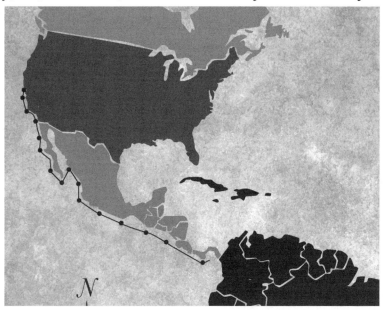

cruise down the Mexican coast and Vicki could meet me again in Acapulco, where my parents had scuba-dived fifty years before. I would then take *Valkyrien* past Guatemala, stopping in El Salvador to explore the various Central American estuaries in the Boston Whaler dinghy I planned to tow. I would then cruise past Nicaragua in a couple of days, stopping in Costa Rica for another reunion with my family, then sail the coast in a leisurely way, stopping at various resorts and surfing beaches. Finally, I would sail the boat to Panama with a group of friends and have the final work completed upon her. Then we would all go together when school got out and sail her through the Panama Canal.

This sounded like a pretty great trip: Every couple of weeks I could come home for a week or two with Vicki, and my whole family would join me at times on this extraordinary adventure. I thought that if I could slow our progress enough to do some exploring and spend some relaxed time with my family, this could be one of the greatest trips of my life. Hard to imagine a better, more fun, or more interesting way of seeing and experiencing America, and to be able to do all of this with Vicki and my children seemed like a dream come true. As it turned out, my family did not end up joining me for much of the journey, although Vicki made several brave trips to Mexico, Costa Rica, and Panama.

• • •

We needed a dinghy to get ashore at various ports and a life raft to escape in case of disaster. I decided to buy a Boston Whaler and tow it behind us to serve as both. This might be considered an unusual choice; Whalers can be heavy to pull, might fill with water in rough seas, and could damage the *Valkyrien* from bumping against her—not ideal qualities for a dinghy. And Whalers are not great lifeboats because they offer little protection from wind, rain, and sun. But the Whaler still seemed to me the best option by far to do both jobs. Whalers are unsinkable, even when they are sawn in half. They are also the most fun motorboat ever built. I spent countless childhood hours bombing around the harbor of Hyannis Port on my brother's Boston Whaler, or alternatively, watching Wayne repairing the Evinrude at Hyannis Marine, or merely drifting, squeezing the ball pump, trying to get the engine restarted. (The old outboards on our Whaler seemed to be broken about half of every summer.)

I found a 17-foot Boston Whaler Montauk for sale on Craigslist about halfway up the coast from Los Angeles. She was built in 1967, two years after I was born. All of the original wood seats and trim had been torn out, so I was able to buy her for $2,000. We screwed in a couple of four-by-four wooden posts to strengthen the center console, and rigged up a towline to pull her behind *Valkyrien*.

Back in San Francisco, rain fell on most of those winter days before my departure. I moved aboard *Valkyrien*. Water seeped through cracks and fissures in the deck and the house-top. It percolated through heavy layers of paint and dripped down on me as I typed away on my computer. I picked up a damp towel—everything by then was damp—and lay it across the top of my Dell, to keep the water from dripping onto the keyboard.

The cabin lights did not work on *Valkyrien*, and her two portholes allowed little light in. My cabin was dark inside even on bright afternoons. My first night a particularly vicious winter storm blew through. *Valkyrien* sidled up against the pilings, preventing the faint light of the storm-filled sky from entering. Old sailboats can be spooky at night; the wood groans even in calm harbors. Lines and shrouds rub up against each other, or screech along the mast. I sat reclining on my bunk, typing an email to Vicki. When I shut off the computer I lay in near total darkness, not realizing then that my first night and last night aboard *Valkyrien*, I would be alone. The wind outside the porthole blew hard enough to create tiny little whitecaps of blowing foam in our narrow channel.

Everyone at the wharf seemed terrified of the moment when *Valkyrien* might actually—finally—leave the dock. I knew that they would never, ever say she was "ready." She had sat idle at that dock for years. I think most people thought she would never move—that eventually, she would sink at the dock and be pulled up by a crane, then cut into pieces and taken to a landfill.

If I did not get her moving south, very soon, we would have to give up. The *Pearl* Coalition could not wait. We could no longer afford the high dockage fees in San Francisco, or to lose momentum. So, one rainy day, I decided just to take her out by myself, for a little spin, to see what might happen.

In the early morning, under the still-dark sky and a pelting rain, I started the engine and cast off her lines. *Valkyrien* moved amidships like a huge old retriever, stretching as it rises from a long sleep, and we sidled a bit off the pier. I engaged the engine and drove *Valkyrien* to a nearby fuel dock, filling both her tanks with clean diesel before returning her to the pier single-handed.

This was the first time in six months that I had seen a single boat cast off from that pier. The two or three people working on nearby boats watched me with something close to disbelief. One persnickety Frenchman stepped aboard his boat carrying a long wooden stick. He held it pointed at *Valkyrien*, threatening, and seemed to hope more than anything that I would foul up and bump into his neatly kept, though never-sailed, vessel. The people on that wharf, I realized, loved boats. They loved to talk about boats, and they loved to repair boats, but none of them, it seemed, actually wanted to go sailing.

4. *Poor Troy*

There gloom the dark, broad seas.
—ALFRED, LORD TENNYSON, *ULYSSES*

I asked my friend Troy Campbell from Oklahoma to join me for the first leg of the *Valkyrien's* journey. Troy is one of my closest friends, and may be the most capable man I have ever met. When the boat boys complained to Troy about how wet and cold they got from the water leaking through the deck, he answered, without guile or irony, "Why don't you fix the leaks?"

I first met Troy about fifteen years ago when he answered an advertisement I took out on Craigslist in Tulsa, Oklahoma. I needed someone to crew aboard the *Glide*, my old Casey yawl in Hyannis Port. The advertisement included these lines:

DECKHAND ON WOODEN BOAT (EAST COAST)

Hard work. Must know how to swim. Must be able to improvise.

Not absolutely required, but good if you know something about boats; diesel engine experience a big plus . . . send note why you would be good at this . . . and very hard work.

This job mainly involves preparing the vessel for sail and work on the vessel while she is moored, but you will sail or be in powerboats every single day. This is a summer job. It will most likely not last past September.

Basically a deckhand must be a jack of all trades—you will have to purchase groceries for trips, make sandwiches, coil lines. The following things are done often, so it would be good if you knew how to do some of them, but in fact, you can succeed in the job with no knowledge of any of these things:

• tying fishing knots and bowlines;
• climbing ropes;
• finding things that someone left on board cleaning out a head after a child has pulled the wrong pipe
• cleaning out a bilge;
• changing belts on an engine;
• working with hammers, nails, screws, grinders, amp meters, flashlights, head-lamps, driving trucks, jumping batteries, 12-volt electrical, plumbing pipes, com-pressed air, folding sails, washing clothes, cooking at sea and at home, making BBQ, climbing trees, cutting grass, catching fish on lines and in nets;

- dealing with injured birds, and almost certainly with an owl (I have a raptor rehabilitation license and an animal rehab permit); also, we currently have nine dogs—a huge pain in the tail, to be frank—and you will have to deal with them probably a lot. You will probably have to jump overboard now and then. And there are generally a hell of a lot of children around (often there are at least 15 children aboard the boat.)

Troy was one of the few who answered the ad. I like hiring people from Oklahoma because they work harder than most East Coast folks. People from the Midwest often don't know much about sailing, and are therefore much less likely to question my orders than some snide New England prep school sailor (like me).

Troy grew up in rural Oklahoma. His grandmother was a full-blooded Cherokee who chewed tobacco and watched professional wrestling matches on television in the afternoons, shouting at the fighters and grimacing at every painful hold. His parents loved Troy, but they did not baby him. In the summertime they would drop him off at a piece of land their family owned beside the Cherokee reservation. He and his cousins were left completely unsupervised for two months each year. They prepared all of their meals on outdoor fires, and noodled for catfish. Meat was a rare treat.

His cousins received a "new" (used—but not as badly used as the one they lived in) trailer home in the middle of one summer. Rather than take the time to move the old one out, they set their former home on fire, and then all sat down to watch it burn. This did not go over well with the local fire department. Troy's next-door neighbors had eight children, all boys. Their names were Joe-Bob, Jim-Bob, Sammy, Pedro, T. J., Clinton, Nate, Wade, and Peanut.

The summer that Troy first came to work for me, I was living in Massachusetts and had purchased a huge wooden mast from an old ketch on eBay. I wanted to erect it in my front yard to use as a flagpole, so I asked Troy to go pick it up for me on the boat trailer. When he got back with it, we built a substructure that weighed more than half a ton, carrying and mixing cement from twenty-pound bags. We built steel and cement anchors and laid them out around the flagpole like stays on a boat, holding the enormous mast well in place. We convinced the driver of a telephone company bucket truck to tie the mast to his boom and raise it vertically.

Late in June, a big northeast wind blew in, bending the mast precipitously. We decided to tie a couple more stays to it, but in order to create any real stability, this second set of stays had to be placed high up on the mast and pulled tight. We set up a twenty-foot orange Werner extension ladder on the flagpole, fully extended to about thirty-eight feet. Troy held the ladder while I climbed. The pole swayed in a manner that concerned me. We placed the ladder at a nearly vertical angle, to keep as much pressure off the mast as we could, and to allow me to attach the new stays as high as possible. I stood on that ladder, scared as hell, while the mast swayed back and forth in the nor'easter.

Unfortunately, the flagpole cracked and fell (and me with it). I broke my pelvis in three places and had a rib break off and tear through my lung, collapsing it. Fluid filled my chest cavity so the lung could not reinflate. I had difficulty speaking because of the lack of air going through and past my vocal cords. I recall thinking to myself, even as I lay on the ground experiencing intense pain: This poor boat boy. He will feel guilty that he did not hold the ladder well. And I will exploit that guilt all summer long, because I love practical jokes. I can't help myself.

Troy loved laughing—at me or himself—and the thought of the two of us laughing all summer made me feel better even as I lay on the ground before the ambulance arrived. I beckoned to Troy, barely moving my chin, and whispered something. Troy couldn't hear, so he bent down on one knee and leaned his head down. I think he thought it was my last breath. I whispered in a tone as earnest as I could muster: "Why did you let go of the ladder?"

Poor Troy. He held on to that ladder a lot longer than most men would have. I just could not resist teasing him.

Troy later tortured me at his every opportunity, as well. He once put a thin zip tie on the driveshaft of my truck so that every time I drove forward, the zip tie spun around, lashing the undercarriage of my Ford and making a horrible sound. Each time I heard the noise I stopped and crawled underneath, searching the axles and joints where the driveshaft attached to the transfer case and differential. I could find nothing seriously amiss. It took me a long time to notice the zip tie.

On another occasion, Troy walked into our house, pretending to be upset with himself, telling me he had put regular gasoline in my diesel truck (and I fell for it). A couple of times Troy dressed up in a terrifying Halloween costume and hid in a bush to scare the hell out of me. I didn't tell him that I had been kidding about him not holding the ladder for more than a year.

That first summer, Troy and I sailed up and down New England with Vicki and our young children. On many days we sailed with at least a dozen children on board, along with their parents, my brothers and sisters, cousins, and my mother. Troy became part of our family, and we have remained close friends ever since.

I was excited to have him join me those first few weeks on *Valkyrien*. I knew that I would be safe as long as I could get Troy to sail with me. Unfortunately, Troy wanted to go home the minute he saw *Valkyrien*. He said he had a bad feeling about the boat. He said, deadly serious, that in his opinion she was absolutely not seaworthy.

The new boat boys who had replaced Bryan and Steve told me they were quitting the same day. They slept on *Valkyrien* one last night, saying they would catch their bus home in the morning. I knew I couldn't sail the boat alone, and I was not ready to give up on bringing this schooner to Washington. I decided to use the old captain's trick of leaving port while the crew slept. They couldn't quit very easily once we were at sea. Resolving to push off that night, and using Troy's greatest weakness—his absolute loyalty—I convinced him that he, at least, should not abandon a friend.

We waited until the boat boys fell asleep in their bunks. I had a tough decision to make as to whether or not to start the engine before leaving the pier. I knew that it would take thirty seconds or so to start, and I didn't not want the boat boys sleeping below to awaken and have time to abandon ship. On the other hand, I did not want to end up drifting into a crowded seaway if the engine did not start. I decided to do both at the same time. I had Troy undo all of the lines save one. I started the engine, and we pushed off and headed out into the San Francisco Bay, bound for Panama.

A cold rain began to fall.

The boat boys came running up on deck just as we left the pier, but it was too late for them to quit. And we were all freezing our tails off. I gave my ski gloves to them—an offering of empathy, and to warm their hands, making them feel at least a little bit cared for. To their credit, they both managed rather quickly to get over their irritation at being pressed out to sea.

We had a tough time for the first few hours because the green and red navigation signals on *Valkyrien's* sides refused to illuminate. An annoyed tug pilot, determined to teach us a lesson, bore down hard on us, matching our every turn and ignoring our radio signals.

We snuck across the bay to San Francisco and headed for the Golden Gate Bridge. Around midnight, and sixteen or so nautical miles into our journey, a US Coast Guard Special Purpose Craft–Law Enforcement (SPC–LE) vessel cruised alongside and hailed us. They ordered us to heave to, as we had no navigation lights. I radioed the guardsmen on channel 16[2] and asked them to switch to channel 11.

I told the captain of the Coast Guard interceptor that we were bound for the Pacific, outside the territory of the United States. He did not answer on the radio. Instead, after a quiet fifteen seconds or so, the Coast Guard captain bellowed on his loudspeaker: "Not my problem anymore." He spun his boat around and headed back into the bay.

Mild fog lifted as we sailed beneath the Golden Gate Bridge and into the Pacific, watching rolling waves begin to break as they approached Land's End and we began our journey in earnest, bound south toward Half Moon Bay.

---

2. The emergency channel that is always monitored by the USCG.

5. *Under Way At Last*

*This is one of the coldest days
of this most damnable
and interminable winter.*
—DIARY NOTES OF SAMUEL CLEMENS

Valkyrien's prior owner had installed quite a bit of cheaply built wooden furniture, apparently in anticipation of living aboard. None of these feeble accoutrements could survive a real storm, and I determined to jettison it all at the earliest possible moment.

Troy had taken most of the night watch, and he slept late the following afternoon in the "guest" cabin on the port side, at the bottom of the second companionway. This cabin had a single porthole, custom-built for *Valkyrien*. The bronze frame was nearly four inches thick and covered by a heavy glass, closed tight against water by four screw-type clamps called "dogs." The porthole had been laid only a foot and a half above the waterline. While under sail, the porthole would be underwater much of the time, or half under.

People who work often with diesel engines become accustomed to their sounds. And every older diesel has its own rhythm and clanking. The slightest change in RPMS will waken a watchful crew out of even a deep sleep, often with great alarm.

As we headed out of San Francisco we made an agreement that before the skipper adjusted the RPMS he would always announce it to the crew, so that they would not be needlessly startled and come running on deck while trying to get their scant four hours of sleep.

Given the unique set of circumstances—Troy asleep, a scary window, and lots of useless wooden furniture on board—I could not resist playing a practical joke.

I asked the boat boys to bring all of the slipshod furniture on deck and lay it out just forward of Troy's porthole. Then I searched the charts for a hellish area on the bottom—where the seafloor rose up near the surface, but not all the way. This rise would cause the long, smooth swells to break the surface and slap the boat hard, while not endangering us in any way. I found a perfect spot and drove *Valkyrien* to the lee of this submerged hill. The rollers all around us flowed gently, about ten feet high. But at this acclivity, the waves lifted up steeply and then broke in a cold stream of white water, just after the bottom rise.

We had been motoring at a constant 850 RPMS. The engine had settled into a regular rhythm, and Troy was sleeping peacefully to that beat. But as we slipped up to the breaking waves, the *Valkyrien* was lifted violently and twisted at a steep angle, dipping Troy's porthole well below the water, and turning his room first green, then dark. I dropped the RPMS down to nearly nothing, then quickly climbed up to the deck and dumped all of the furniture overboard. The crash of the wave on *Valkyrien's* side pushed Troy against the wall, his face pressed up against the cold glass porthole.

The engine sounded as though it had stalled, and Troy woke in anxious alarm. As the boat rolled back to starboard Troy looked out the porthole to see the ocean around him filled with pieces of furniture from the boat. He bolted from his bunk and ran to the cockpit, agitated and ready to jump into action. Instead, he saw me laughing and heard the engine go back up to regular running RPMS. It took him a minute to figure out what was happening, and then he roared with laughter—a kind of Oklahoma guffaw that always cheered me.

One of the reasons I love and value Troy, apart from his great sense of fun and his loyalty, is his amazing mechanical prowess.

When Troy was a teenager, he saved all the money he had earned for two summers and purchased the hulk of a yellow Camaro from a junkyard. One of his uncles got a friend to tow it back to their land. One piece at a time, Troy took the engine down. He cleaned every part—each screw, each washer, each nut—with gasoline, diesel fuel, and a wire brush, until they shined. If any part looked worn, he'd get a ride to the local auto shop and buy a replacement. He bought rolls of rubber gasket material and cut all of the gaskets himself to save money. Then, before he'd take the next piece off, he would put the one he had rebuilt back on. By the end of the summer, he had replaced every single bit of worn material in that old wrecked engine.

Troy was fourteen years old.

No one had taught him how to be a mechanic, and no one thought his car would work. But just before school began, Troy borrowed a battery. The Camaro started right up and ran perfectly. It took him two more years to rebuild the body, but the day he got his license, Troy had a Camaro.

No one in Troy's family had ever gone to college, and Troy could see no point in going himself. He wanted to work with his hands, to literally make things better for people. But someone convinced him to take the SAT. He received the highest score in the history of his high school. Troy got a letter from Dartmouth College, asking if he would interview with an alumni who lived in Norman.

Dartmouth offered Troy a full scholarship—tuition, dorm, meals—even some money to get back and forth between New Hampshire and Oklahoma. He decided to give college a try. Troy showed up at Dartmouth with a single suitcase of clothing and three guns. He had no idea that one needed a license to have a handgun in many states on the East Coast. Dartmouth, it turns out, was one of the few Ivy League colleges that maintained gun-storage rooms in each dorm.

Our backgrounds are completely divergent. Troy is a fundamentalist Christian Republican, and he brings those core values—belief in God and in the redeeming qualities of hard work, good judgment, and an open heart—to everything he does. Even under the most trying and chaotic circumstances, Troy was always grateful for a cup of peanut butter under the stars, and able there to find joy in everything.

Troy gave me enormous confidence and a sense of pure fun as we headed toward the Golden Gate Bridge, finally under way.

6. *A Bad Feeling*

THE SHAPES ARISE!
Ship-yards and dry-docks along
the Eastern and Western Seas
and in many a bay and by-place,
The live oak Kielsons, the pine planks,
the spars, the hackmatack-roots for knees,
The ships themselves on their ways,
the tiers of scaffolds,
the workmen busy outside and inside,
The tools lying around, the great auger
and little auger, the adze, bolt, line,
square, gouge, and bead-plane.
*—*WALT WHITMAN,
SONG OF THE BROAD-AXE

Things happened in Monterey Bay that should have caused me to give up the trip.

It all started out harmlessly enough; first, the sea lions.

In fifth-grade science class, our teacher often showed us documentary films. I loved these movies, especially the ones about seals. Many were shot using 16mm cameras, and projected on the tiny Da-Lite tripod screens that always swayed one way or another, giving us a skewed view of the animal world. When I grew up I wanted to go to Monterey Bay and film the seals, and sea lions, too! I could not believe what a magical place California seemed to be.

I had never seen a wild seal in my life. (Before I was born, my brothers and sisters had had a pet seal named Sandy that escaped so many times, he was finally given to the Washington National Zoo. I went to visit him in his imprisonment off Connecticut Avenue whenever I could get a ride, but was never precisely sure which seal was Sandy.)

When I finally turned eighteen and had my own driver's license, I drove across the United States with my brother Chris. We rode straight down from San Francisco to spend the day at the Monterey Aquarium. I vowed to return one day in a boat.

Thirty years later, as I slid *Valkyrien* into Monterey Harbor, I was no less amazed by the seals and sea lions than I had been as a child. They were absolutely magical, and looked to me like creatures from a fantastical world where movement onshore was difficult and lumbering, but swimming in water became an experience with zero gravity and no boundaries.

In Cape Cod you could rarely see more than a few feet through the turbid ocean. But in Monterey, visibility was practically endless. Sailing in the Bay was like cruising through a gigantic aquarium completely overstocked with fish and birds and seals and sea lions, although with surprisingly few people (at least in winter).

We grabbed a mooring to save money on dockage fees that first night in Monterey, and the following morning Troy and I tried starting the engine. The first time it turned over strongly but did not start. This was typical on *Valkyrien*. It usually took a few tries. We waited a bit, then tried again. This time, the engine made a horrible sound and immediately stopped turning over. I checked the oil level and it was completely fine. I tried a few times more, but the battery merely smoked, as the lead terminal posts melted down.

I knew then that we had, potentially, a huge problem. The engine appeared to have seized up; if we could not get it to move, the entire engine would have to be replaced. There was one last possibility—something might be caught in the propeller—so I needed to check that before becoming utterly dejected.

I dove into the clear, cold water and swam down to see if any detritus was jammed in the prop, but the propeller turned freely. Back on board, I looked in the engine compartment to see if anything had stuck the driveshaft. Then I climbed down the companionway and tried to turn the engine by hand. It wouldn't budge. I looked at the exhaust pipes and noticed for the first time that they had been installed on the cheap. The engine was mounted below sea level. The exhaust had a long run, and the pipes ran straight—with no steep elbow to drain back-flow.

There are several ways diesel engines with through-hull, raw-water cooling systems can create reverse suction through the exhaust pipes. Troy and I took a few pieces off the engine and realized quickly that seawater had entered the block through the exhaust, causing the engine to seize. We would have to tow *Valkyrien* to a working dock.

The currents even within the inner harbor of Monterey Bay are terrifically strong, and our Boston Whaler barely moved the *Valkyrien* shoreward. We had moored less than half a mile from the slip, yet that short ride took us nearly an hour before we landed at Breakwater Cove Marina, not realizing that *Valkyrien* would remain there for a month.

Troy advised me to give up the trip. He told me again that he had a bad feeling about *Valkyrien*. Later that day he caught a bus home to LA, making it clear he never wanted to step foot aboard the boat again. I hoped he would come around.

I remained determined to continue the journey, and knowing Troy, felt confident that if I really needed him, he would return. If I had not been sure that Troy would come back, I probably would have given up in Monterey.

In addition to the problems with the engine, many of *Valkyrien's* other systems had deteriorated to the point of near failure. Both of her toilets (called heads) leaked. The forward head did not work at all when we bought the boat, but rather than pay for a new one, we just used the nonworking head as a space to store supplies.

At Monterey, unfortunately, the single functioning head failed. The usual way to find out a head is not working is to use it. We learned after leaving San Francisco that the rubber gasket seals for the hand pump had hardened up from not being used for years. Sewage, under intense pressure, regularly sprayed out of the top of the pump casing so that when flushing, we had to crouch and lean way back to avoid getting sprayed in the eye. Because the compartment for the head had very little room, it was tough to pump and, at the same time, duck away from the dark liquid that spurted out. After every use, the fetid water that sprayed around the room because of the malfunctioning pump had to be wiped down. It was a nasty business.

Cleaning the bilge on most boats is a notoriously difficult and loathsome job. The bilge is the compartment below the floorboards, and is the deepest and most difficult compartment to reach, much less clean. If any of the sewage hoses leak, as was the case in *Valkyrien*, the gross fluids would gather in the bilge and slosh back and forth, caking the entire interior of the boat beneath the boards in feces and urine.

By crawling throughout the head, reaching through passages covered with a particularly filthy grime, I labeled each of the hoses leading from the head and the holding tank, sticking on variously colored tape to identify the different hoses all along their run. The pump, of course, ultimately failed completely. I am continually mystified by my capacity to withstand all sorts of disquieting and discomfiting situations. I can be fairly comfortable sailing through a full gale, yet I am almost completely overpowered by the mere idea of dealing with feces. Especially human feces. I got better at it on this trip, but when I first confronted that head, filled with feces left there by some unconfessed crapper, I felt nearly despondent.

The fact is, I have some weird version of OCD which allows me to be perfectly comfortable when my own office or home is in complete disarray, so long as the disarray is caused by me. If the detritus belongs to others, I cannot stand it. I'm not sure how, then, I'm able to travel on a boat, sharing food and quarters for weeks on end, side by side with a crew of filthy, stinking men. I guess I love being on the water so much that I can sublimate my phobias.

7. Jasper

Oh, what a tangled web we weave . . .
—SIR WALTER SCOTT, *MARMION*

During the sail down to Monterey I had also become increasingly concerned about the condition of *Valkyrien's* masts. In Monterey I took out an advertisement on Craigslist for a carpenter. I asked potential hires to detail their carpentry experience and at the end, to explain how they would create a butterfly joint and a beveled lap splice on a vertical stud. I ended with: "If you don't know what these terms mean, please do not reply."

I got a few replies from carpenters who said they would not work for me if their lives depended on it, but felt compelled to reply because they thought my ad so arrogant and rude. Frankly, I agreed with them. I needed to quickly cut through the clutter and find someone who not only understood the kind of carpentry required, but who was also willing to work with someone like me. The overbearing post covered both issues.

One carpenter replied in the most poorly written dribble I had ever read. Every single word was spelled incorrectly. Even when he used the same word more than once in a single sentence, he spelled it differently each time—a mad kind of phonetics that combined kindergarten spelling with all of the odd rules we learn in second grade, spelling fish "fesh," or "fsh," and then, later, "phish." His wild orthography was utterly unselfconscious and unique.

Rather than being put off, I was intrigued. The author likely suffered from some form of profound dyslexia, and since I knew that dyslexics often make up for deficiencies in one area of the brain by excelling at others, I hoped that the author of the note would turn out to be a man with a profound visual mind who was also great at carpentry. Unemployed, and with an uncrowded schedule, the carpenter, named Jasper, met me at the dock beside *Valkyrien* that same afternoon.

Jasper never asked me how long we would be away or how much he would earn. The only thing I knew for sure about him was he had never been sailing and wanted very much to sail aboard *Valkyrien*. I saw him as an odd but valiant adventurer with a strong sense of loyalty. Vicki saw his determination to sail aboard *Valkyrien* as reckless. She encouraged me to hire crew who knew how to sail.

I have always been extremely reliant on my wife—not so much for the ordinary things that any of us might expect from a spouse, but for things intangible and inchoate. We have been together for more than thirty years, and I count on Vicki's love and faith to carry me through each and every travail I face. When I embarked on this adventure, I had no idea how often and for how long *Valkyrien* would ultimately take me away from Vicki and our children.

Despite my wife's misgivings, I wanted to hire Jasper, and Jasper badly wanted to join the trip. But another Craigslist applicant, also extremely qualified, practically begged me to choose him. I could only afford to pay one person. I hated to turn away a hard worker and to disappoint a young man yearning for adventure. I needed someone who was willing to do dirty work. And Jasper quickly proved himself in this regard.

Earlier in the day the unthinkable happened aboard *Valkyrien*. Somehow, despite the hoses from the head having been completely and visibly disconnected, and a large sign stating in block letters BROKEN—DO NOT USE, someone had defecated in the toilet again. Interviewing the two men together, I raised the issue of the filthy toilet as an example of the kinds of unpleasant-ness they might have to deal with as boat boys aboard *Valkyrien*.

Neither seemed too fazed by the prospect, so I was no closer to deciding which of them would best be able to deal with the reality of a long trip in a leaking boat down to the tropics. While I continued to talk to the two men together, trying to decide which one to hire, Jasper, without explanation, drifted away from the conversation and disappeared belowdecks without saying anything, and I thought, "I wish he could concentrate on this right now because I really like this wacky guy."

A few moments later he stood up in the companionway, holding the filthy toilet over his head (which was the only way it would fit up the stairs). Feces dripped down his arms and onto his shoulders as he walked heavily along the deck, then off the *Valkyrien*, up the gangway, and into the men's room on the dock. All the while carrying the toilet. He remained in the men's room for about 45 minutes. Then he came out, wearing only his underwear. He had washed the toilet, cleaned his clothes, and showered. The formerly filthy head sparkled clean as new.

I hired Jasper then and there, and that was the beginning of a beautiful friendship. In the end, of course, Vicki was right. My life would be so much easier overall if I accepted the wisdom of my wife. But, it seems I am destined to insist on making my own mistakes and learning by experience. Jasper, it turned out, would be intimately involved in some of the greatest disasters of my life. I am not saying that he caused them, but I am also quite sure they would not have happened if Jasper was not my friend.

Jasper showed up at the boat the first day with his own climbing harness. Shorter than most men, he moves with force more than grace, like a man injured in a series of accidents, determined to walk on his own. His head is shaped like a rectangle, perpendicular at its sides and the top nearly perfectly parallel with the ground. His smile gives away his fundamentally boyish nature.

I asked him to take a look at the weak spots in the mast. He looked me dead in the eye and asked if it was safe. How the hell do I know if it's safe? I thought. You're the one with the climbing gear. But I said, "Yes, it is totally safe."

Without another word Jasper tied himself into the main halyard and began hoisting himself up.

I asked, a bit weakly, "Don't you want to check it out for yourself a bit before you go up?"

Jasper looked straight back at me, only slightly confused, and said, "Why would I? The captain is always right."

I discovered later that Jasper had spent a grand total of ten days of his life on a boat. He'd briefly worked for an engineer on a steel commercial fishing rig. The engineer had taken Jasper under his wing and taught him a hell of a lot about big diesel engines. He also taught Jasper the axiom, "The captain is always right." Jasper did not understand that the engineer was passing on this cliché as advice about how to act on a boat. Jasper took him literally. He never questioned a single order I gave while aboard.

Jasper has a photographic memory for everything he has ever seen. He could not add or subtract reliably or balance accounts, but he could take apart and put back together any diesel engine, without a manual, even if he had never seen it before. He knew not only what it should look like, but what it must look like.

He had essentially been abandoned as a child to fend for himself. An odd neighbor taught him how to recognize the bark of the Pacific yew tree, which he could cut and sell to a nearby vendor who resold it at great profit to a local pharmaceutical company. Researchers determined in the 1960s that yew trees produce what is now called Taxol—a powerful anticancer drug. He lived for the most part outside of the official economy. He heated his house with a woodstove built out of a discarded oil tank he had retrieved from a junkyard. Jasper used windfalls—trees he found felled by storms near roadsides—for powering the stove. Several times highway workers nearly had him arrested. Eventually they became fond of Jasper and would call him when a really good tree came down.

Jasper was possessed of the oddest charm I had ever known. I used to go regularly to a hardware store near the harbor in Los Angeles. The store had a gigantic sign over the central cash register that read in black block letters DO NOT EVEN THINK OF ASKING TO BORROW ANYTHING. Everyone who worked at this shop was famously rude. One day, as Jasper and I walked through the store, he picked up various items. The employees told him to put things down. Jasper ignored them. Jasper's behavior attracted the attention of every employee, and they gathered about him, watching. The customers—used to the confrontational style of shop employees—also grew acutely aware of the budding strife. I became so uncomfortable with the tension that I walked out of the store, leaving Jasper to suffer the consequences of his actions alone.

Twenty minutes later, he walked out of the shop carrying a gigantic cutting tool, the pride of the store. I immediately considered how far I could distance myself from him before the police arrived. A moment later the meanest of the managers came running out, holding a long length of chain. "Hey, Jasper, you better take this, too, in case you need a longer piece." Somehow Jasper had broken through the icy facades of men that captains and sailors alike had avoided for years. The manager actually told Jasper to keep the tools overnight, and offered him a ride back to the boat. Sourcing tools and hardware is one of the most difficult jobs in a long sea voyage. I realized instinctively that if Jasper came along with us, we would find everything we needed, no matter what.

As if to accentuate the dubious nature of my choice, when Jasper reported for duty the next day, he carried at his side a large, curved, carbon-steel, double-handed Japanese sword (his most expensive and prized possession). Before climbing onto *Valkyrien* Jasper asked my permission to step aboard while carrying a weapon. I looked at him, with as serious an expression as I could muster, and told him that he could, but that it must be stowed immediately. Jasper proceeded to the main mast where he strapped his sheath tight to the base. I asked him why he was tying his scabbard to the mast, and he looked at me, a little confused by my question, and said in deadly sweet earnest: "So that I may defend my captain to the last." In fact, I would be profoundly sorry that Jasper wasn't with me later in the trip when the pirates came.

Oftentimes, in the middle of conversation, if seated, Jasper would lay his head down on top of a table, or if we were standing, he would simply lie down on the floor and shut his eyes. A few moments later he would be snoring, and often a bit of drool would slip out of his mouth, slide over his lower lip, forming a tiny puddle. The first time he did this I thought he was making fun of me for being boring. I realized quickly though, that he had fallen deeply asleep. He might lic still like this for ten minutes, or ten hours. Then, if I were still around when he woke up, he would continue our conversation at the exact point where he had left it. I asked him about his narcolepsy and he said to me genuinely, "What is narcolepsy?" I let it go.

With Jasper now part of the crew, he and I immediately went to work on the masts. We sawed through *Valkyrien's* decks and chopped out huge chunks of rotting wood from the gallery down to the captain's quarters. We rewired the starter and the generator. We got the new GPS installed on deck and made the radar work.

Finally, we prepared to remove the seized engine.

8. *Prop Pullers*

Tell me about despair, yours,
and I will tell you mine.
—MARY OLIVER, *WILD GEESE*

Before we could remove the engine we would
have to disconnect the transmission and slide it
backwards. But the propeller shaft blocked the
transmission from moving aft, and the propeller
blocked the prop shaft from moving aft, so in
order to remove the engine, we first had to take
off the propeller. I felt like the old woman who
swallowed the fly.

In a modern motorboat, where servicing the
engine has been built into the design plan, one
can often open a huge hatch above the engine,
unbolt eight nuts, disconnect some wires and
hoses and a link to the transmission, and then lift
the motor out with a chain. Dropping it back in
place is nearly as simple.

This was not the case with *Valkyrien*. Lifting
the engine meant removing a section of the cabin
roof and then cutting through the floor above the
engine, just to start. Then the engine had to be
disconnected from all of the wires that controlled
it and all of the hoses that fed it. We had to close
off and plug the water-intake hose, then remove

all of the control wires and the fuel and oil lines.

Nowadays, when a large prop is taken off, boats are first lifted out of the water. Two or three men can then work with a front-end loader chained to the prop. Bulldozers and backhoes can pull with thousands of pounds of pressure and keep the bronze screw from damage by hitting the ground when it slips off the shaft. Yard workers on dry land toil together using hammers, propeller pullers, various chains, and even pistons to pull the propeller off the shaft. You may be wondering why is it so damn hard to take a propeller off in the first place. The answer lies in the fact that no one wants a propeller to come off while at sea. When a shipwright installs a propeller, they fasten it in such a way that it is nearly impossible to detach.

The local shipyard would have charged us at least $1,000 just to lift *Valkyrien* out, and much more to remove the propeller and engine. I didn't want to pay that kind of fee, so Jasper convinced the yardmen instead to lend us a hand-operated "prop puller," a vintage contraption cast before World War II, that weighed about eighty-five pounds and was usually operated by two people working in a storage area of the yard. Jasper and I would instead have to manipulate the tool underwater, in scuba gear, to save the $1,000 boat-lifting fee.

Intrepid divers swim year-round in Monterey

wearing heavy wet suits—which makes the water bearable—but the thick neoprene restricts movement and renders any real work underwater at that time of year challenging.

We tied on several life preservers to keep the prop puller from sinking, then spent hours fastening it onto the propeller and shaft, which were the absolute maximum dimensions that this puller could manage. The propeller was 46 inches in diameter, with three blades of solid bronze. Essentially a prop puller works like a pair of scissors: When you pull two ends together on one side, the other side opens wider.

The tolerances for locking the puller in place were within a centimeter, and the eighty-five-pound puller became increasingly difficult for our numbed hands to maneuver. We tightened the puller. Then tightened it again. And again. But the prop did not move.

We worked throughout the afternoon, most of the time submerged, exchanging scuba tanks every hour or so, or kicking over to the pier to swap tools. We worked until our lips became numb and blue and we could no longer move our fingers. Still, we could not get the prop off. We floated a huge sledgehammer, tied to life jackets, over from the pier, to assist the puller. The two steel handles used to turn the nuts on the puller are designed to withstand intense force. By evening, though, we had broken both. The nuts on the puller were more than two inches around, and we had no wrenches even close to that size.

Jasper and I knew we had failed, but we refused to acknowledge our hopelessness. *Valkyrien* had so many old tools aboard, we figured there must be something we could use to turn those huge nuts.

We remembered a gigantic pipe wrench—at least 50 inches long, probably built in Ohio in the 1930s. We could barely lift the wrench, so setting it on the propeller puller was possible only by suspending it in place. We tied the massive wrench to nylon lines from the deck and lowered it down to propeller level, roughly horizontal to the prop shaft.

Now and then a friend would pull us out of the water up onto the dock, and help us waddle up to the men's showers where we would fill the neoprene wet suits with hot water. We needed a landsman to turn on the shower valves because wc wcre afraid of scalding ourselves, as we no longer had the ability to sense water temperature in the showers.

Over and over, we swam back to the dock, waddled up and stood in the men's room hot showers, filling our wet suits with warm water, then hobbled back down the pier and into the cold bay and across the slip to the stern of the boat, then down again to the prop.

Various tools—wrenches, knives, pliers, pincers,

a huge sledgehammer, and the preposterously gigantic pipe wrench—festooned the area around the propeller, dangling from assorted colorful flotation devices, including life rings, foam life preservers, and vests. Our work area darkened as the afternoon wore on, and our dive lights, flashing around as we moved, created an odd, almost whimsical discotheque effect.

The whole while I struggled to hold the precarious apparatus in place, I remained terrified that it would actually work. We had torqued down enormous potential force against the propeller. I knew if it ever slipped free the prop would be launched off the shaft as though fired from a cannon. Eventually, even using long improvised breaker bars, we could tighten the bolts no further, and began hitting the breaker bars with a sledgehammer, over and over, and still it would not move.

As night fell, we were finally on the verge of giving up once and for all. I said to Jasper, "Well, just one more hit."

Using a hammer, we twisted the bolts down just one-eighth of a turn more than we had in the past. Twisting the nuts was a harrowing job because we could sense the enormous force on the propeller, the prop puller, and the shaft, and knew that when the prop finally moved it was going to tear off hard and fast. We figured it would kill either of us if we were in the way.

I had heard stories about prop pullers that had launched propellers straight through the sterns of nearby vessels. Yard workers lost fingers and hands and parts of their shoulders to prop pullers.

I gave the puller one final twist, and bang! I witnessed the loudest underwater noise I had ever heard in my life. I thought for a moment that I had snapped off the stern of the *Valkyrien*, and prepared my head to be struck by fast-sinking debris. But when the bubbles cleared the propeller was gone. *Valkyrien* floated safely and Jasper and I drifted serenely, uninjured. Jasper told me later that the prop had hurled loose like a fighter jet catapulted off the deck of an aircraft carrier.

We slept well that night, and in the morning made an easy dive down, finding the shimmering propeller half-buried in the muck on the bottom of the harbor. I tied the old propeller to a rope and Jasper hauled it up—victorious—to the floating dock.

It was only after staring at the prop on that floating dock that we realized *Valkyrien's* propeller was backwards. It turned counterclockwise, which is the opposite direction that most propellers turn. Left-turning props go only with left-hand engines, which manufacturers make only for boats with twin engines. If dual props spin in the same direction, the boat will tend to turn to the right. The helmsman must then disrupt the turning force by oversteering to the left. The left-turning-engine-and-propeller combo as part of a dual-engine system prevents this.

Back when the Detroit 6V53 was built, a few of the engines were constructed to turn to the left. These would be sold paired with a normal clockwise engine. My guess is that someone tore down an old boat and sold the left-turn engine at a discount to the owner of *Valkyrien*.

We had a hell of a hard time finding a backward-turning 6V53 engine in good-enough shape to justify installing it in *Valkyrien*. We searched the internet, walked through junkyards, and talked with bus companies and every old machine shop we could find. No one had a 6V53 that turned backwards. Finally, we found some sellers in Pennsylvania who had a backward 6V53 in a crate. It had probably come from the US government in a surplus sale and never been used. The negotiation was tricky because the sellers knew we needed a left-turn engine, and we knew that if they did not sell it to us, they would never be able to sell it. We worried and bargained, and in the end we bought the engine.

When we got the "crate" engine replacement out to California, we could not find a GM-certified mechanic who was not booked up for months. We finally located a guy who said he could do the job. Of course it gave me pause that he was apparently the only diesel mechanic in Northern California whom no one would hire, but we needed to get moving.

The new engine was designed to replace any Detroit 6V53, in any application, whether it be a tank, a bus, a backhoe, or a boat. But boat engines are much different on the outside than engines that power land craft. Instead of radiators, older marine engines have a series of components bolted to the side of the engine that use seawater for cooling. There's one system for the engine block, one for engine oil, and a third for transmission oil. We had to remove all of the specialty marine parts and coolers from the broken engine, then attach them to the new engine. Our mechanic had no idea how to do this. Jasper figured it out mostly by instinct.

I asked Jasper how he did it, and he described to me, in a childlike but brilliant way, that the diesel lit on fire and when the fire came, it made a big boom—that was part heat and part boom. And every time we put more diesel in, the heat and the boom had to leave. Jasper explained that we had to attach the pipes in a line so the engine could separate the heat from the boom—otherwise the engine would get too hot. The boom would leave by making the propeller turn, and the heat would leave through the pipes into the ocean.

In the end, Jasper installed all of the key components of the engine, locking everything in place employing huge bolts and pry bars. Jasper used a tiny set of cards to measure precisely how perfectly lined up the transmission was to the engine (it had to be within 1/32 of an inch in a full circle—and Jasper made it so).

Finally, it was time to try to start the engine. The ignition had burned out, so we started the engine by placing the positive and ground battery leads manually onto the starter.

A small group of people (mostly men, out of work) had been toiling on the boat engine to various degrees over the last month or so. They sat in a circle on the floor joists, each looking down at the engine. Communally we held our breath as I touched a screwdriver to jump electricity around the starter solenoid. The starter clicked and threw a wide arcing spark, then began turning hard. I held the screwdriver in place for what seemed like forever—probably around thirty seconds—as the fuel made its way from a plastic tank, through a small fuel pump, and into the injection pump.

Then, sudden but smooth, the engine caught and roared forth. We all cheered. Midwinter had come and we wanted to get out of the North Pacific as soon as possible. We ran the engine for several hours that evening and determined to leave first thing in the morning. The wind had been building all week, and it occurred to me that perhaps I should delay the start of the next phase of our trip.

• • •

I had become depressed over the long days spent working on the engine—so disappointed in myself for missing out on the lives of our children, and for abandoning Vicki to the daily responsibilities of carpool, making dinners, helping with homework, and all that needed tending—but mainly I missed being present in their lives and simply being with them. I wanted to be a father and husband they could count on, and here I was spending my time focused more on this voyage than enjoying their everyday lives. Some days I told myself that Vicki and our children might be having an easier, smoother, less chaotic time without me around, but I knew they missed me and wanted me to come home soon.

Valkyrien baffled me. I had spent so much time away from my family and friends, but I still could not admit to myself, let alone my family, that the voyage simply was not possible. I confided only in Vicki about my misgivings and the decrepit state of *Valkyrien*. For a long while I had been trying to figure out how to cancel the trip altogether.

Vicki and I spoke every few days. She assured me that she and our children were doing well, filling me in on their swim meets and football and basketball games, their weekend activities with friends, laughing when she shared her latest stories about completing her own book about teaching.

Vicki also sensed that I still needed to work on this boat. She understood that I had begun to identify myself—my own value and competency as a person—with the success or failure of this voyage. While she knew this was irrational, she gave me room to try to figure this out on my own. I'm sure Vicki would rather I had quit then and there, but *Valkyrien* had taken on a great deal of meaning to me. I needed the boat far more than the boat needed me. Vicki knew that if I quit then, leaving the boat in Monterey Bay, she would have me back, but that a vital part of me would remain with *Valkyrien* for a long time.

I have a lust for wandering, particularly out on the sea. From our home in Los Angeles we drive along the Pacific Coast Highway every day, and each time we do I stare out at the sea and wonder. Vicki knew that I had to sail *Valkyrien* farther.

9. *Maxey*

*Tell me, what is it you plan to do
with your one wild and precious life?*
—MARY OLIVER, *THE SUMMER DAY*

My son Maxey, who had turned fifteen that September, arrived in Monterey from our home in Los Angeles on the afternoon of the day we got the engine started.

When Maxey was two and a half years old, I would take him out with me on the *Glide*, our family sailboat. When we sailed at night, which was frequent, I would stretch a blanket onto the cockpit sole[3] and lay him down on it, folding the blanket tightly over him. From that vantage he could see the wooden wheel, my right leg up to my knee, and then my face from a steep angle. Above it all was the sky, which on August nights filled with stars and the Perseid meteor shower. When we returned to the mooring in Hyannis Port, I would tie our little dinghy a few hundred yards off the beach and slip into the water.

Maxey would climb down and place his arms around my neck and ride in on my back.

---

3. The floor of the cockpit.

Bioluminescent marine plankton would congregate in the warm harbor waters during summertime. The action of the seawater swirling around my arms and passing across my shoulders excited the microscopic creatures, causing them to emit a blue-green light, which passed from one tiny organism to the next, creating an echo of our path as we wended our way toward shore. We always began the trip with me swimming underwater for two or three strokes, Maxey holding on but completely submerged. He became almost as comfortable in the water as he was on shore.

By the time he was three, Maxey could move anywhere on the sailboat by himself. He would climb up onto the boom, then slide into the bag along the foot of the mainsail and fall asleep in the afternoons as we sailed together. The following year he got in the habit of jumping overboard whenever and wherever we were, as soon as I shouted, "Maxey, jump." (In this way we practiced man-overboard drills, and he became accustomed to going from boat to ocean and back, even in heavy seas.) When Maxey turned seven, he began refusing towels. Drying off in the wind made him tougher. By the time he was ten, Maxey could pull himself into the boat, along the lee rail, in a fairly stiff breeze.

Maxey also loves climbing trees.

Ten years earlier, while visiting the Solomon Islands, I met the two islanders who saved my uncle and his crew after a Japanese destroyer rammed their PT boat during the Second World War. Eroni Kumana, aging and still living in a grass-roofed hut on an isolated island, greeted me at a dock on Gizo, the small island the Japanese had used as a naval base during the war.

Eroni traveled with his son, whom he had named for my uncle Jack. I showed Maxey, who was about five years old at the time, the photographs of Eroni's son climbing a palm tree to retrieve several coconuts for lunch. Maxey loved the picture and asked me dozens of questions about how the young man climbed the tree with no branches and no ladder. He marveled that Eroni's son could swing himself to the top of the tree, holding on only to palm fronds.

"Are they really that strong, Dad?" Maxey asked. I said that they were, as long as you only pulled straight down on them; if you bent them by accident, they would likely break.

A few years later we visited my mother in Florida and Max spent the entire Easter week trying to climb palm trees. About halfway through he asked me how the climbers kept their feet from coming apart. I told him that I recalled Eroni's son wrapping a burlap sack around his feet, in a sort of half knot. I had not realized how essential this was to palm-tree climbing.

Maxey tied a strong towel around his ankles, and soon was able to climb the tall straight palms in South Florida. He used a similar technique later, climbing on the bowsprit of *Valkyrien*, locking his feet together around the arches at the low side of the sprit, as he wriggled outward.

His friends say that Maxey is part fish. I don't know about that, but he is a strong swimmer, and as comfortable on a boat as he is in the water. I missed our children so much, I convinced Vicki to send Maxey up to join me on the boat for the sail along Big Sur. Vicki knew that I needed to share at least a part of this trip with my son. She knew how much Maxey and I loved to sail with one another on the Cape, and that he could handle a turbulent sea. Maxey loved to swim and to climb trees. I put these two loves of his to a severe test off of Big Sur.

I was so excited to see my son and show him *Valkyrien*. I picked him up at the small airport in Monterey. We watched a rather dull sunset— never a good sign before a sea voyage—and then ate fresh fish beside the pier. I fell asleep so happy to have Maxey near to me.

The National Weather Service radio announced storm warnings that night. Maxey and I have sailed in all kinds of weather, so I didn't heed the warnings. I was determined to sail the 77-foot schooner down the 90-mile coast of Big Sur, with my fifteen-year-old son and my wacky friend Jasper as the only crew. We would leave at dawn the following morning.

10. *The Cliffs of Big Sur*

Would it have been worthwhile,
To have bitten off the matter with a smile,
To have squeezed the universe into a ball . . .
—T. S. Eliot, THE LOVE SONG OF
J. ALFRED PRUFROCK

I awoke the next morning, tired, excited, and concerned for the safety of my boat and crew. I knelt down on the floor beside my bunk and said a prayer, asking St. Christopher to protect us and to help me guide the *Valkyrien* safely past the rocks. I walked through the interior of the boat, checking packages and equipment, and generally making ready for the blow coming in. Then I climbed the companionway to the cockpit and walked the deck, looking for anything out of place, trying to make her as shipshape as possible.

The harbor and wharf appeared dark as I marched along the deck, checking lines and halyards. I looked out at the breakwater—difficult to distinguish against the dark sea in front and behind it. The sun had begun to lighten the night sky, but the brightest stars remained visible above the horizon. Twilight is a magical time in a harbor—filled with so much potential—

particularly at the beginning of a trip before a storm, where joy and terror are equal possibilities.

We had not yet raised the sails on *Valkyrien* in a big wind, and I was concerned about how they would do. Modern racing sails are made of woven Kevlar—the same material used to make body armor and military helmets. Older boats' sails are usually made of Dacron or some form of Mylar strips or canvas, sewn together using an especially strong thread and a powerful sewing machine. When they are first "bent on," new sails can be so stiff that it takes a few strong sailors to fold them up properly (called flaking) at the end of a day. *Valkyrien's* sails were so old that they could be twisted in hand like an old bedsheet.

Valkyrien carried a heck of a lot of sails, though. She had one huge mainsail, a smaller second main (also called a main staysail) tacked to the forward mast, and all the way forward on the bowsprit, *Valkyrien* flew as many as four jibs.[4]

---

4. Throughout the United States, and in England, local sailors have their own names for various types of sails. The jiboom (also spelled jib-boom) is variously called the "club jib," the "jib club," or the "staysail." The cables that hold up the mast are called "shrouds" in many places. On Cape Cod we call them "stays." On the Cape, cables chained to the sides of the boat are the "side stays," while the stay at the very bow is called the "forestay," and the one on the back is called

With all sails raised, *Valkyrien* would show a lot of canvas—at least eight separate sails including a main top gallant staysail and a main royal staysail. Maxey knew the names of every sail. Jasper knew the name of not a single sail. The approaching storm would mark Jasper's first day of sailing.

We pushed off the dock as the sun began to lift over the horizon, refracting through the mist from the waves, creating an astonishing orange glow. Whitecaps formed in the harbor, and a small-craft warning was issued. I had been taught to always sail during small-craft warnings on Cape Cod; what better way to prepare oneself for an emergency than to sail intentionally into one? But my need to test myself was less of a motivating factor than my need to begin the journey.

Wind blew strong through the harbor, heeling the boat slightly as we made our way past Fisherman's Wharf toward the harbor mouth. The motor ran well, and the boat moved nicely along, but when I turned the bow into the wind to exit the harbor, I felt the *Valkyrien* slow as she began to slog through the wind and waves.

The first hundred miles of the coast south of Monterey down to Point Conception were the

---

(cont.) a "backstay" (I like the name "backstay," because even people wholly unfamiliar with sailing can quickly grasp the idea of a backstay).

most dangerous we would have to pass in the United States. Sailing off of Big Sur is a dream for every sailor because of its stark beauty—but it also presents a serious danger, because the wind generally blows toward the shore, and every inch of shoreline is either rock or cliff. Big Sur has not a single safe harbor along its entire hundred-mile length. If the boat were to lose power, we would be pushed hard by the wind and waves toward that cliff-rock coast.

I should have waited out the storm.

As I turned west past the Monterey Bay Aquarium, the waves built higher and higher, approaching six feet at Point Cabrillo, but we were still within Monterey Bay, which was protected from the full strength of the Pacific wind. The swells continued to build as we moved out toward open ocean, although they were farther apart. Before we passed Point Pinos, the largest waves stood at about the height of our mast spreaders—twenty feet above the sea, and growing larger.

Maxey pulled up the main and then the second mainsail, and then the smallest jib. I turned the *Valkyrien* south, and as the sails began to fill with air, she picked up speed. We cruised amid swells gigantic beyond any I had ever sailed. The waves towered over our spreaders, and we began to lose our wind at the bottom of the troughs. The big Pacific rollers were topped by five- and six-foot wind waves that broke and sprayed white and black as we cut along.

Suddenly, a powerful gust laid the boat hard over on her side. The wave behind us pushed us forward, sliding down its face. For a moment, as we skidded into the trough of this gigantic wave, no wind hit us at all, and *Valkyrien's* four tons of lead, bolted to the bottom of her keel, bounced us straight back up like a child's inflatable punching toy. But just at the moment the boat caught equilibrium, another gust hit us as we rose atop the next giant roller.

Bang!

The mainsail tore in half, and then the halves shredded into more pieces—all of the tatters snapping back and forth like a cowboy's whip. I shouted to my son, but he could hear nothing over the roar of the torn sail. He moved toward the first mast to try to pull down the remnants. Just as he reached the main, the second main tore as well. It ripped first, separating a seam with a loud zipping sound, then shredded.

We had lost the mainsail, and the second main, and we were being pushed inland by wind and waves. I retained confidence in the smallest jib—extraordinarily heavy, and a perfect storm jib—and it kept its shape. But with only a single sail, and that one way out in front, the boat was pulled hard downwind toward the cliffs onshore. To counterbalance that pressure up front, I turned the boat back and forth, shifting between a straight rudder and hard to starboard.

I thanked God for the new engine. Despite the wind and waves, and lack of sails, that brand new Detroit saved us, giving the boat enough forward momentum, and adding just enough pressure against the rudder, to hold us off the rocks onshore. We could not move much farther out to sea, but we were not being pushed closer to shore, either. We rode a delicate line, and I knew as long as the engine held, we would make it south to the sandy beaches below the rocks of Big Sur.

The waves grew even larger as we were pushed south. *Valkyrien* raced down the sides of these waves, the increased speed causing her to turn back up into the wind. I had to spin the wheel quite madly in various directions, trying to maintain a semblance of a straight course while avoiding the push of the waves toward the rocks.

In the midst of my steering woes, the engine, tossed so many different ways, conked out. Some connection in that long fuel hose had moved and caught air and the engine was done. I realized, with increasing despair, that we could not possibly chase down an air bubble lost in seventy feet of hose, amid that storm.

Maxey pulled down the shredded main and tied its remnants to the boom. Then he moved forward to the second main, and did the same, his face and body whipped by the shorn bits of Dacron. He stayed at the job and got the sail tied down.

On one big wave, I failed to correct sufficiently and we swung hard toward the wind. Our stern was hit by the following wave, which washed over the boat. My son looked up at me as though I had lost my mind and shouted, using his hands and mouthing the words: "DAD! WHY . . . ARE . . . YOU . . . DRIVING . . . SO . . . BADLY?!"

I held up the *Valkyrien's* bronze steering wheel, which had torn completely off of the steering shaft and slipped into my hands. With no mainsails, no engine, and now no steering wheel, we had lost control of the boat.

Although not a sailor, Jasper grasped the gravity of the situation immediately. He looked at the waves and the cliffs of Big Sur and down at the busted-off steering wheel, and without a word, he disappeared below.

Well, that's unfortunate, I thought. I could use a hand up here.

A minute or two later, Jasper came running back up with the largest vise-grip I had ever seen. Also a can of WD-40. The vise-grip was badly corroded, but Jasper loosened it with the WD and mounted it hard onto the steering shaft. With one hand atop the vise-grip and the other helping to hold it in place, I was able to turn the shaft and make minimal adjustments to our course.

We were still being pushed toward the rocky cliffs onshore, and Maxey and I both understood, without saying anything to each other, that the fix on the steering wheel had bought us time, but that unless we could put sails up enough to jibe the boat, we were going to crash against the rocks.

11. *High Seas*

I will drink
Life to the lees
—ALFRED, LORD TENNYSON, *ULYSSES*

If I did not yet fear for our lives, I had great concern that the boat would not survive the day.

Maxey came to the cockpit to talk to me. Together, we looked at the wind, the waves, and the shoreline. Maxey said, "Do you think she could make it around the point if we could get her turned around?"

"I think she could hold it—but not by much," I replied. "And if we continue much longer on this angle, she will not be able to claw it back, even if we do get her turned. The only way we can save *Valkyrien* is to pull up at least two more jibs."

My son and I both knew what this meant: I had put his life and the life of my wholly innocent friend Jasper in jeopardy. Maxey knew who he was dealing with. He was not surprised that I had sailed with him into the storm. But he was upset that I had brought along Jasper, who had no way of knowing the risks I would take.

Maxey had learned sailing through years of training, but he also had a visceral understanding of sails and lines and wood—all the mechanisms of sail—so he understood immediately what had to be done to save the *Valkyrien*. Simply put, someone would have to crawl out to the end of the bowsprit, attach the halyards, and release the ties on two more jibs. The widow's net that stretched beneath the bowsprit would likely catch him, if he fell, but he could easily be swept out of that netting.

At this point, the *Valkyrien* had become a very wet boat. She rode up these gigantic waves and when she reached their peak, the entire front of the boat thrust into space horizontally—so far out, in fact, that I worried her spine might snap.

I recalled the American cruiser, the *USS Pittsburgh*. Caught in a Pacific storm, *Pittsburgh's* bow jutted out beyond the crest of the waves and literally fell into the sea. The heavy cruiser became forty feet shorter in an instant. The *Pittsburgh* cruised through the storm, with no lives lost. She had been designed for battle survivability, with waterproof bulkheads. Her well-trained crew and gutsy captain brought her safely home.

I did not have the same faith in *Valkyrien's* design tolerances in her current condition. I thought of how long she'd been sitting in that polluted waterway, and the age of her timbers, and I wondered how much rot decayed her keel. I thought of the pressure of the masts, so many thousands of pounds, driving down into her and working her seams further open with every crash of the waves.

Her physical condition notwithstanding, my main concern at that moment was how, exactly, to get to the bowsprit to raise the other jibs. Every time *Valkyrien* crested a wave and shot down the other side, her entire bow disappeared underwater, driven deep into the next wave. The balustrade, a few feet high around the foremast, disappeared below the sea when she fell down the biggest waves—nearly forty feet of *Valkyrien*, over and over, with each wave, dissapeared— completely submerged. I turned and checked on our last resort—the trusty old Boston Whaler Montauk. We had purchased a brand new engine for the Whaler, and I remained confident that if we had to abandon ship, she would be able to carry us safely through the enormous waves, even with the high winds atop them.

But I was by no means certain.

Towing a dinghy in a storm can be a terrible mistake. I have many friends who have simply cut away their dinghy midway through a long storm. These boats, dragging behind, can be lifted high up a following wave, then race down the wave face like a mad surfboard to come crashing hard into the stern of the pulling boat, slowly smashing the two vessels to pieces.

Before we left port I had tied a bridle with two

bowline knots around the stern of the Whaler. Then I'd passed a heavy ship's line in another bowline around the bridle and tied some big knots and a life jacket onto the heavy line. The idea was that the heavy line with the knots would create drag (like the tail on a kite), which would slow the Whaler enough as it raced down the waves that it would not strike our stern. The bridle rig would keep the trailing line in the center of the Whaler, which theoretically would keep it riding straight.

Other friends have had dinghies flip and dive; their bow, turned sideways, dips below the water, then the overturned dink dives down like a fishing lure. The dragging line then becomes so taut that it actually "sings," vibrating like a plucked violin string.

If either occurred, we would lose our emergency boat.

The towline from *Valkyrien* that held the Whaler was two inches thick, nearly two hundred feet long, and absolutely taut. Most of the time I could not see the Whaler at all—just the rigid towline slicing and disappearing into a gigantic wave behind us. When we arrived at the bottom of a wave, invariably I would see the Whaler cresting the wave behind us. Then, the little fiberglass boat would drop toward us, skipping and skimming along, barely touching the water on the steep wave face.

I figured we could probably escape death on the Boston Whaler—but the only way we could save *Valkyrien* would be to raise the sails on the bowsprit. I knew that Maxey was the only person on board who could climb out on the bowsprit and untie those sails so they could be raised. In these conditions, I was the only one who could steer the boat by holding the vise-grip.

The waves tossed the boat about, threw us on our sides and often buried nearly the entire boat underwater. Keeping her from being utterly swamped had become a tricky business.

I asked Maxey if he thought Jasper could make it out on the bowsprit.

Maxey replied with strength: "No way, Dad."

"Maxey, will you do this?"

"I don't think I can, Dad."

"I know you can do it. This is the hardest, the toughest thing I have ever asked of you. There are a very few people in this world who could save this boat now, but you can."

The humongous waves lifted *Valkyrien's* stern crazily high out of the water as the bow dove in. Both of us were wondering the same thing: What would it be like out at the end of that bowsprit during the long moments when the entire sprit plunged below the ocean's roiling surface?

I looked at my son and thought about how much I loved him. Maxey's green eyes looked stunningly handsome in the wind and waves.

His hair, soaking wet, flashed around his head. I knew he had never been stronger. And he could keep his head in a storm. But I was terrified for him. I also felt though a huge satisfaction that my son would receive this test. I truly believed that he was in no danger—Maxey would not fall into the sea, and even if he did, he could tread water in those waves until I pulled him out. I was glad that tomorrow my son would wake up and know that he was capable of doing things that most men could not do. It scares the hell out of me now that I thought this way then.

We watched several cycles of the waves, and practiced holding our breath from the time the bowsprit disappeared below the water, until it came flashing out again. These were very long periods. Tears came into my son's eyes. He looked at me with anger.

"Dad, how could you put us in this position?"

I looked at him, unable to answer.

"Dad, how can you ask your own son to do this?"

"I don't know Max. I am sorry. I do not know why I do things like this. But I have done them my whole life, and it will not end here."

I paused for a long moment, looking my son straight in the eyes, my heart bursting with love for my brave and clear-headed boy.

"Max, you have to go out there," I said. I pointed at the end of the bowsprit, as it dove again into the sea. "I need you to go out there and ready those sails."

Maxey looked at me once more, hard this time. Then he turned and faced the waves towering over us.

He took off his life jacket and threw it below. We both knew it would only get in the way. Then he crawled out along the deck. He took a deep breath while holding on to the forward mast, watching the water race across his knees. Then, as the boat began climbing and the bowsprit lifted out of the water, he made his way forward, using the stays and sheets as hand holds.

I watched Maxey knowing that he would surmount all of this.

Looking back now I am horrified that I sent my son on such an errand. I have never asked Maxey to do something that I would not readily do myself. But I do not wish him to do all of the things I am willing to try. And I am glad now that I have passed beyond the asking.

Maxey leaned down, then straddled the bowsprit. He tightened his legs around it and tensed his thighs, then stretched his arms over the sprit and locked his fists below it. I saw him lift his head and take a giant breath as the bowsprit dove into the water and disappeared with him on it.

I held my breath with him, as he disappeared under the water. I counted slowly to myself: 1-2-3-4-5-6-7 . . . It felt like a full minute, but was probably closer to fifteen seconds before I saw him again, still clinging to the bowsprit as it lifted up and out of the water. I saw Maxey take a quick breath, then shimmy his way farther out toward the end. He grabbed another breath before plunging once again into the green and black water, vanishing below a lion's mane of frothy white.

Again I counted and watched. I checked my knife. If Maxey fell in, I would cut the towline and jump into the water. Theoretically he would rise up somewhere quite close to me, and we could then follow the towline to the Whaler and climb aboard. After we got the Whaler going we would pull close to *Valkyrien* and convince Jasper to jump overboard.

It wasn't a very good backup plan and it was our ONLY backup plan. I hoped to hell we wouldn't need to try it.

Maxey made it out to the first jib, then smartly climbed beyond it to the furthest sail. He knew we would need at least two jibs and that the first one, when up, would block his retreat.

To raise the outermost jib Maxey needed to release the halyard clipped to an eye on the bowsprit, then lift it up to the head of the jib and clip it back on. This would almost certainly require the use of both hands, and he would need to be submerged several times just to get the halyard clipped on. Even with the halyard on, his job was only half done. He would then have to shimmy back down along the bowsprit and release the sail ties holding the jib. The knots we used on the ties were designed to be released with one hand, but Maxey carried a knife just in case.

I watched as he climbed out and over the first jib, then, gripping the bowsprit with his thighs and feet locked, he unclipped the halyard. As *Valkyrien* lifted atop a wave, Maxey deftly locked the halyard down to the top of the sail. Then he shimmied his body in reverse, pulling off sail ties as he slid backwards.

With each tie that he removed, the jib began to rise more freely and whip back and forth with a sharp towel-snapping sound, striking him on the top of his head and across his shoulders. To protect his face, Maxey kept his head buried in the parts of the sail that were still tied. Unable to see, he moved only by feel, taking a gulp of air whenever he sensed the tip of the bowsprit going under.

I could feel Maxey's powerful determination as he strained to lock his elbows and knees tight to the bowsprit, his forehead down, dragging along the wood. He slithered aft around the inner forestay and deftly clipped on the number-two jib, then released its ties and inched back to the bow. The bow, which had at first seemed an absolutely terrifying place as it dove below the sea into each trough, two or three feet deep below water running down the decks, now seemed as safe as home base. Scuttling along the deck to the foremast, Maxey quickly pulled each jib the last of the way up, cleating off the halyards to the belaying pins on the fife rails.[5]

The change in *Valkyrien's* attitude was immediate. She began to respond to my steering. As *Valkyrien* lifted atop a huge wave I turned the vise-grip over and over, to port. *Valkyrien's* wheel took eight and a half turns to move the rudder from full starboard (all the way to the right) to full port (all the way to the left).

The huge schooner, flowing down the wave with her forward sails all full, obeyed her rudder and turned slowly to the left, finally coming through the wind and back into the waves. We slogged our way, slowly, lumbering back toward Monterey. We made it around Point Lobos and soon after, I began to catch glimpses of the green fairways at Pebble Beach above the rocks.

The seas calmed only a little as the afternoon wore on, but I knew we would make it back. I

---

5. *Halyards* are the ropes that run up and down the mast and are used to raise or lower the sails. The *fife rail* is a sort of tiny balcony that wraps around the base of the mast. The balcony rail is holed every five inches or so, and a wooden peg, called a *belaying pin*, is stuck in each hole. The pins are used to tie the halyards in place.

sent Jasper below to run the bilge pumps and try to figure out how to get the engine operating again.

I had wanted Maxey to see Big Sur from the sea. I had also wanted my son to experience the dangerous side of sailing. Most fathers seek to protect their children from unsafe conditions, but I consistently put my son in harm's way. At the time I thought the experience completely worthwhile, formative, instructive, and reasonable.

Now, though, sometimes at night, just before I fall asleep, I think of Maxey struggling on the end of the bowsprit to save a decrepit boat, and my body shudders. I fear the side of me that forced him.

12. *Experiential Sailing*

I want to run away . . .
and I want to stay. Amen.
—FROM "THE HYMN OF JESUS" IN THE
ACTS OF JOHN

Darkness came early that time of year, and we sailed downwind into Monterey Bay in falling light. As the seas flattened out inside the Bay, Jasper got the motor running, and I drove *Valkyrien* into the flat water between the break-walls. Maxey brought the jibs down and tied them well, and I turned the boat back toward the marina.

We were tired and cold and fairly miserable, but glad to be alive and on a floating boat. I gave her a fair amount of throttle as I prepared to make the left turn to the dock. But when I turned the vise-grip to the left, I heard the sharper sound of metal against metal, and the pressure came completely off of the rudder. *Valkyrien* did not turn at all.

I pulled the throttle back to neutral, then slipped it into reverse, with the prop still spinning forward. *Valkyrien* was making nearly 6 knots, and headed straight toward the eastern breakwater. And she would not turn!

Maxey looked up at me as though I had lost my mind. I leaned down and tore the cover off the gearbox, exposing the worm gear, which torques the rudder to either side. The black disc and screw looked almost brand-new, with thick grease covering everything. I spun the wheel back and forth and everything seemed fine, except that when I got to the halfway point, all of the tension came off the rig.

It took me a minute to realize that the arm on the right side (the arm that pulls the rudder to the right) had come unbolted. The bolt was a full inch and a half thick, and had fallen into *Valkyrien's* bilge, submerged below the worm drive. If I could not get the bolt back in place, I would not be able to turn *Valkyrien* left, and we would hit the breakwater.

I reached down but could not get my fingers to the bolt. I struggled further and smushed the side of my face against the thick grease on the edge of the worm. My fingertips brushed the bolt, but I could not pick it up. We raced on toward the breakwater and I shouted to Jasper. He rushed up with a huge screwdriver, which I jammed into the bolt holes, temporarily attaching the arm to the rudder post, and turned the wheel hard over.

The rudder responded, but *Valkyrien* was not turning quickly enough. Because the propeller was spinning in reverse, it was removing water pressure from the rudder that normally causes the boat to turn. We were continuing on straight toward the rock wall.

The only way to get the boat to turn away from the wall was to give her full forward throttle. But by this time we were only a boat length or so from the rocks. It would be a very risky maneuver to accelerate the huge schooner directly toward the break wall. Especially when the boat was refusing to turn. If I did not floor it, *Valkyrien* would certainly hit the rocks. If I floored it and she made the turn, she would be fine, but if I floored it and she did not turn quite enough, she would be totaled.

I grabbed the throttle and floored it—full force forward—headed straight at the rocks. For the third time that day, Maxey looked at me as though I had lost my mind.

For a long moment she did not turn. But as she gained velocity, the water pressure against the rudder slowly forced the stern away and the boat began to change her path. We slid past the break wall, so close we could clearly see the submerged rocks only inches below *Valkyrien's* side. We passed by, unscathed.

That night we tied up to the dock back at Breakwater Cove Marina. My friend and colleague from The *Pearl* Coalition, Bob Nixon, stood waiting at the end of the pier, grinning, wearing his trademark green sweatshirt and yellow Camp

David hat and shaking his head. I had called Bob on the cell phone to give him an accounting of our trip thus far. Nixon had been filming a shark show in San Francisco. He rented a car and drove straight down Route 101 to see us.

I teased him, asking if he was visiting friends in need or merely checking on his investment. Bob had rented a hotel room, which we shared that night with Maxey. All of us slept well.

Nixon is my oldest friend and the finest story-teller I have ever known. Bob left school to study falconry under the legendary British falconer Phillip Glasier, and later convinced me to become a master falconer. Bob makes environ-mental documentary films, and has won six Emmys and been nominated for an Oscar. Bob is a true adventurer. He has made films in the most uncomfortable deserts, jungles, war zones, and urban environments around the world. He worked on several films with the legendary primatologist Dian Fossey. Dian agreed to give Bob the rights to make a film about her life, but instead of money, she made Bob promise to spend a year of his life doing conservation "on the ground."

Bob coproduced the movie *Gorillas in the Mist*, Dian's life story, and a few months after its release Bob moved to Washington, DC, to build a grassroots environmental group to clean up the Anacostia River. Bob committed to spend a full year in Anacostia, that was more than twenty-five years ago, and he is still there. The Anacostia flows through the poorest neighborhood in the nation's capital, and was perhaps the most polluted river in America. He worked with about twenty young people from Anacostia each year. During the first ten years, twelve of his volunteers were murdered in drug- and gang-related violence. But alongside Bob, the team continued to work, and pulled more than seven thousand tires out of the river. Together, they began the long and often frustrating process of cleaning up a neighborhood and changing their lives.

Bob learned the story of the *Pearl* from residents in Anacostia. He became involved and enticed me in. Five years later, we found ourselves on the end of a wharf on a stormy winter night in Monterey Bay.

For some reason, my unconscious mind brings songs and poetry into my head that reflects my thoughts, feelings, and concerns. When I was a child my brothers and sisters and I were forced to memorize a poem or present a biography each Sunday night. I retain bits of some of these poems, which come out now and then to let me know what I have been thinking. If I'm missing someone, I may notice that I have been humming "Oh My Darling, Clementine." On darker days, words from Hamlet's first soliloquy come up fairly often ("Or that the Everlasting had not fixed his canon 'gainst self-slaughter").

I noticed that the night before departing on a trip, that I was humming the second phrase from the old Roy Rogers song, "Happy Trails" ("Until we meet again"). Most of the time I don't catch it; a tune or some words will come into my head, and move off as softly as they appeared.

That dark night in Monterey Bay, as the rain pelted down, I kept finding myself humming Louis Armstrong: "Don't know why, there's no sun up in the sky . . . stormy weather."

The following day, the marina authorities asked us to move to a slip. We spent only one night in that docking space. The marina had built beautiful slips, much more rugged than the wooden docks we were used to on Cape Cod. Sixty-foot slabs of reinforced concrete formed the sides of each berth. Iron cleats, each more than a foot long, were sunk into each corner of the slip.

The only available spot was the berth that lay closest to shore, just on the edge of a steep subsurface hillside. The depth reduced sharply, from about 26 feet in the marina to nine feet deep on the outside of the slip, and only two to three feet deep on the inside at low tide. I worried that in an extreme low tide *Valkyrien* would lay aground even inside the slip. The marina authorities assured me though, that the slip could more than handle her draft.

At the time I thought the worst thing about the slip was the danger of running aground while landing. *Valkyrien* drew around eight feet, and she would be only a few feet from a hard grounding at all times while berthed there. To my surprise, entering turned out to be the safest thing about this slip. The unusually steep grade, combined with the Pacific swells that made their way into the harbor, made for a surprisingly dangerous evening.

We tied up with some of our strongest two-inch lines about an hour before the tide turned at dead low. I asked Jasper to climb to the top of the mast to check one more time for rot and to make sure that all of the halyards were running easily through the blocks. He put on his harness and tied his knife to the outside of his belt. I had never spent time with someone who not only always carried a sharp fighting knife, but also kept it at the ready. Jasper found constant uses for his blade.

Of course, I was concerned as hell about him climbing up the mast after all of the stresses we had put on the boat the day before, but Jasper was certain it would be fine. When he got about three-quarters of the way to the top, though, the tide switched direction.

The boat keel rested only a couple of feet above the seafloor, and at that moment of tide and current change a sharp wind blew in, led by a gigantic swell. The shape of the breakwaters actually steered the swell directly toward the beach behind *Valkyrien*. As the first line of swell passed below us, it lifted the floating dock, and *Valkyrien*, and as the wave met the topographical rise on the seafloor, it stood up tall, turning *Valkyrien* almost on her side.

The mast, with Jasper near the top, leaned over so far on its side that Jasper swung out and dangled over the top of the boom of a different boat, berthed beside us! As the wave passed, *Valkyrien's* lead keel righted her quickly, catapulting Jasper out in the other direction.

The huge lines holding *Valkyrien* to the dock tore at their cleats. The bowline, with a breaking strength of well over ten thousand pounds, tore apart, snapping loudly. The two pieces slingshot in opposite directions.

Valkyrien turned her hull first to the right, then back to the left, like Gulliver, tearing his bonds when he first awoke, surprised. She pulled the gigantic cleats out of the reinforced concrete. The cleats, ripped from their mountings, clattered across the little pier, then swung, striking the side of *Valkyrien* as she leaned the other way. She rolled back then, and another shrug, sundering the concrete floating dock on the opposite side of her slip.

I looked up at Jasper, horrified. I thought the mast would snap and he would fall thirty feet onto the boom and deck of the neighboring vessel. Instead, just as the *Valkyrien* spun across centerline, Jasper released the halyard holding him up and dropped to about eight feet off the deck. He gripped the line hard then, stopping himself with one bounce. Jasper reached his right hand across his stomach and in a smooth motion, grabbed his knife in midair, flipped it open with a snap of his wrist, and deftly cut the line holding him to the mast.

Jasper fell hard to the deck, landing on his back. He tumbled across the deck, and suddenly, almost like a cartoon character freed from gravity, he jumped nimbly to his feet and leapt down to the concrete dock. Jasper is strong and stocky. I knew he was capable of feats of great strength, but he is not elegant. I will never forget that moment. Jasper achieved one of the most graceful performances of athleticism under pressure I have ever witnessed.

When he looked up and saw the genuine concern and absolute admiration in Maxey's eyes and my own, Jasper seemed embarrassed.

That first night in the slip, a gale blew in and brought with it a storm of rain, lightning, and sharp thunder. We moved quickly to tie *Valkyrien* with longer lines around nearby pilings rather than the cleats. It raged all night, as we took turns on watch through the darkness, making adjustments to the lines as the tide came in or the wind changed direction.

All of us, including Bob, found it an exhausting night. I called Vicki from the marina and told her about the storm. It was difficult to impart the sheer fright we felt when we all thought Jasper was going to die, falling from the mast—and that somehow this nighttime storm was almost worse than the wild day at sea. I kept imagining the *Valkyrien* breaking free of the slip and absolutely crushing the relatively puny fiberglass boats crowded in narrow berths all around her.

I felt two distinct forms of fear in those days. The first occurred more rarely, but was absolutely raw, cutting through my skin—the fear of harming my son or my crew. I rarely consciously worried for my own safety back then. The second type of fear was more insidious, and it was related to my fear for the *Valkyrien's* safety. Despite her nearly dilapidated state I had become so involved—mentally, physically, and spiritually—in the endeavor that I began to weigh danger differently. I took risks to get *Valkyrien* south that I would not take today.

I had invested all of myself in this voyage. Imagine driving an old Ford along a beautiful mountain road, to your mother-in-law's home, with your children in the backseat. Snow begins to fall, and becomes a blizzard. At some point you realize driving is too dangerous, so you pull over somewhere safe to wait out the storm. Perhaps if you'd known a storm was coming, you would have canceled the trip, or waited until the roads were cleared before you would pass.

Sailing a long way in an old boat is a lot like driving a car amid a snowstorm. The competency of the captain or the driver makes a huge difference—up to a point. When a storm grows too big, there is little or nothing a captain can do to save a ship; you simply have to stay in port or you are risking too much. The captain's trust is to weigh the chances and the consequences and in the end, bring his boat and his crew safely to their destination.

While in port I constantly ran through various scenarios in my head, trying to determine whether to sail, or wait it out. And when sailing I spent much of my days figuring out when we should return to port. I had much less confidence in my decision-making on these matters than did my wife. I was afraid that I had placed so much importance on completing the trip that I would make a mistake and sail when I should have stayed in port.

Vicki knew what I did not: that as a person—a father and a husband—my value was in no way connected to *Valkyrien*. Vicki never mentioned this to me—I would not have had any idea what she was talking about in any case. It is so funny to me how problems that are desperately complex and unfathomable to me are understood with complete clarity by my wife and dearest friends.

So often after getting through an ordeal they point out the obvious—and I say, "Well, why didn't you just tell me this in the first place?" They all laugh. My friends know that we could avoid a lot of angst and heartache if I could learn these lessons by reading or thinking or being told, rather than experiencing.

It is my very fortunate lot in life to have gained a wealth of experiential learning. Not all of my friends are as enthusiastic about sharing this form of education with me. A few no longer like to go sailing when it is raining.

13. *Kevin*

Half a league onward.
—ALFRED, LORD TENNYSON, *THE CHARGE OF THE LIGHT BRIGADE*

Maxey flew home at the end of the long weekend. Nixon returned to his filming. I missed them both immediately. *Valkyrien* was hurting after the storm. Jasper and I made repairs to her, squeezing Loctite on every bolt we could find. During a break, I called my friend Kevin Ward and asked him to come out to join us.

Kevin is a disruptor. He graduated with honors from Harvard despite being kicked out of boarding school. In addition to English, he speaks Farsi and Arabic. He's done many things in his life and is one of the finest thinkers I know, but despite—or maybe because of this—he is rarely employed, at least in traditional ways. So I was not surprised that he jumped in his old Subaru, drove to the Denver airport, and took the next plane out to Monterey.

We set sail off of Big Sur the following daybreak, an epic California winter morning of clear blue, cloudless sky, and were carried by a gentle breeze over smoothly rolling swells and barely cresting waves along the cliffs, sailing easily through to the following night.

That evening, a school of dolphins swam in to play in our bow wave. Their darting excited the bioluminescent plankton, which marked their paths in streams of green light. Bioluminescence in the Pacific can be so bright that the fighter pilots during World War II used the green light trails left by navy fleets to find their way back to their aircraft carriers after nighttime raids. PT boats, in enemy waters, rode with only a single one of their three engines running to reduce the signature of the bioluminescence that lit them up as targets for the predatory Japanese destroyers.

We sailed that night amid a quiet storm of underwater sparklers and fireworks, all various shades of luminous green. And I thought of those days when my son was younger, and he would swim in from the mooring with me, at night, watching the tiny blue-green creatures quietly light the sea around us.

I was glad to have Kevin spell me at the wheel of *Valkyrien*, but concerned by his usual blasé attitude. Kevin's demeanor suggested tranquilizers more than mere tranquility. At first I thought he had gotten high. I knew that the throttle-control cable on *Valkyrien* was wound a bit too tight (we had installed it ourselves, and the cable ended up being a little too long, as a consequence of which the skipper had to lean forward uncomfortably, holding the throttle in place for hours on end). Then I noticed that he had tied down the throttle into position with a white ribbon.

No matter how convenient it might seem to him, I couldn't countenance the danger and un-seamanly nature of his laziness, so I told Kevin to remove the ribbon immediately. He did so reluctantly, although being the rascal he is, he would later surreptitiously replace the ribbon with a thin strand of nearly transparent monofilament fishing line.

Later that evening I took down the sails as we prepared to enter Morro Bay. I climbed below and removed the ladder to gain access to the engine compartment. I had by then gotten rid of the hot-wiring system of starting the engine and replaced it with a starter solenoid. But the mechanism for exciting the solenoid had quickly burned out, so the solenoid, which manages the starter, had to be powered up by hand. I had rigged two twelve-gauge wires to this new starter mechanism. By touching them together, they closed the circuit to the solenoid, which in turn closed the circuit to the batteries and engaged the starter. It was almost as easy as using a key, but had the advantage of forcing the captain or crew to open the engine compartment and always look at the engine and fuel filters when starting the engine. It certainly made me much more aware of the mechanics inside the engine room.

Unfortunately, though, this arrangement left me quite blind to what was happening on deck and in the cockpit at the moment the starter engaged.

That evening, the engine started right up but made a terrible screaming sound. I leapt up the companionway (climbing along the side walls because I had removed the ladder) and lunged into the cockpit. I shifted the throttle as far as it would go, reducing the flow of fuel to what I thought was a bare minimum, but the engine continued to make a horrible screaming sound, and when I looked at our stern, a huge cloud of dark, nearly black smoke obscured the aft deck. (I did not see the fishing line Kevin had tied to the throttle, which kept the fuel flowing at cruising speed.)

Horrified, I jumped back below and climbed over the engine to shut it off manually. I knew that the black smoke meant the diesel fuel was not being fully combusted, and with almost no fuel running through the engine (or so I thought), I knew somehow something awful had gone wrong again.

I went through the fuel lines section by section. We checked each fuel tank and all of the oil levels. We changed all of the fuel and oil filters. We checked the coolant levels and the raw-water intake hoses. I was reluctant to run the engine a second time, lest we do more damage, but everything seemed fine, so I touched the ignition wires and the engine started screaming immediately, pouring out more black smoke.

At that point, I became almost wholly despondent. A flash of so many of the things that had gone wrong with *Valkyrien* over the last few months ran through my mind—tearing the sails, the steering wheel falling off, the engine burning out, pulling the propeller, the boat boys quitting in frustration, and the ever-present leaking. For a few moments I felt utterly defeated.

But I was the captain of a vessel at sea, so I dealt with the situation at hand. We raised the sails back up and sailed into Morro Bay, coasting up to a mooring far out at the edge of the mooring field. I hated to pay the enormous cost of a diesel mechanic, but could find no other option. I found a fellow who was willing to come out, at a four-hour minimum fee. We waited two days for him. When he finally arrived, before starting the engine, he went through the fuel system as we had, checking all of the fluids and hoses. Everything seemed fine.

He was a bit thrown off by our ignition system, but said that our ragout of hot wires culminating near the starter could not cause the black-smoke problem. Then he started the engine and looked genuinely shocked at the grating scream of the diesel. He rushed up to the cockpit, stared at the horrendous black cloud forming, and shouted at me to shut it down immediately. He stood there, dumbfounded.

After thinking things through, he checked the exhaust pipes and the outflow while I swam down with a scuba mask to the through-hull pipes, where cooling water entered the boat, to check for blockage. Everything seemed fine.

Finally, the mechanic climbed up to the cockpit and joined us. He looked as puzzled as we looked sad and distressed. We could not afford to buy another new engine. The next level of trouble-shooting—which would require taking the engine apart—would be difficult, time-consuming, and expensive.

I looked at the mechanic, who was staring intently at the throttle. He leaned forward and reached out slowly. His eyes had caught the glint of fishing line, holding the throttle in the open position. He snapped the line off, with no small measure of violence, and pulled the throttle down an additional inch.

We started the engine again. It sounded per-fect. No more black smoke. No more hideous shrieking.

I looked at Kevin, severely irritated. He stared back at me. We glared at each other for about thirty seconds, then we burst out laughing. Kevin and I have been camping together since we were teenagers. Both of us had made so many ridiculous mistakes in our lives that this one, in the scheme of things, was not even worth more than a sideways glance.

I remain loyal to old friends essentially no matter what they do.

We can be pissed off at each other, or even angry, or despondent . . . it does not really matter. We're stuck with each other, and we will be friends forever.

14. *Into Stranger Waters*

As though to breathe were life.
—ALFRED, LORD TENNYSON, *ULYSSES*

Kevin, Jasper, and I set off again that afternoon, sailing past Point Conception in a light breeze, flying six sails. We cruised lazily along the Santa Barbara Channel off the straight coast of California, slipping past Platform A, which in 1969 caused what was then the worst oil spill in American history. The oil rig had been painted light blue, sprouting with cranes and lifting booms, and looked like a gigantic prehistoric water bug, consuming something just below the surface. Anacapa and California's Northern Channel Islands hung low on the horizon to our right, and we sailed by Carpinteria, Ventura, and Oxnard on our way to Malibu.

Sailing in New England, shoals abound, and the terrain varies almost from mile to mile. The entire bottom of the ocean from the beaches out three hundred miles to Georges Bank was, not so long ago in geologic time, dry land. The Laurentide Ice Sheet covered New England in ice two miles thick. For eighty thousand years the ice pressed against the continent, forcing the edge down. When the ice receded, the sea flooded in. The actual New England coast is three hundred miles out at sea; that is where the continent ends. And the sailing there is so excellent in part because the terrain and views change constantly, as though one is off-roading in a jeep. Along Cape Cod, just on an afternoon sail, you could depart outside of a kettle pond and into an inland waterway not unlike Florida's coast, past a stream, then through an inlet protected by a breakwater and a barrier beach, then around a series of shoals out past giant boulders to a rock ledge—and that is just the first five miles. Sailing in New England never requires a purpose. Useless curiosity and courage are at the heart of cruising, especially in New England.

Southern California, relatively speaking, has almost nothing to offer the casual cruiser. The continental shelf is often within a few miles of shore. When sailing south, if you look to your left, you see an unbroken white line of surfing beach, and to the right is open ocean—unbroken for two thousand miles. If you stay twenty-five miles out, there is virtually nothing to hit except some other boat. Cruising southern California requires a destination.

We cruised close to the shore along Zuma Beach and around Point Dume and Paradise Beach and the Malibu Pier, looking at the beach houses through our binoculars. The wind blew steady at just below 10 knots. *Valkyrien* passed by Santa Monica Canyon and the pier at Venice. We dropped the sails and pulled in beside the municipal pier at Marina del Rey. We had some of the finest, most calm, simply delightful sailing days, and I began to feel the possibilities for this trip really becoming what we had planned: a challenging but beautiful beginning of a real *Pearl* Museum in Washington, DC.

I had a little difficulty getting permission to land at the LA County dock, because I was required to show the vessel's registration. The Coast Guard was almost hopelessly backed up at that time, so we had been waiting on a registration since we'd closed on the boat at the end of December. I showed dock officials the registration for the *Glide* (a very different boat—about twenty feet shorter, and with a black hull). The official said, "She looks bigger; is that really fifty feet?"

"Well, I don't know who measured her; maybe they just looked at the deck?"

The officer shrugged and allowed me to keep *Valkyrien* on the dock for a week.

I still had not found a second boat boy for the sail to Panama. I interviewed four young men on the evening of our sixth night on the dock. One was drunk, another, an apparent stoner. I asked him if he had smoked marijuana recently. He looked at me, and said, as though it were both reasonable and an achievement, "Not since lunch."

I hired him, along with two of the others. When I assess crew I tend to see their potential more than the reality. Also, I had no alternative. They were surprised when I told them we would leave at sunrise.

The following morning my friend Daniel Voll joined me an hour before sunup, at the Burton Chace Park municipal pier. Daniel is a gifted writer, but even more than that, he is a man who thinks deeply before he talks. Lack of loquaciousness is a well-appreciated character trait at sea. Daniel has the great gift of talking only when he has something interesting to say.

We waited a few hours for the boat boys. Two of the three I hired showed up—the pothead and a geeky computer kid who still lived with his parents. The geeky kid's mother drove him to the dock, and after getting a good look at *Valkyrien* and her captain, she beseeched him not to sign on. This young man had lived an extraordinarily pampered life. Though not well-off, his mother had taken constant responsibility for all of his needs. He had no idea how to care for himself. Later, when we were out at sea, he refused to clean a cast-iron skillet. I dropped him off in Mexico.

On the other hand, Kit, the pothead, turned out to be one of my luckiest hires. He had decided to stop smoking weed for thirty days, and so signed on to *Valkyrien* for thirty-one. (I had a pretty good idea of how he was planning to spend his last night on board the boat.)

I did not have particularly high hopes for Kit at the outset. Every time he ran down the deck, he seemed to stub his toe on a pad eye or cut his fingers on some sharp corner. He could not tighten a screw without tearing the grooves on the head. His tender hands couldn't take the rough rope work of sailing. On the third day, he asked me for a Band-Aid. I handed him a crushed roll of duct tape, its silver threads almost black with dirt. Kit protested; it was too dirty.

Shaking my head, I unrolled the first circle of tape, revealing the clean silver duct tape beneath. Somehow, slowly, steadily, he caught on.

Each day without marijuana Kit seemed to grow smarter and more mature. He ate scoops of creatine at breakfast and dinner, and his arms and legs grew strong. On the fourth day he stopped complaining that his hands hurt. The next morning he had wrapped his palms and most of his fingers with duct tape and pulled up the sails without being asked.

His toe had become badly infected from smashing it over and over again against the same wooden block on the port side of the deck. He cut the fingers out of a rubber glove and slipped them over the injured toe. Eight days into the trip his hands became calloused. After two weeks, he had the swollen hands of Popeye, and could pull in a salty line in the dark without a word. (Recently, I heard that Kit has become a millionaire selling his own brand of legal medical marijuana in numerous California counties.)

The first night, several miles off the coast of Palos Verdes, Daniel and I sat in the cockpit below an absolutely clear and star-filled sky and I listened to him speak for hours. He told me how he had left his home in Indiana and become a journalist, and how he tracked down and interviewed war criminals in the former Yugoslavia, and American spies in Iraq. These were interesting, even exciting stories, but I loved most when he spoke about his own father and working their old family farm near the Mississippi. This was truly one of the finest nights aboard *Valkyrien*.

Two days later, we arrived in San Diego. My wife Vicki drove down with our children to see me off on the next leg of the trip. I had been missing Vicki a lot, and I was grateful that she had driven all the way down to say good-bye. What I really wanted was for them all to come with me, even though I knew that was impossible. Certainly if I had known all that would take place over the next year of trying to get *Valkyrien* through Panama, I would have sold the boat that morning and driven home with my family.

My daughter Summer lifted off the bow line and tossed it aboard. Then she ran down the pier and took off our stern line. I smiled, acknowledging how smartly Summer handled the lines, but so sad to be leaving my loving daughter behind. She pushed our stern off the dock as Vicki stood there with Noah and Maxey. I called out "See you soon, my loves," and slowly motored down the channel.

I looked back every few moments, hoping that the worst part of the trip lay behind me. But part of me knew we were now leaving the United States behind, traveling into strange waters, and that anything could happen. The three of them stayed by that dock, like Nantucket families seeing off a whaling ship, until I passed out of sight.

15. *Brave Men Run in My Family*

He works his work, I mine.
—ALFRED, LORD TENNYSON, *ULYSSES*

When Vicki stood beside me on the dock in San Diego and our children were running around the boat, all seemed right and good with my world. But as soon as my family left, I began to question everything. I'm not good company for myself. As soon as I am alone, negative and disquieting speculations tend to run through my head.

Was I one of those men? A Running Man? Is that what I was doing on this journey—running? And if so, from what, and why? *Valkyrien* was now sailing well enough on her own that I began to wonder more pointedly about my own life.

For the first fifteen years of my son's life (fourteen for my daughter Summer, ten for my daughter Noah), I was around nearly all of the time. I worked in steady jobs that required me to remain at home for long periods of time, without traveling. I prosecuted criminals in Philadelphia as an assistant district attorney. Later, I taught English as an adjunct professor at Boston College, and, with my friend Charlie Lord, I headed the Urban Ecology Institute (UEI) at BC.

At UEI we created an enhanced biology curriculum for public schools in Boston and neighboring cities. We presented a continuing education course for public high school science teachers, pairing them with a mentoring professor at Boston College. As part of the program, we set high school students up to do field studies. Most students began the program by figuring out the species and number of birds that lived around their school campus. The field studies became more complex as the students got better at collecting and interpreting data. Some advanced to the point where they were trapping coyotes and doing radio-collar monitoring of coyote bands living in the city.

We were among the first enhanced science programs to insist that children with developmental disabilities be fully included and integrated into the work. At first teachers thought this would be impossible. But even children with quite severe cognitive impairments can see a bird in flight, and they often notice things, particularly in nature, that those of us with more fully functioning brains miss.

My family and I spent summers together in Cape Cod, and skied on school holidays. When I wrote my World War II book, *Danger's Hour: The Story of the USS Bunker Hill and the Kamikaze Pilot Who Crippled Her*, aside from the few long stints I spent researching in Japan and around the United States, I worked at home in my office, writing.

Did my children think of me as an absentee father? I assumed for the most part that my absences were relatively easy for them—certainly easier than the few times Vicki would travel for her work and I was left at home to take care of them.

During one long trip, when Vicki was away lecturing for a teacher-training program, I purchased a dozen frozen lasagnas, and we ate lasagna every day for lunch and dinner. My children could not believe I was willing to eat lasagna every day rather than cook something. We were all beyond grateful for Vicki's return. The truth is that I actually loved the frozen lasagnas, but I longed for Vicki terribly. When we are apart I suffer a nameless ache, like some part of me is missing.

At times it was a mystery, even to me, maybe especially to me, why I was so obsessed with *Valkyrien* and the *Pearl* project. I often lay in my bunk at night, asking myself what the hell I was doing and why I was spending this time away from the people I cared about most. Why was I absenting myself from my wife and the life of our family for such an extended period? Was the *Pearl* project really worth more to me than the precious time it took away from my family? It certainly was true that the struggle of the slaves who escaped on the *Pearl* was more important than any single flag-football game. But did the creation of a memorial to those slaves justify my missing out on events in my children's lives that were irretrievable?

The answer, most certainly, is that missing time with Vicki and our children, their stories around a dinner table or a kiss goodnight, was a mistake. I knew all the time I was away that I was making a choice that I would regret forever. It is true that I was home and with my children more than most fathers—I am lucky in that I could afford to be— but I missed out on many moments in their lives because I was down in Central America on that boat.

I could say I don't know why I did it, and largely, that is true. A truer answer might have to do with how, particularly for a certain kind of person, working for a full day to loosen a single bolt could be more satisfying than walking with my truly beloved wife through the woods or taking my children to the movies. That sounds terrible, I know, and maybe it is, but when that nut finally slipped, and I could unscrew it with my finger and thumb and slip it off and hold it before my eyes, and see the shiny silver threads and know that some man had tightened that nut down fifty years before and it had not moved one bit since, I am carried away, filled with a strangely satisfying joy and a not uncertain, though inexplicable, pride.

Yes, the guilt of being away from my children always mixed into that moment. My children are beautiful, smart, strong, kind, and filled with love. My wife and I remain deeply in love, and yet I loved to sail away. Even though I sink, I am not sure I will ever get to the bottom of this. Of course the joy I speak of—unscrewing a nut—is easy to understand: It's the difference between a complex life of relationships and obligations and a life of simple duties and tasks, and on a boat! That part is not tough to get. There is something deeper, though, and darker, I suppose.

I can become disconnected from peace and serenity so easily. An afternoon sail, if, say, a storm blows in, can quickly become, almost sub-consciously, a test of my fitness as a man. When I camp or ski or sail or dive, in the back of my mind, every act I attempt is a referendum on my fitness to be alive—a measure of my courage, and my value. I do well in these tests. Although claustrophobic, I can, by praying and concen-trating, remain deep inside a mud bank, twenty feet below the ocean's surface, in zero visibility, for an hour, or until my tank runs out of air.

Partially because I am so filled with self-doubt and partially because I like winning, I tend to put myself in situations in which I am tested, often. My sense of self feels validated through risky behavior that I survive only through courageous acts. These acts become stories, often very funny stories, which substantiate my place in our family—where truly great acts are commonplace among my parents and siblings. And it can take a lot even to be noticed when you are one of eleven. I am happiest when near the water—not, I think, because water is such a touchstone for spirituality and love, but because water, to me, offers constant challenges, where I can be tested each day and be found fit to live.

I was drawn to the call of *Valkyrien* and to the intense nature of this particular journey. Whether facing the perils of a sudden storm or the constant demands of this vessel, I felt useful. A challenge at sea requires that I set aside the restlessness and despair that so often controls my mind—my choices, my life—and focus on what needs to be done in that one moment, then the next moment. Despite the chaos—and I do have a chaotic life—on a boat there is a sense of order. All of the rules are defined. I know what I need to do to keep the boat afloat for another day. If I do not sink, I have done what I need to do—what I have set out to do.

My father once said, "Well, we all have fathers." To me, this is a profound statement of what all of us go through in dealing with life on life's terms—and growing up. I think about this, and Maxey, and why I asked him to climb out on a frail bowsprit during that storm to change sails.

Maxey is now in his early twenties. He will graduate this year from college, and has a job at a serious firm in New York. To some, our lives may seem very different. Maxey does not need the same physical challenges and ordeals in order to feel fully alive, or worthwhile, nor do his sisters, Noah and Summer, but I know that he will never hesitate to dive into stormy seas to rescue me or anyone he loves. Summer will become a public school teacher later this year, in Oakland, California, empowering young minds, building character and confidence and instilling hope. Noah is a creative leader and will start college in the fall.

Maxey, Summer, and Noah are competent and fearless—they climb and ski mountains, raft challenging rivers, excel in all sports, and yet, like Vicki, they are grounded, content in themselves. They approach life confidently; they do not require the constant ordeals and benediction of the sea. Maxey, Summer, and Noah understand that we are all tethered to this world by the thinnest of lifelines, and they are always ready to reach out a hand. My children will never be limited by the expectations of others. Vicki has always lived completely independent of the thoughts and judgments of others.

Vicki has joined me on so many adventures. I have seen her sick and shivering, on the banks of the Usumacinta River along the border of Mexico and Guatemala—a trip we did without a guide company. I have seen her hungry and tired after a long night's sail through New England squalls, and I have watched Vicki time and time again rally to the side of our children when their small bones broke or their heads needed forty-six stitches or when they required guidance and comfort. But I have never noticed Vicki scared on a boat. Vicki has the most astonishing gift of enjoying life fully without needing to take physical risk or create drama. Vicki is willing, at any moment, to help me better understand myself, with love.

The other day I asked my son, in a text message, to say a prayer that I would find something I had lost. He sent a note to Vicki saying that he did pray for me—but instead of locating that item, he asked God to allow me to realize how much he, his siblings, and Vicki truly love me. Vicki, my constant companion in adventures big and small, at sea and at home, is always helping me recognize myself—not through danger and challenges, but through love.

Somehow our three children have found a channel between our two lives; between sailing through storms and navigating through reflection on their own lived lives. The fact that our children do not need to feel heroic in order to feel totally loved and beloved, fills me with a rare joy.

They are free. They are free from the torment of inventing a life of threatening adventure in order to feel worthy. They are free to live. I hope so much that, despite my mad dashes into stormy seas, I have also helped them to love.

And so, despite the regret of leaving my beloved family behind in San Diego, I set my sights on Panama and sailed south. And in the process, my relationship with this noble yet broken, heroic yet struggling boat continued.

16. *Mexico*

I have looked upon those brilliant creatures,
And now my heart is sore.
—WILLIAM BUTLER YEATS,
THE WILD SWANS AT COOLE

Jerry, the surveyor, had told us *Valkyrien's* fuel tanks could carry more than four hundred gallons of fuel, and she would make at least five miles per gallon. In fact, the tanks held less than two hundred gallons of fuel, and she made only about two miles per gallon, so our fuel capacity quickly became a huge issue, in light of the fact that for much of the trip we were without sufficient wind.

Diesel fuel tanks can be shockingly expensive, and installation adds another big cost. *Valkyrien* offered few places to install the tanks easily. Any replaccments would necessitate the services of a marine architect to make sure that the weight of the fuel—about eight pounds to the gallon—would not completely throw off *Valkyrien's* critical balance. We would also have to hire a skilled welder (and it can be tough to convince a skilled welder to create an arc inside a highly incendiary fuel storage area). At first we tried to make do with what we had; later, I tried various schemes to hold more diesel.

My first idea was to purchase diesel fuel from passing foreign-flagged vessels, rather than taking the time to go into port. I figured that the captains of those boats would be willing to sell to us because we would pay them cash, and they probably charged all of their fuel supplies to the owner's credit card. I think I was probably not far off in that regard. These huge vessels plied the waters off the shores of Mexico for months on end, often with crews that had no connection to Latin America or the United States. I thought it would be interesting to have some interaction with them.

The first boat we hailed was a Russian fishing vessel with a Polish flag. When we pulled beside her, a friendly, shirtless American hailed us in a perfect East LA accent. His face was covered almost completely in dark tattoos, which trailed down his neck and then along his arms, spreading to his chest in a violent series of images that seemed a dark mix of Hieronymus Bosch and the symbols of a San Pedro Valley gang.

He immediately grasped the opportunity for profit and ordered the mostly Slavic crew to action. The dark-inked American had a powerful but disturbing influence over the captain and crew as he supervised the unloading of the fuel. He ended up charging us about six dollars a gallon, roughly double the prevailing price. I didn't argue, although thereafter gave up on my idea of purchasing fuel from passing freighters.

We motored slowly down the unvarying desert-like coastal plains of Baja, always backed by dark volcanic mountains, sliding inside of Isla Cedros and Isla La Natividad off of Punta Eugenia, where Baja California Norte meets Baja California del Sur.

Mexico created a biosphere zone on the coast near Punta Eugenia, which is now a UNESCO World Heritage Site. The pristine coast there is visited by Pacific gray whales, California sea lions, and even the blue whale. It is also home to four species of endangered sea turtle.

We sailed past several two-liter plastic soda bottles that had been painted pink and green. I vaguely recalled a long-ago biology teacher saying that sea turtles were often trapped by fishermen who made bottles look like jellyfish. Fishermen suspend heavy weights and gillnets below the colored bottles. When the sea turtles show up to investigate, they become tangled in the nets. The turtles are often able to catch just a breath of air, pulling with all their might against the weights—and so, slowly, as they weaken, the turtles are pulled under and drown.

I halted *Valkyrien* at the next set of bottles and headed out in the Whaler with Jasper and several sharp knives, wire cutters, and needle-nose pliers. We found six or seven traps and freed the turtles from each one, then pulled the prohibited turtle snares into the Whaler. I planned on bringing the traps to the first village we passed so I could inform the authorities.

On the way, we came upon a bigger agglomeration of plastic bottles, this trap floating menacingly, perhaps five feet around. Five turtles struggled in the webbing. Two more were already dead, steel wire, laced throughout the trap, having sliced through their tough skin like a garrote, tearing their forearms to the bone. We set the living turtles free even though I knew that freeing an endangered sea turtle from dying in a trap is a violation of US law. One irony of the environmental movement is that citizens who take action to save any endangered animal face prosecution in every nation.

Years later my brother and I freed a drowning sea turtle caught in a trap off Cape Cod, and we were investigated by NOAA. It is still illegal for a child to pick up a blue-jay feather in every national park. Some wildlife officials use the rules to harass citizens (like me) who seek a more personal interaction with nature.

Authorities in the coastal villages of Pacific Mexico have no mandate for protection and actively support the trappers, making life miserable for Good Samaritans trying to save the turtles. In fact, after pulling the last trap into the Whaler, we were accosted by an angry group of fishermen who threatened to call the police on us. We sailed on in a hurry, farther down the coast, stopping at a small town where we were confronted by the local sheriff. He asked us if we had stolen the fish traps.

"You know damn well these are not fish traps," I told him. "These are traps for turtles. And this one here had seven turtles stuck in it, two of them dead."

The uniformed sheriff ordered me to turn over the traps to him at once or I would be arrested. Reluctantly, I passed him the tangled trap, trying to tangle it even more while handing it over. We pulled away from the little seaside fishing village, filled with self-righteous anger. I looked back at the little concrete block bodega restaurant at the corner of the wharf. The board in front advertised turtle eggs and turtle meat for sale. When I read the sign, I reconsidered my position. I remember thinking to myself as I looked back at the little bodega, Really, how can we expect to force our will and our values on the rest of the world?

As long as they were not selling to an international market (which is largely shut down, at least for deliveries from Mexico), how could I so self-righteously complain? This limited killing of turtles for local consumption in Baja is perhaps not too bad. The Mexicans have many more serious challenges to deal with before they can justifiably utilize law enforcement resources to address the illegal capture of a few sea turtles whose meat will be sold to local townspeople.

We sailed on. After our jaunt with the turtle traps, *Valkyrien* had drained all but the furthest diesel tank forward, and the Whaler, too, was low on fuel. Luckily we continued to have fair winds, though light, and were able to sail into Cabo San Lucas two evenings later.

17. *The Harbor at Cabo San Lucas*

Errand into the Wilderness
—TITLE OF A BOOK BY PERRY MILLER

Valkyrien's anchor was a gigantic antique Danforth, weighing about 125 pounds. The anchor was fastened via a galvanized steel shackle to the anchor chain. The chain itself weighed about five pounds per foot. The anchor was lifted and raised by a rusty iron windlass powered by two electric motors salvaged from a World War II bomber. A cogged wheel, attached to the motors via chain drives, turned the windlass.

While in San Francisco, I tested the windlass, and one of the drive chains snapped. It turned out that the size of chain that fit the cogs was no longer made. We couldn't figure out a way to cut off the wheels without damaging the windlass, and after driving around to dozens of machine shops, we finally found someone who would make us a chain. I remained skeptical about the dubious replacement drive chain and successfully avoided anchoring all the way down to Cabo.

In Cabo, though, we had no other options. I sailed *Valkyrien* in as close as I could to the beach without running aground, in about fifty feet of water, and lowered the anchor. The replacement drive chain on the windlass snapped almost immediately, and the windlass spun out of control, free-wheeling as the huge anchor dropped hard into the water, pulling with it hundreds of pounds of anchor chain that clattered across the deck and through a chock, racing down to the bottom, the steel chain screaming and chattering all the way.

We had no way of stopping or even slowing the chain as it fell into the sea at three or four feet per second. Jasper and I jumped away from the runaway chain, fearful that it would maim us or drag us overboard, taking us down to the bottom with it. Almost immediately, we struggled to our feet, leaning in, and with mouths agape we watched helplessly as the chain sped off the boat. Both Jasper and I knew that if we couldn't figure out a way to stop the chain, we would lose our anchor.

Almost at the last moment, Jasper grabbed the largest screwdriver we had on board—nearly two feet long and half an inch thick—and stabbed it into a link. His long days tramping through the woods and throwing his hand-hewn knife at trees paid off. As the lanced link passed through the chain guide at the edge of the deck, the screwdriver jammed, stopping the chain from running all the way out. We tied the chain in place with a couple of bow lines, and began to wonder how we would ever lift that anchor and chain back aboard.

Danforth anchors were state-of-the-art in the 1940s, developed as a quicker and easier way to anchor World War II landing craft. Until the Danforth, anchors had basically remained the same shape as the one frequently seen on the tattooed arms of seamen around the world. The older anchors relied on weight more than anything else to hold boats to the seafloor. Danforth anchors were built with flukes that could dig into a sandy bottom and, once set, hold boats well. In recent decades several new anchor designs have been manufactured, all of which hold vessels more reliably, in nearly all conditions, than the Danforth.

The principle defect with the Danforth is that if the wind shifts, the boat swings around and instead of holding the Danforth in the sand, pressure from the boat can actually lift the anchor out. Also, if the helmsman does not intentionally set the anchor, the flukes can start to drag along the ground, creating lift, almost like the wings of a plane, preventing the anchor from grabbing. In those circumstances, the boat will slowly creep away, often without the crew realizing it. The issue is so problematic that modern GPS systems are often set to sound an alarm if the boat moves more than one hundred feet or so from the anchoring point.

The best way to ensure that a Danforth anchor will hold is to drop a huge amount of chain onto the seafloor; this tends to keep the flukes low and digging into the sand.

At this point, floating above our pendent anchor, we faced a set of issues:

1. Our anchor lay about one hundred feet below us, and attached to a chain we could not possibly lift.
2. We had just entered a crowded harbor.
3. We were low on fuel—so low that I figured we could reliably count on only a few hundred yards of power.
4. We needed the fuel to land at the fuel dock. Certainly we could not land at the dock under sail.
5. I could have laid out more chain, which would have helped the anchor to hold, but we had no way of getting the chain back aboard. Chain is expensive, and difficult to come by in Central America. I did not want to lose more chain, so I resolved not to let any more chain out.

We lay floating in the harbor of Cabo San Lucas with an anchor suspended, one hundred feet below the surface of our bow, dangling above the sandy bottom, or dragging along the seafloor, with no motor and very little wind (our sails were already down).

I resolved to set the anchor on the *Valkyrien* without turning on the engine and without releasing more chain, nor using the motor. We put up our sails and headed in toward shore. The closer we got to the beach, the shallower the harbor became, until finally the anchor began rubbing hard along the bottom. We loosened the sails as the anchor bounced and, finally caught, holding us on a sandy bottom in forty feet or so of water, a few hundred yards off the beach. We readied the sails so they could be pulled up instantly if *Valkyrien* began to drag.

An hour or so later, just after dark, I swam ashore and purchased fresh food, then swam out to *Valkyrien* again, and climbed aboard, stretching out on my back and resting by the helm. The harbor was unusually dark for a moonlit night. The wind blew at only 1 to 2 knots. But later, near midnight, the wind shifted. *Valkyrien* turned a slow circle and began pulling the old anchor in the opposite direction from which it had been set. The anchor lifted out of the sand, smoothly and easily. The tide raised us up, carrying the anchor a few feet off the sandy bottom. The new breeze pushed us north across the harbor, with the anchor still dangling below us like a giant fishhook. The wind drifted us into the deeper water of the bay. No longer dragging, we were simply floating along, the chain far below the boat but also far above the deep bottom.

My first thought, of course, was to raise the sails to gain some control over *Valkyrien*. I checked our direction, and as it seemed we probably would not hit any other boats, I decided to wait a bit. Drifting in that harbor at night was both ridiculously dangerous but also remarkably relaxing. We meandered slowly past several gargantuan motor yachts. They were anchored so far out and away from everyone that they did not use security codes on their Wi-Fi systems (which must have been outrageously expensive, using some sort of satellite hookup). Pirating their internet, Jasper and Kit and I dashed off emails to friends and family each time we floated by a mega yacht. *Valkyrien* drifted slowly back and forth, pushed by a gentle wind and slight tides, throughout the night. I knew that in the morning we would have to somehow lift the anchor aboard, and I dreaded the task.

The next morning Jasper and I passed a 12-foot rope through the anchor chain, about fourteen inches below the top rail of *Valkyrien*. Jasper and I then each wrapped opposite ends of the rope around our shoulders, while crouching like a body builder getting ready to do a heavy squat. We then stood up, pulling the chain a foot or two up onto the deck. Kit crouched beside us, holding a second line with one end cleated down. We were able to lift the anchor just enough for Kit to tie his line through the lifted chain and tie it off, raising the anchor about fourteen inches. We repeated this process in the wet heat of the harbor a foot or so at a time, until we got the sixty or so feet of chain onto the deck and the anchor to the side of the boat.

The most difficult part of the process—probably because we were so tired at that point—was lifting the anchor itself over the side gunwale and up onto the deck. We got the flukes of the anchor alongside of the boat but the shaft angled down, and the chain lay completely out of reach as it wended its way to the guide on the bow. To get the anchor on board, we had to carry the anchor and fifteen feet or so of chain in a single lift. This was an awkward load, and the three of us collapsed from the effort—drinking many bottles of Gatorade afterwards while lying on our backs on the deck, nearly unable to lift our heads or get up.

Without an anchor, the boat, of course, immediately began to drift. We were too tired to stand. Every couple of minutes one of us would summon the strength to raise our head sufficiently over *Valkyrien's* bulwarks to see that we were not in any immediate danger of collision. But we called it pretty close. Several times *Valkyrien* meandered within a boat-length of some moored vessel. The wind was barely blowing, so that we wafted quietly through the harbor while regaining our strength.

We lay there for twenty minutes or so. At first I didn't move because I was too tired to stand. But even after I had the energy, I lay in the bow, not wanting to face the reality of trying to start the motor.

We were nearly completely out of fuel. I wasn't sure we would have even enough to start the engine. Once started, I would drive *Valkyrien* to the fuel dock in the crowded inner harbor. If we ran out of diesel in the inner harbor, *Valkyrien* would likely smash into dozens of tightly parked boats. The engine cranked over and started beautifully. I spun the wheel and held my breath, with a sickening sense of the imminent possibility of doom and humiliation. All night I had worried about this moment—the time between starting the engine and arriving at the dock. If we ran out of fuel I would be powerless to stop *Valkyrien* from drifting, bumping and smashing into every boat in that crowded little harbor. *Valkyrien* turned toward shore and we chugged closer and closer. My worry turned to relief though as I pulled *Valkyrien* gently up to the fuel dock, safe and sound.

Bob Nixon had planned to meet me again in Cabo, and as we passed the fuel pumps I saw him in his standard border-crossing uniform—a blue Brooks Brothers button-down Oxford shirt and worn khakis. He already had his wallet out to pay for what was going to be an astronomical fuel bill. I can't put into words how happy I was to have Bob along again; no one was more fun on a hard trip than Bob.

After fueling and filling *Valkyrien's* water tanks with potable water, we headed back out to the mooring field and reluctantly prepared to drop the anchor and chain back over the side. First we pulled about 120 feet of chain onto the deck, then tied the chain off at the bow and humped the whole thing over the side. Very quickly we had the anchor in the sand with 120 feet of chain. Dropping the anchor was a commitment, like Irish boys throwing their hats over a wall. Getting it up is the hard part. We had fully committed to getting the windlass working.

Jasper and I swam to shore, then took a taxi and walked through the light industrial districts, searching for parts to repair the windlass.

I had picked from Jasper by then then how to enter a shop and gain help. We would walk into the machinery space together in our work clothes, not saying a word or looking at anyone nor ever smiling. I would stop in front of a lathe and watch two men working a piece of metal, then make an offhand and unintelligible comment directed only at Jasper.

Jasper would not respond except to nod his

head at something in a pile of metal that looked slightly out of place. All of the men working in the shop recognized that the one thing Jasper noticed should not have been left in that pile. Perhaps someone would be in trouble. Or, perhaps someone had just been saved from being in trouble. Sometimes we would walk through shops for twenty minutes before anyone spoke to us, saying something like, "What do you need?" At which point we would shrug and say something noncommittal, like, "We are looking for some square bar."

SHOP MASTER: "Why do you think that you need square bar?"

JASPER: "So it fits."

SHOP MASTER: "We can grind it down."

JASPER: "Well, you could, but I'm not sure you can make it square with just that lathe."

SHOP MASTER: "I definitely can. I do that all the time. How long does it need to be?"

JASPER: "Well, it is going to have to be welded. Do you know anyone around here

174

who has something big enough to hold a weld at more than 500 kg?"

SHOP MASTER: "We make deep welds here all the time."

JASPER: "Well, if you have some round bar, about 1 ¾–inches thick."

SHOP MASTER: "I don't have it, but I can get it."

ME: "When?"
(The fact that I have not yet spoken and I am only interested in deadlines shows that I am the boss and the one with the money.)

SHOP MASTER: "Well, today is Saturday. It's too late to order it already. Monday is a holiday, so I can order it Tuesday, and we will probably have it here Wednesday or Thursday morning."
(The shop master thinks that this timeline is not merely reasonable, but actually quite impressive in its efficiency and overall timeliness.)

ME: "That is too late. We have a broken piece, and the owner of the boat will be here tomorrow. We have to fix it before he gets here."

SHOP MASTER: "Well, you could go to San Eugenio. They are tearing down a building there. Maybe you could get them to sell you a part of the fire escape. It is steel. In fact, it's square bar—I think."

ME: "What time does the bus run to Eugenio?"
(I do not ask where to find the bus. It is clear I already know where the station is, so I am not rich enough to take taxis. Also, I am Jasper's boss—but I am not the boss. I must report to someone. I rush him, not because I'm in a hurry, but because I will be in trouble if I don't get this fixed in time. I share something with the workers—a vague sense of fear at not getting enough done for the boss.)

SHOP MASTER: "Never mind the bus, my nephew will drive you."
(We then get into a 1983 blue Nissan, which rides about three inches above the crumbling roadway. After finding nothing at the torn-down building, we convince the nephew to drive us to four more places until we find square bar. Jasper then

produces a portion of a bough of a tree he picked up before we left Los Angeles. He had whittled the little branch until it fit perfectly into the slots on the windlass. We would grind the steel bar, and weld corners on it until the bar measured the exact same dimensions as the whittled wood.)

This is not exactly how it went that day, but it is a fair-enough approximation of our general method for procuring difficult-to-find items.

When *Valkyrien* was built in the 1920s in New Zealand, packet schooners were not equipped with electric motors to lift their anchors. Originally, the windlass was driven by hand, with two humongous crank handles, made of iron or steel, 1¼-inch thick and squared off to lock into the windlass. Two sailors working together would turn the windlass manually with the cranks, lifting the anchor.

Of course, it's likely no one had lifted *Valkyrien's* anchor manually in decades. We had no idea if the old system would work. But when we took the windlass apart, the grease looked good, so we stood hopefully in that welding shop. Eventually Jasper convinced the shop master to let him do most of the welding himself.

We walked a few blocks before jumping back into the cab. Kit picked us up in the Whaler, now fueled, and we inserted the two gigantic cranks into either side of the windlass and began turning. It worked perfectly. In the following weeks we suffered a bit each time we lifted the anchor, but Kit grew stronger and we managed.

We left Cabo the following morning bound south toward Manzanillo. Threats of bad weather, bad fuel, and a leaking boat faded from my mind whenever Bob was aboard. We laughed and laughed throughout each day. Bob is a master camp-chef, and in the end, no matter how bad a trip is, if the food is good, the trip cannot be terrible. Bob supplemented whatever we found in the galley with fish we caught from a line off our stern. We ate lobster tails with rice and baked beans. He cooked eggs fried in bacon grease beside a grilled steak for breakfast. And then we shared old stories of camping and fishing, trips together and raising our children.

18. *Kit Drinks the Water*

*There is something in the clear blue
warm sea of the tropics,
which gives to the stranger
a feeling of unreality.*
—RICHARD HENRY DANA, *TWO YEARS
BEFORE THE MAST*

Unfortunately, we had almost no wind crossing below the Sea of Cortez. We had to run the engine the whole trip. The 6V53 on *Valkyrien* is a two-stroke engine; most modern engines are four-stroke. The major difference is that the cylinders in a two-stroke engine are directly lubricated with engine oil and tend to burn more oil. The *Valkyrien's* engine burned nearly as much oil as diesel fuel, and as we cruised by the entrance to the long bay at Puerto Vallarta, we poured in our last five-gallon drum of oil. Ordinarily we would simply drift, waiting for the wind to come up, but Bob was on a tight schedule. We had to buy more oil to keep the engine running so we could get down to Manzanillo in time for Bob's flight.

Puerto Vallarta sits miles inside one of the largest bays in Central America. The sea was calm. We had little prospect of wind, so Bob and I decided to take the Whaler on a 170-mile trek in search of 40-weight engine oil. The two of us drove the full eighty-five miles into Puerto Vallarta then hobbled inland, tired out by the long, bashing trip in an open boat. We stopped at every fuel station and agricultural supply shop we could find, buying ten-gallon buckets of heavy 40-weight oil. Finally we filled each of the gasoline tanks in the Whaler to the brim, then headed back out to sea to find *Valkyrien*.

The Whaler had no navigation equipment save its nearly fifty-year-old compass. We had told Jasper and Kit to keep *Valkyrien* running, south-southeast, at about 4.5 knots, so we would know where they'd be. With the sun setting, we made it out of the sweeping bay, but we saw no sign of our ship. We had already traveled about seventy miles by then, and the Whaler had only enough fuel to cruise about ninety-five miles in total: no way we'd be able to make it back into the bay at Puerto Vallarta. I stopped the Whaler to experience a moment of shining calm. We quietly approached an extraordinary collection of seabirds at rest beside each other as evening fell in this lonely spot of the Pacific Ocean.

In our rush to purchase oil, Bob and I had missed the paradise of land birds in the jungle that surrounds Puerto Vallarta. I am a licensed master falconer, and have observed birds in many settings: jungles and swamps, mountainsides, heavy forests and across plains, on seas and parts of the ocean. Not one of these experiences prepared me for the moment of our approach into this collection of indignant seabirds, roused by our Yamaha outboard.

A single gray gull struggled up out of its slumber, followed immediately by line after line and then great groups of seabirds taking to the air. Gliders, dark frigates, and others, lured by the visual and auditory phenomenon of our boat, flew directly toward us, joining the brown pelicans with their striking golden heads and more gulls by number and species than I have seen before or since. Thousands upon thousands of birds took to the air, all seeming at once curious, angry, or alternately oblivious to our presence in their realm. This was not a peaceful moment—nor was it disturbing. We simply had one long astonishing shared experience at sea, the kind of thing that happens so often for sailors, which when described to landsmen can neither be translated nor understood as likely or possible, or even to have existed.

We stared at the birds, amazed, but knowing that each moment the birds flew, the sun sank. After several minutes the entire mad avian collection drifted off toward the horizon and disappeared, leaving us in total quiet. The sun always seems to fall more quickly in the tropics, especially when you are on a small boat in a big sea, far from shore. Darkness approached.

Bob and I wondered whether Jasper and Kit would turn *Valkyrien* inland to look for us, or stay on the course where they were supposed to meet us. We knew that with nightfall, fear would be telling them to head inland. I said to Bob I don't think that is how Jasper operates.

So we stayed on our course, and as the stars began to appear overhead, we saw *Valkyrien's* sixty-eight-foot mast on the horizon. We made it to her side with a few miles of fuel to spare and poured the new, clean oil into the engine, which made everyone happy.

A day or so later I dropped Bob in Manzanillo and he caught a flight back to Washington. I sailed on with Jasper and Kit. Vicki and Wes would join us three hundred miles down the coast at our next port of call—Acapulco.

Dehydration occurs astonishingly rapidly when sailing in the tropics. One of the first signs of advanced dehydration is lightheadedness, and difficulty reasoning. Quickly following the onset of these symptoms comes paranoia, distrust of shipmates, and a strong sense that drinking anything will make matters worse. During the first few hours after one rehydrates, a flu-like nausea can become so overpowering that even walking is difficult.

I had ordered Jasper and Kit to put aside three two-gallon bottles of water each morning, which we then mixed with a huge portion of powdered Gatorade. We put our names on our respective bottles, and every few hours each day we would check in with each other, showing how much we had drunk. I took dehydration very seriously, but it amazed me, despite my precautions, how quickly any one of us would become completely unreasonable about fluid intake.

Jasper grew bitter and argumentative after only a few hours of not drinking. One day he told me that he was busy working on the engine, and would drink when he climbed out of the darkened compartment. By late that evening he flat out refused to drink anything. Kit and I yelled at him, to no avail. I slapped him as hard as I could in the face, but this also had no effect. Finally, I punched him very hard, and he agreed to drink if I would promise not to hit him again.

I immediately assented, and we watched through the night as Jasper finished a gallon of water mixed with electrolytes. The next morning, fully hydrated, Jasper apologized to both of us. After that, we made a solemn pact that if any two people ordered the third (even me) to drink, he would have to drink until the other two said "Enough."

This worked well until we were approaching Acapulco, and Kit refused to drink any fluids at all, no matter how we cajoled him. We drove straight up to the fuel dock. Kit, confused and dizzy, stepped off *Valkyrien* and walked down the pier without tying any lines. I tied up the bow and rushed after him.

When the dockworkers saw Kit in his disoriented state, they insisted on calling for an ambulance. I knew that Kit just needed to drink something, so I threatened him.

"If you do not begin drinking immediately, I am going to leave you here, and you will have to find your own way home. You will likely be arrested and spend at least one night in jail."

Kit looked overjoyed at this news.

He said, to me in absolute earnest: "Really, Max? Thank you so much! This is really good news! So, I don't have to get back on the boat as long as I don't drink any water, right?"

I said, "No, Kit, that is not right. You must drink the water, and if you do not drink it now, Jasper and I will force you back on the boat and we will never let you off again."

Kit looked crestfallen, but managed, despite his haze, to see the determination on our faces and began drinking. By late the next morning, he was back in his right mind, and we had a few laughs about it when my wife Vicki and my friend Wes finally arrived, at the dock in Acapulco.

19. *Vicki and Wes*

Come live with me, and be my love.
—CHRISTOPHER MARLOWE, *THE PASSIONATE SHEPHERD TO HIS LOVE*

As *Valkyrien* nudged against the fuel dock Vicki stepped aboard and threw her arms around me. The thought of falling asleep with my wife in my arms for the next few nights gave me an extraordinary feeling of peace.

Wes had flown from Los Angeles with Vicki. Wes and I met many years ago when Vicki and he were teaching fellows at Harvard. Wes grew up in Norman, Oklahoma, and his kind demeanor and openhearted accent belied a keen intellect and incisive wit. Wes had shaved his head for the trip and arrived looking like his Cherokee ancestors (minus the scalp lock). Two of my greatest friends in the world are Oklahomans descended from Cherokee who won full scholarships to Ivy League colleges.

At Harvard, Wes won the Rockefeller scholarship and used the funds to travel to Ghana, where he worked for a year in a small village eating fufu, a sort of soupy mixture that is also used, unadulterated, to repair leaking gas tanks or popped tires. A year of eating fufu might have been tough, but Wes will readily confess that his three days aboard the *Valkyrien*, apart from the company, was the worst trial of his life.

We set sail again the morning after Vicki and Wes arrived, our crew consisting of the two of them, Kit, Jasper, and myself. A strong wind came up that night and waves crashed over the bow, socking the foremast beneath a couple of feet of water. The waves rolled fierce, though nowhere near as steep or as tall as the gigantic Pacific waves we had encountered near Monterey.

Working in the dark, I reset the sails and tried not to betray my alarm. I did not realize at the time just how miserable our guests were. Vicki, sick with the flu and violently nauseous, never complained. And Wes, more stoic than any man I know, never let on that he was concerned. They both displayed extraordinary stamina and calm. Most people would have been terrified beyond action. The rain and wind, combined with the lightning and thunder and the fact that the seas south of Mexico offer little hope of rescue in an emergency, made for a scary crossing.

The following morning we skirted the north-western edge of the Gulf of Tehuantepec and landed at Salina Cruz, in the far south of the Mexican Coast. Salina Cruz is a town that should not be missed by anyone who savors visits to landfills or the scent of dead animals left to rot on dusty roads. Salina is entirely artificial.

One hundred years ago some officious bureaucrat determined that Salina, a blank spot on the map, would be a good place to construct a port city to serve as the Pacific Coast station of the new national railroad crossing Tehuantepec. The government built seawalls and port facilities in the early 1900s, but the hoped-for bonanza of cross-continent shipping never materialized, and the Mexican government has deferred maintenance on most of the port. Built to be a great rail terminus, it has become literally the end of the line.

The harbor had no facilities. We pulled up to a "pier," little more than a collection of half-submerged boards tilting in various directions as we stepped across them.

Vicki and I walked together into town searching for fuel, to little avail. The sadness of the vacant streets, abandoned buildings, and short-haired starving dogs spilled into my heart the doom that is particular to the tropics and keened my awareness of the emptiness I would feel at Vicki's departure. I needed to find fuel, but I knew that once we had filled *Valkyrien*, Vicki would return home.

I never know what to do during the hours before Vicki leaves. Demented butterflies flit around in my stomach, bringing with them a slight nausea and nervous energy. This feeling sneaks up on me. I walked along, fully intent on finding fuel, and suddenly realized that my sense of well-being had nearly collapsed. I have left Vicki so many times for travel, and yet every time before I go I become completely afraid. It is similar to the anxiety that some of my friends feel about taking a flight. I have a vague sense that without Vicki something will go wrong. I can experience this sense of Vicki's absence anywhere in the world—in a storm at sea or at a Broadway play. When I am with Vicki I feel grounded, in the present. Vicki brings to me a contentment, and I need our connection. And yet I continue to get back on the boat. My restless soul carries me away.

We walked along the narrow streets that day in Salina and watched the smoke rising in varied locations from the burning of rubbish. Finally we located a small truck stop and paid a group of men to bring us a collection of fifty-five-gallon diesel drums. They rolled the drums along the street, 18th century style, then down the dilapidated dock.

We pumped the fuel through the smallest hand pump I had ever seen; filling a single drum required hundreds of strokes. We took turns pumping, and concentrating on that tedious work, I lost track of my surroundings, lulled in the tropical heat. I did not notice as a dozen Mexican military guards, each carrying an assault rifle, marched down the pier until they climbed aboard *Valkyrien*. The guards stopped our fueling and clambered all over the decks, searching for drugs. (I don't know who would ever smuggle drugs south from Mexico, but I did not ask.) They were polite, as we were in turn, and after looking at a lot of papers, they allowed us to continue on our way.

Vicki and Wes remained with us long enough to run satellite checks on the weather and ensure we were well-provisioned for the last portions of the trip (southern Mexico was more than halfway to the Panama Canal). Wes, a master on any computer, checked every major weather service and the cruising websites, and he also asked the locals about possibilities for heavy weather. Conditions sounded ideal.

It was with a great measure of sadness that I watched Vicki and Wes feel their way along that ramshackle dock. They headed home as I made ready to embark again, south. Vicki had been so encouraging about this undertaking, urging me to continue on, but I don't think I had ever wanted to give up the trip more than I did while watching Vicki make her way down that rickety pier.

I had been away from home too long. I missed my children, and the *Glide*. I missed sailing around Nantucket Sound. I feel comfortable in New England. On Cape Cod I am surrounded by family. I know where I am off Hyannis Port, even at night, because I recognize the cadence of so many channel markers—six seconds on the light at the end of the break wall; the Morse code on the HH Buoy, four seconds of red on the old bell at the entrance to the channel. Hodges Rock, Hallets Rock, Half-Tide Rock, The Spindle. For someone new to the Cape, these are all navigational hazards to be reckoned with—dangers lying, partially obscured. But for me they are the welcome signs that I am home. I had been away now from waters I knew for a long time. Each day we sailed anew into unknown seas, with unrecognized dangers. I wanted to go home.

I reasoned with myself that the trip was nearly over. As an experienced sailor, I never quip "What could go wrong?," but I figured that the rest of the trip—through the warm tropics, with a proven engine and good sails—would go more smoothly. Within eight days we would be in Costa Rica, and I would be able to fly home for a couple of weeks, after which Vicki would fly down with me and our children and we would sail together into Panama. Lonesome, standing alone beside that stinking dock in Mexico, I figured I could stick with it after all we had been through.

I had no idea that the trip was about to get much worse.

20. *The Gulf of Tehuantepec*

In the tropics one must
before everything keep calm.
—JOSEPH CONRAD, *MARLOW IN HEART OF*
DARKNESS

The passage across the Gulf of Tehuantepec is the most treacherous section of the coastal trip to Panama. The Gulf is one of the windiest places on Earth, at least during the winter months. Cold fronts moving across Central America are funneled into the mountains between Mexico and Guatemala and are essentially slingshot across the bay. Winds often blow 20 knots, but during weather events, which are not infrequent, they may blow 40 knots or more, causing huge westbound waves to drive out to sea, hammering sailboats hundreds of miles offshore.

Experienced cruisers with blue-water boats will tell you that 250 miles out at sea is the minimum safe distance. I knew *Valkyrien* was a strong boat, but I would certainly not cross the ocean with her, and I would not sail her that far offshore. The next best choice was to sail the entire bay while staying about a quarter-mile from shore. The wind jumps a little bit at the beach, creating a narrow line of safe navigation that winds along the edge of the shoreline, where the water is just deep enough—at thirty feet—for sailboats.

La Niña had been active that year, which somewhat weakened the effects of the gigantic wind tunnel, and we did not begin this portion of the trip until late March—well after the windiest days of December through February. According to the reports Wes had gathered, we had a safe weather window, and so we headed off along the Gulf shore with the wind steady at about 20 knots. That is a hell of a lot of wind when you are sailing, but was considered fairly calm for the Gulf of Tehuantepec.

Nevertheless, the narrow band we sailed along the coast was really the only smooth line on the long haul across the bay. Just a kilometer or so further offshore, winds were gusting over 30 knots as we sailed along that desolate desert shoreline, past the tiny fishing village of San Mateo del Mar. Most young people have left the villages along the Gulf for life and jobs in Oaxaca. The old ones remain, living as subsistence fishermen, in simple poverty. They care for their boats and tiny homes, eating their own daily catch.

I looked across at the villagers staring out at *Valkyrien*, each of us perhaps thinking of the lives of others, and I was happy with my choice to continue the journey. *Valkyrien* beat hard, her sails pulled tight to stay on the safe side of the wind line. The wind blew beautifully strong, beckoning on a heading that would keep our course on a perfect reach directly across the bay. This was precisely the wind and weather schooners were designed to sail. I stared out at the rolling waves. I wanted to sail with that wind. I have never shied away from a fresh breeze. On Cape Cod when the wind is like this, we say, "It is blowing like stink out there." And it was blowing like stink.

I turned the wheel right a bit, falling off, to a broad reach. *Valkyrien* cruised out of the narrow band of calm and into the wilder seas of the Gulf of Tehuantepec. The next five hours were perhaps the greatest sailing I have ever experienced. We crowded on sail, and *Valkyrien* swept along well over her hull speed, often making 14 knots. The sail felt more like a Nantucket sleigh ride, with the stars overhead, and eight- or nine-foot waves that allowed *Valkyrien* to surf but never took control of her.

With the advent of Doppler and even newer forms of satellite radar, weather prediction has improved stunningly over my lifetime. Nevertheless, some storms, particularly in storm-prone areas, are not efficiently predicted.

This was one of those times.

A few hours into our dark crossing, about twenty-five nautical miles from the Guatemalan border, the sky turned absolutely black, and rain fell in thick, driving sheets. The heavy rain was followed a few minutes later by thunder and sizzling zigzags of lightning, first on our starboard, then, suddenly, everywhere.

We were surrounded by powerful lightning bursts whose thunder shook the frames of *Valkyrien* to her keel. People think that it is the mast that holds the sails, but the mast is really only there to stiffen the cables. The stays and shrouds, comprised of stainless steel, are what really hold everything together. Without these stays, the whole boat will break up.

The short, almost inconspicuous cables that tie into the sides of the bowsprit are essential. If these cables fray or come loose, the entire rig—both masts, and all of the sails—can come tumbling down. If you lose one of the cables, you lose the bowsprit. Without the bowsprit, you lose the forestay. And if you lose the forestay, then the masts will begin swaying forward and back, like a wedge, digging themselves deeper into the boat and trying to split her apart.

For this reason extra-strong cables are used on the bowsprit. Many bowsprits on older sailing boats are buttressed with thick chain—the same size the boat uses to hold the anchor. And these cables and chains are secured to the ship's sides in a manner that makes it nearly impossible for them to come loose. In carpenter's terms they are "through-bolted," which means that instead of screwing in an ordinary eyebolt, the carpenter actually drills a hole entirely through the wall. Then she forces a huge metal bar, threaded at both ends, through the hole. Finally, the carpenter slips thick stainless-steel washers over the bar and then slides oversized stainless nuts on either end, and tightens down fiercely on the threads. The double bolt holds the rig precisely in place. The only way that bolt can come out is if the washers literally fold in on themselves, against the nut. A heavy stainless-steel bolt, washer, and nut combination can hold the engine onto a 747.

Unfortunately, instead of using two double-thick stainless-steel washers, which cost a few dollars each, our carpenter Jerry had chosen the cheapest, thinnest washers he could find. That night off Guatemala, the jibs pulled hard, bending the bowsprit to starboard, like a taut bow. I thought to myself, *My God, if that thing snaps, we could lose the whole rig.*

That evening, and into the night, the jibs pulled against the bowsprit, and the sprit in turn pulled against its cables. The cables pulled against the through-bolts. And the through-bolts pulled against those cheap Chinese washers.

In the midst of the storm, in the dark, at the bow, and unbeknownst to all of us, the washers slowly worked themselves into a bend, then suddenly folded up about an hour after dark, and ripped through the holes drilled into the side of the gunwales. A gigantic cracking BOOM! raced across the ship, like the sound of a double-barreled shotgun fired right beside me.

The bowsprit snapped about six inches in front of the deck, and both jibs pulled out to the side, then backwards, collapsing halfway into the sea. The jibs acted like parachutes, stopping the boat by filling with water. Each jib remained connected to the foremast by the forestay and halyards, so when they filled with seawater, most of the stress the heavy sails exerted pulled at *Valkyrien's* weakest point: the top of the mast, multiplying the pressure at the mast-foot like Archimedes' lever.

Before the bowsprit snapped, the forestays were helping to hold the mast in place. That help was the key to keeping the entire rig held up. Now, instead of helping, these stays were actually pulling the masts down, and sideways, with enormous force. The huge bowsprit fell into the sea and snapped in two pieces. A mess of cables, ropes, and netting tangled the broken spar, smashing it repeatedly against *Valkyrien's* side. It made a loud cracking sound as though we had hit another boat. Sometimes the pieces struck the hull below the waterline, sounding more like a muffled boom, as though we had struck a rock.

The foremast, freed of being held forward by the forestay, immediately snapped backwards.

The main mast then fell backwards too, and the main boom fell to the cabin top, nearly smashing my head, and the helm. This loosened the back stay, and left both masts free. The untethered masts began swaying back and forth, beginning the slow process of gnawing through *Valkyrien's* hull, gradually splitting her open. The terrible wind continued to blow, turning the stays and shrouds into a sort of mad harp, a ghastly pitch that grew higher and louder as the winds increased. The noise echoed, haunting the boat.

I let go of the wheel, ran forward, and dropped the two mainsails, to take some pressure off the masts. *Valkyrien* slowed to a crawl. The waves, which had been so kindly when we were cruising at 12 knots, began battering us as the boat slowed. I rushed back to the cockpit, then peered into the cabin where Jasper and Kit stared, amazed.

Valkyrien stood in a brutal storm, her forestays all untethered, and her masts swaying danger-ously back and forth. Two jibs and huge portions of the bowsprit dragged along the starboard side, carrying rope and cable and netting along with them. The two mainsails, down but not tied, whipped back and forth out of control. The boat rocked forward and aft, and side to side. Huge waves smashed against her port side, and swept the decks. Heavy rain slashed at my eyes and pelted my skin, striking in sheets and often in hardened beads. Frequent lightning strikes accompanied by shattering thunder struck and rolled down upon us.

Jasper and Kit crouched together, in shock as the boat buffeted about, with no sails and no motor, entirely at the mercy of wind and waves. Jasper started the engine, but the boat slammed side to side violently, lifting the propeller out of the water, over and over, revving the prop.

I became quickly concerned that all of the sloshing would disrupt the flow of oil from the pan, and cause insufficient lubricant in the cylinders, so I asked Jasper to shut the engine down. Then I told Kit to take the wheel, and Jasper to put on a life jacket and come to the bow with me to set a forestay and pull the jibs on board.

I leapt back up the companionway into the cockpit, then crawled forward on my belly along the deck, watching the destruction unfold as the changing winds and seas cast the *Valkyrien* in wild disorder. The jibs dragged through the water, seized by the waves and caught up in the various cables from the bowsprit. The weight was pulling the boat to the starboard side, bending the masts, and often nearly stopping us short.

At other times, the jibs might, singly or in unison, release all of their water, and for a few moments fill with air and lift out of the brine, cracking and snapping with relentless ferocity. The broken pieces of the bowsprit had tangled with the jibs, and when the jibs rose out of the sea, like kites, they sometimes carried the bowsprit pieces up with them. The *Valkyrien*, freed of that massive drag, would pick up speed. Then, bent by the wind in her newly flying jibs, she leaned over, and the heavy blocks of broken sprit would catch and dive back into the ocean. The sails would pull back under, jerking *Valkyrien* over to starboard again, stopping her hard. The huge waves smashed against her stalled hull, as they would strike a rocky shore—shaking her, covering her, beginning to swallow her up.

Scientists have not determined why certain songs can become stuck in our heads, nor why this phenomenon occurs at any particular time. But sometime that night I began singing to myself the lyrics of "The Wreck of the Edmund Fitzgerald." I found the song a welcome distraction and an impetus to act correctly as a sailor and captain. I also found it amusing. Often when I worked at the bow, far out of earshot of the crew, I shouted the song as I struggled with the lines:

> *The wind in the wires made a tattletale*
> *sound,*
> *as the waves broke over the railing . . .*

I waited for Jasper and Kit to follow me up on deck, watching the jibs and stays and pieces of sail tearing apart, momentarily transfixed

199

by the madness unfolding all about *Valkyrien*.

I stared at the rows of drenched belaying pins and for a moment thought of Douglas Fairbanks, the legendary hero-captain, swinging from the halyards, using the belaying pins as knives to tear his enemy's sails, while preserving the safety of innocents.

This is not how things went aboard the *Valkyrien* that night.

I had to be extremely careful with every move that I made on deck to keep from falling overboard. Jasper and Kit did not appear. I spun around to face the stern, still lying on my belly, with my legs pinning me against the railing and the house top. Then I reached over the coaming, into the cockpit, and held tight to the companionway. I shouted out to Jasper, but he couldn't hear me. I leaned my head into the galley and told Jasper again, loudly, to jump up and grab the wheel, and ordered Kit to come with me to get the sails down.

Neither man moved.

"Jasper, you have got to be fucking kidding me. We need to get this done. Now!"

Jasper did not say a word.

I jumped into the galley, face-to-face with my crewmen. I saw a look in Jasper's eye that I had not seen before, and realized immediately that reasoning was useless. He would not climb on deck in that storm.

Thinking that it would be better for it to look like this was my idea, I ordered Jasper to go below and check the engine, and instead told Kit to come up and hold the wheel while I moved forward. I climbed up the companionway to the cockpit and turned around. Neither man had moved.

"Kit, quit fucking around and get your ass up here." I spoke harshly, punctuating each word.

Kit did not move.

"Kit, I need you. I need you to come up here now, and grab this wheel."

Still, Kit did not move.

I climbed below and stood only a few inches from him. I spoke each word with staccato emphasis, not shouting, but loud and clear and filled with command.

"Kit," I said, "this is a tough time. A very tough time. This is a difficult storm, no doubt about it. The bilges are filling with water, but we can't turn on the pumps unless the engine is running. And we can't turn on the engine until the boat settles, or the engine will be destroyed. The masts are untethered, and each time we move, they jerk back and forth. They are driving through the bottom of this boat, and with each wave that strikes us, the masts pry the planks a little further apart. They are causing us to break apart. If we let this continue, we will sink.

"Look below. Water is beginning to pour

through the deck in places it never has before. *Valkyrien* is starting to open up. I can prevent this—but I can't do it unless you get up there and hold the wheel while I move forward to reset the masts."

I continued: "Kit—thirty years from now you will be telling this story to your children. Come with me, Kit. Together we'll save this boat. And in thirty years, when your children ask you what you did at this time of great difficulty, you won't tell them that you stayed below, that your fear took you, that you refused to help. You'll tell them instead that you took the wheel and sailed through the storm, through the lightning and the thunder and wind and waves. You'll tell them you did this great thing!"

Kit looked me straight in the eye and said he was sorry, but there was no way he was going back on deck.

21. *Making Lists*

*I caught myself listening on tiptoe
for the next beat of the boat,
for in sober truth I expected the wretched
thing to give up every moment.
It was like watching the last flickers of a life.
But still we crawled . . .*
—JOSEPH CONRAD, *MARLOW IN HEART OF
DARKNESS*

My great captain's speech having failed
miserably, I jumped back up to the cockpit and
made adjustments to the wheel, then jumped
below again. I told Jasper that he didn't even
have to come into the cockpit to help me. He
could sit on the ladder and reach one hand
back. From that position he would be able to
see *Valkyrien's* direction to the wind. He could
hold her steady enough until I finished with the
sails.

I helped Jasper put on a life jacket. He pleaded
with me, telling me not to go.

"I'm going, man. It's the only way. Give me
your knife."

Jasper, with a solemnity that I found both irritating and charming, rather dramatically placed
his most prized possession in my palm.

Normally, in a storm, a crewman working on the bow hooks his harness to a safety rope so that if he's swept over the side, he won't be lost at sea. Other crew can grab hold of the safety line and pull him back aboard. I thought that if the debris tangled in the safety line I could be pinned under, unable to move, and so decided not to tie myself in.

Waves washed over the entire boat. As I grabbed Jasper's knife, I heard the clump of falling wood and turned my head forward, looking at the mast hole.

Masts are seated on a platform of hard wood called the "mast step." The masts exert enormous pressure on the bottom of a ship, and, when untethered or moving back and forth, they can quickly work a hole in the boat and push themselves all the way through. The mast step is supposed to disperse the pressure of the mast to a wider area on the bottom of the boat. The mast then passes up through a hole cut in the deck. This hole is framed with especially strong wood. Wooden wedges are hammered in along the sides of the mast, holding it stiffly into the frame, jamming the mast tight into position, immovable. These wedges make the mast and deck essentially a single piece of wood. If the wedges are ever removed, however, the mast will move independently of the deck, and the destructive power of the mast colliding constantly with the deck will tear the boat apart.

All of this was now happening on *Valkyrien*. Our mast had begun twisting and deforming the deck, and thus, widening the mast hole. The wedges had fallen through. Now the mast was free to move in whatever direction the wind pushed it. This would vastly accelerate the deterioration and ultimate destruction of *Valkyrien*. The hole was widening further every minute. I had to get the sails and bowsprit out of the water and stabilize the mast before the boat became critically damaged.

As I peered into this hole, I felt the dark energy of fear run from my neck and down my arms, electrifying my hands. The boat was coming apart. I was scared as hell. The first thing I had to do was to stop the damage from spreading. I had to quiet my fear.

I have learned to walk through scary predicaments mostly through a life of long practice. I begin by thinking about how I would like things to be, ideally, and then consider in detail the way things are. Then I make a mental list of everything I can do to bring the situation closer to the ideal. This mental work usually takes me out of the fear, at least long enough to think through the issues and decide what needs to be done. Once I have a list, it is a simple matter to work on each item, one by one.

1. Tie down the mainsail to stop it from flapping around.
2. Tie down the forward mainsail.
3. Replace the forestays using halyards. Climb to the bow, take the halyards from the forward mast, and tie them to the deck. Then tighten them down hard. The halyards run from the top of the mast, just as the forestays used to do. If I could tighten the halyards down hard enough, they would hold the masts in place—at least through the storm.
4. Pull the pieces of the bowsprit and the two jibs back onto the deck, or cut the mess loose.
5. Raise the storm jib. (I kept the storm jib ready, and had only to release a single tie and haul up on the halyard.)
6. Find a mallet and knock all of the mast frame wedges back into place.

That was it: a list of six things, all of them relatively simple. All doable. Making this list, going through it in my mind, imagining myself at each stage and walking through the steps, helped enormously. The process calmed me.

Jasper sat in the companionway, stretching awkwardly backward so as to keep a part of himself in the cabin, and one hand on the wheel. The main boom clattered back and forth just above Jasper's head while the sail snapped and whined and spilled into the sea, then back up on the boat, bursting with wind.

I had no time for further delay. I pulled in the boom as tight as I could, then I looked up at the mainsail snapping crazily and thought, How the hell am I going to tie that down?

I remembered my uncle telling me when I was a child and we were racing his Victura: "Move like a cat . . . move like a cat." I do not like cats, but I moved on all fours up to the main mast with that idea in my head, carrying a line I found coiled on the balustrade.

The closest edge of the sail sounded like a dozen whips snapping all around me, crack-crack-cracking, over and over. I spread my arms wide and leapt atop the main boom, linking my hands around it and pressing with my knees, like wrestling a fighting dog to the ground. I passed the rope between my hands, tying it tight as a cowboy would a steer, and as I cinched down the knot, the sail calmed. I was able to wrap the line around and around, lashing tightly to the boom, finally immobilizing the sail.

In just a few minutes I had the mainsail tied hard so it no longer moved. Check One. Time to move forward to get the second main. Dark clouds completely blacked the sky. All deck lights had been extinguished. No moon shown through. Not even a hint of a star. I could barely see at all—even a few feet ahead of me. Harsh rain fell in horizontal sheets that stung my cheeks and forehead. The boat made the terrible sounds of wood coming apart.

I sang out Gordon Lightfoot as loud as I could, though no one could hear me.

> *And every man knew, as the captain*
> *did too,*
> *T'was the witch of November come*
> *stealin'.*

I made my way to the forward mast, by feel as much as by sight, crawling along the deck and holding my breath when the waves rolled over me. Every few seconds a bolt of lightning exploded near *Valkyrien*, creating a brief, surreal moment of daylight and clarity that was immediately followed by a darkness that seemed even more Stygian than what had come before.

When I reached the mast, I looked at the base where it passed through the deck. Several more wedges had fallen through. I could see a pale light emanating from a tiny LED flashlight that had fallen off a shelf near the fuel tanks. I had never before seen any light escaping through the tight mast hole from the cabin. I became afraid again. I thought: I am too late. And I thought then about how stupid I was to have tried to sail across this bay. I wished the storm would end, but I knew it wouldn't.

I thought of abandoning the ship, and wondered whether Kit and Jasper could handle spending the night and perhaps several days, or more, aboard the Whaler. If we lost power on the Whaler, the storm and wind would probably push us two hundred miles out to sea. We might never be found. How could I have done this to them?

For a few moments I froze, hands shaking. I did not know what to do.

Pinning my thigh against the mast, I looked at my hands. I stared at them and said to myself, "These are my hands. I know these hands well. I am on a boat, and the boat is sinking. It may be too late to save her, but it is too early to abandon ship. I can move with these hands and do the right things. Take the sails down, stow things away. Stabilize the masts. Make her shipshape, and stay with the boat until morning. Reassess if things change. But for now, I do everything I can to keep *Valkyrien* afloat. I know these hands. I can move through this, one step at a time. Move through the list."

I pulled the sail in tight and cleated off the boom, then leaned forward, gathering as much sail as I could hold, and wrapped my body around the boom, and tied the violent sail down. Then I shuffled aft along the boom, leaning over and hugging it again—I tied the second knot. The sail shook much less now, and I continued wrapping rope around it until finally this main, too, lay steadfast.

Check Two.

I moved to the tip of the bow where the bowsprit had shattered. I wrapped the halyard around the wreckage of the sprit still attached to the bow, holding my breath each time *Valkyrien* dove beneath a wave. I thought of Maxey in that earlier storm. I tied a bowline, then slid behind the front hatch and back behind the mast, and I pulled as hard as I could on the halyard.

The new rig worked like a miracle. The moment I tightened down, both masts stopped about 80 percent of their movement. Much of the sound of wood moving hard against wood dissipated, and the boat smoothed out markedly.

I quickly moved forward and tied on a second halyard. Each time we struck a wave, the masts bent forward, causing the halyards to slacken. But I took in the slack behind each wave until the masts did not move any longer. The boat continued to pitch and yaw, and waves broke over the bow, submerging the deck and roiling over me. But I felt great relief at stabilizing the masts.

Check Three.

A pile of wreckage hung off *Valkyrien's* bow. These ropes and chains and cables and netting, powered by the wind and the waves, slammed the heavy broken bowsprit against the side of the boat, jarring *Valkyrien* with every smash, halting her in the sea, and tipping her sideways. I had to get hold of some piece of this shambles and begin pulling it in. I figured if I could grasp one line and brace myself sufficiently, I could, bit by bit, bring the whole mass aboard.

This was by far the most dangerous task for me that night. Cables that had been stays tangled amid jib sheets, and sections of rope work from the widow's net, stretched across the deck in a dark maze of materials which shifted with each wave rolling across the deck, arced and looped, half hidden in the blackness and the roiling sea, like a horrendous fish trap, waiting to seize me under. I felt like a canny raccoon trying to get a piece of food out of a box he knows is a trap. Each time I reached out, I risked a snag that could pull me overboard.

I leaned down and forward to grab a piece of the wreckage pitched atop the deck, but the next wave ripped me away from the mast and tumbled me down the deck, in amid the wreckage and hard across the safety lines. My leg and thigh slipped over the side and into the sea, but I grasped the toe rail, and the safety lines stopped me from falling completely into the ocean. The wave rolled past and I climbed back aboard and crawled to a safer spot before the next wave crashed over the bow.

After a few breaths, I tried again, reaching down into the debris. I got ahold of a piece of heavy line entangled in all of the cables, wood, ropes, and sails that banged against *Valkyrien's* side. I pulled on that heavy line, inch by inch, dragging the mess up and onto the deck. I forced Jasper's knife through the jib halyards, which released the tension in those dragging sails and let them trail behind us. Then, working my arms like a fireman holding a trampoline, I wrestled the jibs aboard. Finally I pulled in the gigantic piece of the bowsprit and tied it down tight along the inside of the gunwale.

Check Four.

Once out of the sea, this detritus no longer pulled at the masts, turned the boat, or twisted her hull. We smoothed out even more.

But I had created a quagmire of debris on the bow that threatened to ensnare me, hold me underwater, or pull me overboard at the slightest misstep. I moved carefully forward again and raised the storm jib. This sail was able to further stabilize *Valkyrien*, and she became ever more able to hold her course. I moved back to the jibs and unhanked the first one, rolling it up tight before half dragging it back to the galley.

Check Five.

The bow had stopped diving. Waves no longer smashed across the deck but merely spumed over the sides, which seemed almost relaxing by comparison. I rolled the second jib and passed it into the galley, then returned one final time to the center of the deck, checking the braces I had made, then pulled tight the makeshift forestays a bit more.

I made my way back to the cockpit and into the cabin. Kit returned to the cockpit and took the helm. Jasper and I carried scrap wood from the carpentry room, and using a hammer and mallet, we jammed as many bits of wood as possible into the frames holding the masts, which succeeded in halting the last of their movement.

Check Six.

I am afraid a lot, partly this is because I put myself in frightening situations. But I am afraid at home, too. I'm afraid when my phone rings late at night. I am afraid of green pants in the dark. And I am often afraid in a storm.

My close friends and my brothers and sisters say that they have never seen me afraid of anything at sea. The truth is, I loathe my own fear and try very hard to hide it. I think a good captain should never seem afraid. Fear on a boat is contagious, and if seen from the captain, can be destructive. It is best to put that kind of fear aside.

But I also carry with me a general level of anxiety that is more accurately called fear. This fear is my near-constant companion. It has been with me for as long as I can remember, even when I was a child. I have always wanted to be rid of it.

I think one of the reasons that I am so willing to place myself in physical danger, is that experiencing fear of a certainty—some thing that certainly may hurt me, or even kill me, helps me to deal with, to live with, to bear and become less molested by, the fear I carry with me to nearly every sanctuary. Perhaps the only times that I feel the complete absence of fear are those that I spend in the embrace of my wife and my children. Most of the time I do not consciously experience the sensation of fear. I am, I suppose, like a goldfish, having no idea of the existence of water, until I splash out of the bowl.

I have heard it said that fear is an absence of faith. I don't know much about that, but I do know that I pray a lot harder when I am in danger on a boat than when I am lying on the couch at home. There are some who may find my account to be merely the recollections of an adrenaline junkie. I do not deny that I enjoy the sense of adrenaline pumping through my veins, but I'm not interested in skydiving. Sailing is different.

A couple of hours before dawn, Jasper and I started the engine again. The power it generated allowed us to run the bilge pumps. Seawater had come up over the floorboards in my compartment and seeped down through the deck, soaking everything in my cabin. The lightning drew further away, the rain let up, and soon the moon came out, though the wind and the waves remained. In the clear moonlight, the scudding of the foam across the sea appeared beautiful beyond all imagining. We were making 1/2 knot, headed toward a harbor in Guatemala.

Exhausted, I said good night and stepped below, taking with me one of our two-gallon bottles of springwater. In my cabin, I took off my clothes and poured the water onto my face and down my body, clearing much of the salt away. I had nothing dry, so, dripping wet, I pulled my water-slogged sleeping bag over my body and fell into a deep sleep.

> *You are the meaning deepest inside things,*
> *that never reveals the secret of its owner.*
> *And how you look depends on where we*
> *   are:*
> *from a boat you are shore, from the shore,*
> *   a boat.*
> —RAINER MARIA RILKE

22. *Jasper Gets into a Scuffle*

*What would be left of our tragedies if a
literate insect were to present us his?*
—EMILE M. CIORAN

The storm passed an hour after dawn. The wind
and waves fell away, the rain stopped, and the
sea became completely calm. The night had been
shivering cold, but by ten a.m., anyone up on
deck stood drenched in sweat. The bow had been
split in half. The coamings on either side of the
snapped bowsprit moved back and forth slowly
with the steady swaying of the boat. This in turn
pressured the deck, which subtly changed shape
with each movement.

We needed to stabilize this area. Jasper and
Kit wrapped a ratcheting cargo strap from my
truck around the broken bow. When we cranked
down hard on the ratchet, the bow came together,
firming up *Valkyrien*. We chugged along,
repairing what we could, tightening stays, and
cleaning up spilled cargo the rest of the day and
into the night.

Early the following day, we pulled into
Guatemala's tiny Puerto Quetzal. In order to purchase fuel we had to officially enter the country
and have our passports stamped. But Guatemala

did not yet have customs officials stationed at Puerto Quetzal. We were told they would be on their way soon.

We topped off *Valkyrien's* tanks. The cracked flow meter on the dock's fuel pump no longer measured how much fuel flowed, so the dock-master "estimated" that we owed him $800 for a paltry amount of fuel.

The customs officials finally arrived, but told us they were too hungry to do their work. They told us in an informational, but instructive manner that the nearest restaurant they could afford was a couple of hours away. Catching on, I suggested that I pay for their lunch at the local restaurant. They agreed. Once I put a free lunch on the table, several more customs officials mysteriously arrived.

While they feasted, we rechecked *Valkyrien*, working through the areas of the boat that were unreachable while sailing. We unfastened the bronze shackles and pins that held the snapped bowsprit to the whiskerstays and the bobstay, and took apart the dolphin striker. The three of us worked together to tighten the halyards we had set to act as forestays, and retightened the side stays and backstay. Then we gave *Valkyrien's* storm-tossed interior a thorough cleaning.

I called Vicki and told her about our adventure. Summer had just begun and my children were about to finish school. I had been away a long time and needed to go home, but before I could leave Central America, we had to find a place to make repairs on *Valkyrien* and store her until the fall.

Vicki went straight to work, calling nearly every marina between Guatemala and Nicaragua. There are very few yards on the Pacific Coast of Central America with facilities that will allow them to lift out a boat as large as *Valkyrien*. Those with sufficiently powerful lifts are designed for commercial vessels whose owners will pay a fortune to get their boats back to work. Every day ashore for a commercial boat is a day of lost income. These yards had all the work they could handle, and none of them wanted to risk lifting *Valkyrien* and having her fall apart on them. As a consequence, every quote that Vicki received was outrageously expensive.

Finally, Vicki found a small estuary in El Salvador at the Rio Lempa, which at one time had had a marina with a lift that could pull *Valkyrien* up. She could not get anyone on the phone there, but we decided it was worth a try. The inlet to the estuary was one of the most dangerous on the Pacific Coast. We figured few commercial boats would risk those waters, so we were likely to get a good deal at that yard.

After lunch, the half-dozen or so customs employees dutifully looked at our documents and had us fill in numerous forms. Finally, in the late afternoon, they stamped our passports and allowed us to leave. We cruised along the coast of Guatemala, and then El Salvador, seeking a haven where we could leave *Valkyrien* safe and sound during the summer months. I wanted to go home, to spend the summer with my wife and children, sailing in the relative safety of Nantucket Sound.

Vicki purchased plane tickets for Jasper and me to fly out of San Salvador. Kit's flight left the same day. We cruised through the night, and in the morning came upon the Lempa shoals, blocking what would otherwise have been one of the finest natural harbors in Central America.

The entrance to the Estero Jaltepeque is blocked by a horseshoe bar laden with detritus carried 250 miles down the Lempa River from the Sierra Madres in southern Guatemala, then through Honduras and half of El Salvador. Every filthy bit of trash discarded into the stream beds of San Salvador eventually flows down the Rio Lempa. Huge fallen trees, rocks, and sand wait to snag passing vessels, and the shoal itself is constantly moving and changing position with wind and tide. We sailed well off the coast to avoid it.

In order to enter the bay, passing sailboats have no choice but to run a narrow unmarked channel about eight or ten feet deep at low tide (though the depth changes, and little hills develop each day, which can make the water even shallower).

We called on VHF channel 16 which is monitored at a local bar. The bartender put us on hold, then asked the patrons if anyone wanted to guide us in for $20. A local Salvadoran agreed to show us the way.

We waited in safe water until the start of high tide. As the current switched direction and began flooding the bay, a small hand-built wooden boat appeared atop a wave. It disappeared a moment later, in the trough, and we marked its progress through a mile of heavy breaking waves—not big by the standards of the bay, but for us, at eight feet high and breaking over a shoally ground, these types of waves were new, and scary.

The pilot, a local Indian named Alejandro, pulled up near us, but I could not understand what he was saying, so I dove off of *Valkyrien* and, much to his amazement, climbed into his little boat to receive directions as specific as possible about how to cross that bar. Satisfied, I swam back to *Valkyrien* and we followed our indigenous bar guide through the waves. At times *Valkyrien* surfed breaking waves for several hundred yards, like a gigantic surfboard manned by Lilliputians. Twenty minutes later we passed through the narrow entrance and into the estero.

We found a small marina/hotel north of the entrance to the estuary, the place where the VHF radio was wired to the bar. I tied up to the marina dock, walked ashore, and ordered lunch.

The lifting facilities had closed down, but I spoke with some dock workers who said that a local man on the island across the estero had a couple of moorings in front of his house available for a small fee. I needed to meet him, make a deal with him to care for *Valkyrien* while I was gone, and keep her safely moored, all before our flight departed that same evening.

I tried not to appear in any hurry, because gringos in a hurry pay a much higher price than people who don't have much to do and no place in particular they need to be. I didn't tell the bar men that our flight was leaving later that afternoon. Instead, I made arrangements with the bartender to have customs meet us and give us entry visas later in the day, then we jumped back in the Whaler and drove across the estero to a completely different world.

On the hotel side, a colony had developed of people who were trying to live as though Salvador were a normal country with normal rules of behavior and public safety. But on this, the other side, lay the real El Salvador, mud huts with tin or grass roofs, electricity enough for one television and a DirecTV dish. These locals experienced the internet on small cheap cell phones and heard gunfire every night.

We met Cesar, a lean ambitious man, determined to lift his family out of poverty. He agreed, for a very reasonable price, to take care of *Valkyrien* on his mooring until I returned. He would clean the bottom, run the pumps, and do carpentry work. In this way, I felt I was also doing my little part, taking business away from the foreign-run operations across the water and giving it to someone who really needed it.

Cesar was a bit surprised when I asked for a ride to the airport in an hour, along with his phone number and email. As soon as we sealed the deal, Jasper and I rushed back across the estero to the hotel to check in with customs and have our entry visas stamped. We then motored *Valkyrien* over to one of Cesar's moorings, tied the Whaler up behind, and walked Cesar through *Valkyrien*, explaining her various systems. After paddling ashore in Cesar's canoe, we climbed into a 1980s vintage red American sedan owned by his neighbor, who rushed us to the airport. When we got there, I became concerned when I saw that Jasper had brought only his carry-on luggage. I knew that he had come aboard *Valkyrien* with two humongous bags of tools, so I made him open his carry-ons for me to view.

Seeing what he'd packed, I said, "Jasper, you cannot bring a compound bow on board the passenger compartment of an airplane."

Jasper got really mad. He didn't generally get angry more than two or three times each week, but I always became aware of how strong he was when he was ticked off at me.

I took away his compound bow and had a cab drop me off in San Salvador at some kind of mall where I went in search of a cheap piece of luggage I could throw Jasper's tools and his bow inside. But when I got back to the airport an hour later, I saw no sign of Jasper.

Jasper often did things his own way, and I was so tired of him disobeying specific directives (mostly things I had told him not to do) that I considered simply boarding my flight and going home. I wanted to get home to Vicki and my children. But my conscience worked on me as I sat waiting for the boarding call.

I could tell that the energy in the airport had changed. All of the police seemed to be on extra alert, and higher uniformed officials walked briskly through the passenger areas, talking quickly but quietly to each other and shaking their heads. I realized that Jasper must have been arrested.

I walked up to a guard and said, "I am with the American you are holding. May I see him?"

The guard asked me how I knew someone was being held, then quickly corrected himself to say he did not know of anyone being held. He told me to wait there, and he walked vigorously away.

A military officer arrived and escorted me to a back room in the immigration area. I explained that my friend Jasper had a number of disorders and disabilities which made it very difficult for him to understand customs and rules, and that I had taken him to El Salvador as part of a special program for people with these kinds of disabilities.

I did not tell the official that Jasper was the only person in the world I had ever encountered with this particular type of disability. I thought it quite possible that Jasper had fallen asleep while being questioned by the officials. And I thought that if he had lain down and gone to sleep, snoring, in the middle of a formal questioning, that the Salvadorans who, like police everywhere, value respect, might have become considerably angry. Especially because it was sometimes very difficult to waken Jasper during a bout of narcolepsy.

The senior officer told me Jasper had tried to get on the plane carrying a hammer and a Skilsaw, among a great variety of other tools. And when they took his baggage, Jasper had gotten into a scuffle with them. One should never try to take away a carpenter's tools.

I forced Jasper to apologize individually to each person at customs and baggage, and they agreed to let us on our plane. I was really angry until I realized that Jasper had never been on a plane before. His passport was brand-new. He had never left the United States, and *Valkyrien* was the greatest thing that had ever happened to him in his life. My relationship with *Valkyrien* was more complex.

The *Valkyrien* and I sailed together. From the cold of the North Pacific in February through the long hot days of tropical torpor, we continued our journey. I had helped her to harness the wind and the explosive power of compressed diesel. She had helped me to escape and to apprentice to a life on the sea. Together, we stayed afloat through storm and wind and gloom of night. I left her, happy to be going home and looking forward to the next leg, which would take us through the Panama Canal.

23. *Life in the Estero*

You see I rather chummed with the few mechanics there were in that station, whom the other pilgrims naturally despised—on account of their imperfect manners, I suppose.
—JOSEPH CONRAD, *MARLOW IN HEART OF DARKNESS*

I returned to the United States without further incident, and spent a calm summer in Hyannis Port, sailing and scuba-diving with my wife and our children, catching fish and eating family dinners with my mother, my brothers and sisters, and their many children. We played Capture the Flag and touch football, and spent most of our time together as a family.

I worried about *Valkyrien*—she needed constant attention to keep from sinking. I felt so far from El Salvador and the trials of *Valkyrien* that I almost forgot that I would soon have to return.

But return I did in the late fall, to continue my journey. Jasper had secured full-time employment that summer, and so could not rejoin me. Instead I hired a couple of hipster gringos who worked with me mostly as ship's carpenters. The hotel we stayed in beside the estero was perfect—not too expensive, a nice swimming pool, rice and beans and fish for lunch, a few US tourists, but mostly Salvadorans. The owners looked as though they had walked straight out of a xenophobic film about the wars in Central America. They wore black suits and never removed their sunglasses.

Sadly, and with intense irritation, I realized that very little of the work Cesar had promised to do had been done. Cesar had spent most of the summer speeding around the estuary in our Boston Whaler, apparently charging people for rides. He struck a log, crushing the gears in the lower unit of the outboard. Now the engine made a terrible sound, like someone hammering broken glass. She ran at half speed. This made the Whaler much less appealing as a last resort in case of a storm.

I heard that at one point in the summer Cesar had actually let the *Valkyrien* sink down into the mud of the estero, but then with the help of many family friends, got her bailed out at low tide and refloated her, still attached to the mooring.

It sickened me, thinking about all the money I was spending on *Valkyrien's* host of problems. Nixon and I were self-funding the journey by this point. The engine no longer started, the rudder had come loose, the worm drive did not function, and the generator had failed. Real dollars were hard to come by in that part of the world, and I loathed the feeling I got when I pulled money out of my pocket, especially when it actually left my hand. For some reason charging things to a credit card back in LA was not nearly as hard. Rental cars in Salvador cost about a hundred dollars a day, so, to save money, I purchased a decrepit thirty-one-year-old faded purple Mexican Ford for about $600. It was one of the smallest trucks I had ever seen. I think it would have fit in the bed of my Ford.

I had lost my wallet and driver's license just before returning to El Salvador, and had somehow left my spare credit card at home. Fortunately, the front-desk clerks at the hotel remembered me, and as a returning guest they gave me a room without securing it by credit card. I handed over my entire cash reserve, about $2,000, which they kept in a safe-deposit box behind the front desk. The management was comforted by the fact that I clearly had cash to cover my bill.

Two grand is a huge amount of money in El Salvador, and at first things went very well. But each morning as I stopped by the front desk and withdrew more of the cash from my safe box—the big outlay for the truck, $50 to pay a carpenter, $200 for fuel, $100 here and there to buy wood—I sensed the hotel staff growing more and more concerned. This coincided with my work on the boat intensifying. Each day I returned to the hotel grubbier and greasier than the day before, and with a little less money. I could feel their growing unease.

After two weeks, I had blown through all of it—no cash left, no credit card—literally no money at all. I convinced the hotel to grant me a room and food for a few extra nights, which they reluctantly did, even though I'm pretty certain they all thought I was going to make a run for it.

While moored in the estero we spent a huge amount of time trying to get *Valkyrien's* diesel engine to run. Our biggest problem was the starter—not so much that it didn't work (broken starters can usually be rebuilt), but that we had to remove it before we could fix it. The bolts mounting the starter to the engine had locked tighter than any I have ever seen, and were nearly inaccessible. A cocoon of wiring hid the starter bolts in the darkest portion of the engine compartment. Fuel filters and a set of copper pipes blocked access from the rear and side. The starter lay sandwiched just slightly above the oil pan, and nearly touching the water cooler above it. Worst of all, *Valkyrien's* hull walls sloped diagonally to within just a couple of inches of the starter's mounting bolts, making it impossible to turn a wrench more than a few millimeters at a time. The only way I could get close to the starter was to lie down in the bilge. I twisted my chest around and hung under the belts on the front of the engine. In that position I was able to reach through the muck to the mounting bolts.

Each time I moved my arm, or slid it in and

out, I would first run my wrist and forearm along the top of the bilge, which is where most of the oil gathered, and then, lubricated with the foul grease, I would slide my arm between the bilge boards and the engine, to the starter bolts. Despite the lubricant, I cut my arm each time I reached in, and cut it again each time I turned. My elbow fell numb until I could barely sense it.

I did not realize why the bilge was so foul until I had been working in it for about a week. Jasper had repaired the head back in Monterey, but had reversed the pipes so that throughout the trip down the coast, when we thought we were dumping our waste into the sea it was actually going into our holding tank, which had filled with feces, then cracked and overflowed. The walls of the bilge were literally pasted with crap.

The tight workspace forced me to spend time crouched on my left knee, which hurt a bit more each day, until it finally opened up for about a week, expelling pus that turned from greenish black to an almost perfectly eggshell white. I scrubbed the narrow, two-inch wound hard with soap and water each night, finishing with a bath of iodine. Before going to sleep, I washed it finally with bottled water, caulking in some Neosporin before turning off the light.

I had nearly lost a leg to a neglected infection as a child. That, and Hemingway's "The Snows of Kilimanjaro," made me careful with infected cuts, especially in the tropics. But if I had known the true contents of the muck in the bilge compartments, I might have been more careful still.

Many times I thought to myself, "I am stuck in a Graham Greene novel." Fluorescent lightbulbs drew throngs of truncated geckos (truncated, because something had eaten their tail). I spent most mornings in *Valkyrien's* bilge coughing up black dust mixed with various VOCs (volatile organic compounds), from paint thinner, spray paint, carburetor cleaner, starting fluid, glue, used diesel oil, and gasoline. Later, in the purple truck, I inhaled burned radiator fluid, brake oil, and power-steering fluid.

More than anything I breathed in an extraordinary agglomeration of molds of various sizes, shapes, and thicknesses. I realized that molds were like snowflakes—no two were alike. Some were beautiful, like the ones that grew only in partially burned fuel oil. Others were more disturbing, like the dark molds that appeared to be moving. They grew under the bunk where the strange boat boy slept. Others lived in oil combined with cleansing agents banned in the United States in the early 1970s. When these were stirred up by a hand groping for a dropped wrench, they released a gas. This gas knocked you hard, making it difficult to think straight, making you wonder why you would want a wrench anyway, and what was the rush? Might as well lie down in the muck for a while.

Someone always waited topside when we worked in these deep bilge areas of the boat. When they stopped hearing anything below, it was time to wake up the fellow turning a screw.

One of my proudest moments came on the day I loosened the starter bolt that we had been working on for most of two days. Basically I put a wrench on the bolt, then tied a rope to the wrench and pulled up on the rope to turn the bolt. It was a complex maneuver. First, I covered the starter bolt in WD-40 and let it sit while I used a grinder to file down the box end of the wrench. I used a 1/8th-inch drill bit to cut a hole in the open end of the wrench and slid fifteen inches of bailing wire through the hole, then knotted the wire so it made a very strong loop.

I tied a strong rope around a metal pry bar and strung the other end of the rope through the floor, into the engine compartment, and around the side of the engine to the wire loop on the wrench. I slid the open end of the wrench over the bolt, jammed a couple chunks of wood beneath the wrench head to hold it in place, then climbed onto the floor joists above the engine. I bent my knees, and holding the pry bar in both hands, straightened my knees, hauling upward. The rope began to stretch and then suddenly and beautifully, I felt the bolt slip.

It turned easily after that, and we removed the starter and carried it to a shop where they would rebuild it.

With the starter out of the way I offered Cesar $100 to clean the bilge. This was a month's pay in El Salvador. He refused. Later that day Cesar watched as I climbed into the filthy bilge, unscrewing all of the hoses and pipes and fixtures that held the giant holding tank in place. Twelve or fourteen inches of dark sludge sloshed around inside the holding tank, oozing out the cracked top. The only way to get the tank out was to lift it over my head and make a run for the stern of *Valkyrien*. Every step I took caused the crack in the top to open wider, dumping old and recent feces on my head. The sludge plopped on my shoulder, down my arms, and into my eyes. Awful. I made it to the end of the cockpit and dove overboard into the estero, and then swam the tank to shore.

I figured I might one day need that tank again. I had not seen any holding tanks for sale along the trip. I was already so filthy I had nothing more to lose. I also thought that if I cleaned the thing thoroughly, in front of Cesar and his family, he might feel obligated to work more diligently on the boat repairs. It made a difference for people to see the captain willing to do the dirty work, literally mired in crap. I scrubbed the tank myself with Dr. Bonner's soap, inside and out, until the appalling receptacle smelled only of peppermint. Then I carried it back aboard and let it dry in the sun.

I bathed and shampooed myself in the muddy water of the estero for nearly an hour. Standing there, with my bare feet sinking into the silt, I looked up at the stern of *Valkyrien* which rose above me like a giant, unruly horse that had only a moment ago stopped raging. She sat, impassive, not caring at all that she had just covered me in the worst slime I could imagine. I recalled George Orwell's *1984*, in which Big Brother is able to divine our deepest fears, then designs tortures specific to each victim. *Valkyrien* had covered me in one of my deepest antipathies.

After removing the holding tank I needed to clean the bilge. *Valkyrien* had no wash-down system. I tried carrying buckets of water into the cabins, but this proved entirely insufficient to clean the filth-lined compartment. I needed a hose. I removed one of the bilge pumps from *Valkyrien* and attached some long DC wires that I had pulled from the sides of the engine compartment, onto the pump. Then I wrapped the apparatus in a hose clamp to hold the wires in place and tied on a rope. I attached a long hose to the outflow. I let the pump off the side of the boat into the estero and grabbed the free end of the hose, attaching the opposite ends of the DC wires to a car battery. Water flowed forth, and I used the hose to wash the crap down both sides of the bilge. I cleaned the walls with sponges and soap and dug everything out, from each niche and corner, dumping the solid waste into doubled-up trash bags.

In the end the bilge looked completely clean. Scouring it had revealed some of *Valkyrien's* inner beauty. Many of her planks had a triple curve to them. The shipwrights had not merely bent the planks on (steam-bending kauri is a difficult job, to be sure); they had also bent and twisted the planks, so they turned a slow arc from high on the boat's sides down through to the keel. She is one of the most beautiful wooden boats I have ever seen.

I wrote to Vicki:

Most of the Europeans will not speak to us because we speak to the locals (or because we are so dirty). The locals have gotten the wrong end of a short and filthy stick for a long time. They seem more amused by us than anything else, but "confused" runs a close second. I am sitting dockside right now, dripping puke from my thumbs and sleeves, still covered in grease. Spent about 4.5 hours today lying in a bilge as stinking as most of the open sewers in this poor country.

I was left largely on my own in Salvador, gathering wood and hardware and trying to repair *Valkyrien* with Cesar. I will never get past how awful San Salvador was in 2009. In the light industrial area of the city, which I frequented, a tall stone-and-concrete bridge crossed over a slow-running stream. The stream was used by everyone in that district as both a place to clean clothing and a toilet. A number of animals had apparently been thrown over the bridge. I don't know if this occurred before or after they died. The combined stench of rotting flesh, piss, crap, and decaying trash lay thick around the center of the bridge. The foul odor hit me hard the first time I crossed, and I threw up violently over the side. Thereafter I held my breath and ran each time we crossed the bridge.

24. *Pistola*

When despair for the world
grows in me . . .
—WENDELL BERRY, *THE PEACE OF*
WILD THINGS

Weird stuff happens every day in El Salvador. Each day stands out, and yet the days and nights remain numbingly monotonous. El Salvador overflows with weapons left over from the civil war, and is one of the most violent countries on Earth. I drove from the estero to the capital city, San Salvador, nearly every other day to purchase supplies. Each trip we passed by the same dead animals left to rot where they had fallen. The drive took about ninety minutes. One afternoon Cesar and I passed a woman lying beside her broken bicycle on the side of the road, bleeding. This was one of the only sections where the road is actually divided by a full median, and the woman lay in the tall grass between lanes, moaning. I thought she had crashed her bike and I shouted to Cesar, "Stop the truck."

"It is okay; she will be fine."

"Stop immediately."

"This is none of our business. They will help her if she needs help."

"It is my truck. Stop driving now!"

Cesar pulled to the side of the road, and I ran back to the woman who lay alone in the grass. I asked her if she could hear me.

"Si," she said.

Then I said, in my terrible Spanish, "Where does it hurt?"

"My back."

"Tell me, how many fingers am I holding up?"

"Three."

She seemed to be alert, and conscious of her surroundings. An awful lot of blood lay splattered and clotted in the grass. I thought she must have cut her foot or head to lose that much blood. But I checked both and saw no wounds.

"Can you feel my hand touching your hand?"

"Yes."

"How many fingers am I touching your arm with?"

"Two."

I reached down to her feet.

"Can you wiggle your toes?"

She wiggled them well.

I checked to see whether she could sense my hands on her feet and toes and she kept saying, in a nice way, but wanting to rush, "It is my back."

Five or six men and a host of women had by then gathered around us, but none came forward.

"Is anyone here a doctor?" I asked.

"No."

"Where is the nearest hospital?"

They named two towns, both roughly an hour away.

I gathered the men together, and we each slid our fingers beneath her head and back and legs and began to turn her over a bit. That's when I saw the pooled blood. It had soaked her shirt and the grass around it.

Someone said, "Disparador!"

I did not know that word in Spanish, and, terribly confused, I made a gun shape with my hand and said, "Bang bang?"

"Si, pistola," they all said together, nodding.

I ran back to the truck and drove it half a mile down the street, then across the grass median strip and into the parking lot of a lumberyard. I slammed the truck into reverse and backed into a covered loading area. I jumped out and grabbed the heaviest plywood board they had. I threw the wood into the bed of my truck and floored it out of the lot, quickly followed by six or eight astonished employees chasing after me as a thief. I drove the half-mile down the highway to the fallen woman in the oncoming lane (there is not much traffic in southwestern El Salvador). I spun the truck around and jumped out. Four men carried the plywood with me to her side. Then—on three—we all lifted her lightly onto the board.

The woman's sister had come upon our heart-breaking scene and stood close by, nearly hysterical. I helped the sister into the truck bed. The two siblings held hands. Blood seeped across the new plywood board. We took off, with Cesar directing me to the hospital.

Traffic built as I rushed toward the hospital. I cut around other cars, driving in the wrong lanes and honking like hell. The other drivers got pissed off but I didn't care. Then my truck stalled. I turned the ignition, pumping the gas. It wouldn't catch. A group of angry drivers climbed out of their cars and converged on my truck, and I stepped out to confront them. They were taken aback by my earnest manner. I pulled two of them forward to see the woman.

Suddenly they all jumped into action, pushing my truck until it started. Two of the drivers sped around me and broke trail all the way to the little town where the hospital was located. Once in town the traffic became unrelenting, nearly unmoving. I drove on sidewalks. I drove the wrong way down one-way streets. I drove toward oncoming traffic in a serious game of chicken, and was amazed that at the last second the others always moved. Finally, I was chased by three police cars. They caught me at a hopelessly locked bottleneck leading into the town square by a busy outdoor market.

I jumped out of the truck, and the police ran

toward me, shouting. I pointed at the woman in the back. The police saw her sister crying, and the blood, and they took control. They did what police are supposed to do. Two or three ran down the street, telling every car to move, yelling at the drivers until they had half the cars on the sidewalk. Police cruisers turned on all of their lights and sirens, and police on motorcycles cleared the way ahead. We pulled into the hospital courtyard a few minutes later and volunteers carried her in with me, still on the board.

The "hospital" was an old auditorium, something built for town meetings or a Rotary society. It had no air-conditioning and was stiflingly hot inside, and smelled horribly, mostly of chemical disinfectant. The building had no separate rooms—no rooms at all, in fact, merely sheets suspended from the ceiling by long, dark-stained, moldy ropes.

I spoke with a doctor for a few minutes. He told me he thought that she would survive but that I should leave immediately lest I be in some way blamed. I took his advice, and quietly fled the area. Exhausted from stress, we took the long way home, stopping on the side of a mountain road where I found an elderly woman cooking over a wood fire. She sold me three pupusas with cheese and beans for one dollar. I washed my hands in a metal bowl half filled with soapy water, and bought a couple of Cokes in glass bottles for 25 cents each.

We stopped at Super Repuestos and I purchased four very expensive car batteries. I tried, without luck, to find some cable tensioners and other fancy tools and boat stuff. I stopped at the lumberyard and paid for the piece of plywood we had used as a stretcher. And finally, drove back to the estero.

There, I made my way out to *Valkyrien* and lay down in the cockpit, my back against the broken captain's chair. I thought of this woman, shot in the back while riding her bicycle and her family, and said a few prayers. I thought too, of Vicki and our children at home, and how completely different our lives are. You can pull out of my driveway and ride down a single, unbroken piece of asphalt straight to San Salvador, and if you make a couple of small turns, you will end up on the roadside where that woman was shot. We are so connected to Central America and and so much apart from it.

I wanted badly to leave El Salvador, but I also loved it there. I loved everything about the country, except the violence. I loved the food and the people and the dichotomy of law and social norms and the warmth of the climate and the extraordinary storms. I loved traveling up the estero to where Cesar's grandmother lived in a grass-roofed mud hut with no electricity. But, my

God, I wanted to leave. I assured Vicki that all was fine, we were making progress each day. But of course she knew by the sound of my voice that it was time for me to get out.

25. Troy Returns

Believe me, my young friend, there is nothing—absolutely nothing— half so much worth doing as simply messing about in boats.
—KENNETH GRAHAM, *WATER RAT IN THE WIND IN THE WILLOWS*

One afternoon I decided to see how far up the *estero* we could get in the Whaler. Cesar and I sped across the harbor, then far inland until the water ended in a muddy swamp. As we passed farther and farther into the jungle, away from the roads, away from electricity and refrigeration, it was as if we were moving back in time. First the fiberglass boats disappeared. Then we stopped hearing the sounds of outboard motors; all the boats we saw up there were small and made only of wood. Most of the people were either very old, or children.

One old man, an indigene, built most of the canoes in the estero. He agreed to build one for me. He chose a tree in the forest and chopped it down, then hollowed it out. This generational shipwright left a thick part in the stern so I could hook up a 9.9-horsepower engine. He also left a couple of seats, roughly a third of the way toward each end. When he was finished, he presented me with one of the most beautiful canoes I have ever seen.

I had worked day after long day with Cesar, and we were completely sick of each other. I could not stand to be with him after he had refused to stop for the injured woman. And he was a terrible carpenter. Every carpenter makes mistakes. All of us are lazy at times. But you cannot cut a hole in a wooden boat without having the replacement wood on hand to repair the hole the same day. Wooden boats with holes sink. I needed to replace Cesar.

Vicki could sense my desperation in our late-night Skype calls. She knew I would never get *Valkyrien* out of the estero without help. The one man who could definitely save the day was my friend Troy, but he had stepped off *Valkyrien* back in Monterey, having fulfilled his promise, and had no interest in coming back.

Troy worked hard, long hours on complex jobs, managing the physical plant of a large building in downtown Los Angeles. He received ten days of vacation each year. If he came to El Salvador, Troy would have to use up all his vacation time, work harder, enveloped in heat, covered in sweat and soaked in diesel, tormented by mosquitoes and frustrated by the lack of supplies and tools. Somehow, though, Vicki convinced Troy that returning to El Salvador was the only sensible thing for him to do. She told Troy that this was the chance of a lifetime. She told him that he could vacation anytime, and that in twenty years all of those vacations would blend together into a single muddled memory of pleasant comfort. But if he joined me in El Salvador he would remember the trip for the rest of his life. She clinched it by saying, "Max needs you."

Troy showed up flush with cash and a brand-new Visa card from Vicki. I paid my outstanding debts to the hotel and various vendors, and everyone on the estero became much more relaxed.

The minute Troy arrived, I dragged him down to the pier and we jumped into the Whaler so I could show him the estero before the sun set. We skimmed atop the calm waters, at full throttle but going only about half speed, with the engine screaming a rough clank as the driveshaft rattled against whatever gears Cesar had mashed when he struck that log. We raced past the grass-roof huts and rows of brightly colored dugout canoes at the edge of the estero. The beach, like so many others at primitive villages around the world, was covered almost completely in trash. Salvador provides no sanitation services to these villages, and the indigenous people continue to simply discard rubbish on the ground, as they have always done; the difference is that now, because so much is plastic, the trash does not disappear.

We ran a mile or so up the estero and then

turned hard around, tilting the Whaler, angling in a smooth arc, narrowly grazing the deep green mangrove banks overgrown on each side. At Cesar's home they use the mangrove as charcoal in their cooking fires. Pottery shards—many of them from pre-Columbian times—litter the whole area.

We sped back down and out of the estero, awed by its beauty but also worried about what it might look like in another ten years, and where and how families like Cesar's would scrape by. I ran the Whaler past a small Indian village, their homes built on stilts along a narrow bank, then turned west toward the sea. I took the Whaler through the eight-foot standing waves at its bar, into the Pacific, as a full moon lit up a completely clear night sky.

Later, we drove the Whaler back to *Valkyrien*, where I showed Troy the dugout canoe. Troy is a third-generation carpenter, and he marveled at the strength of the wood, and the difficult work of hacking the canoe out of a tree trunk. But he was horrified when he realized I planned to take the canoe with us; dragging it behind seemed a terrible idea, and lifting the heavy canoe onto our deck, even worse. In the end I convinced Troy that we could not leave this artifact behind.

We checked the oil level in *Valkyrien's* diesel, then started up the big engine. I tried the reverse gear, checking the wiring and the genset. Everything worked.

I slept well that night.

Mostly because of Troy's know-how and skills, we were able to get a lot of stuff fixcd on the *Valkyrien* that had been deemed impossible. Locals said the boat would have to be pulled out of the water to have the rudder re-seated, but Troy and I righted it in the water using scuba gear. I had propped up the worm drive with several 2x4s jammed into the sides of the cockpit. We were told that the entire worm gear would need to be replaced, but Troy rebuilt the steering box and magically repaired the worm gear.

Troy also realized that it made no sense to head south with only one hundred nautical miles' worth of fuel, especially as there had been no wind (apart from vicious storms) for most of our time in Central America. The Nicaraguan coast offered almost no opportunities to fuel up.

Cesar had promised to repair the bowsprit, but had done no work on it, and the masts, without forestays, were not strong enough to sail. That was another reason we needed to carry more fuel. I did not want to pay for fuel tanks to be installed, and even standard, portable diesel tanks cost a fortune in Central America.

Troy is a meticulous man, and by the time he arrived in the estero, he had become a bit wary of some of my ideas. Though he was always up for adventure, Troy spent much more time thinking of what could go wrong than about how great it would be just to try. We complemented each other well in that sense. I envisioned great trips; Troy made them succeed. Buying the diesel drums, though, was a mistake we made together.

Troy and I looked at dozens of different potential containers and finally purchased some inexpensive eighty-gallon drums used to transport water to cattle on local farms. I had not seen too many drums that were larger than fifty-five gallons. These tanks were humongous, nearly as tall as me, a few feet wide, and made of a material that would eventually be dissolved by the diesel fuel, but hopefully not before they had served their purpose.

I purchased six of them. This was perhaps my best idea, and worst execution of the trip. Had we spent five times as much money, the trip would have been ten times easier.

We realized that there was no way to safely secure the drums to the decks (each tank weighed about five hundred pounds), so we took some measurements and removed *Valkyrien's* center hatch, then slid all six tanks, empty, into the main saloon. They fit tightly, which was perfect; we wanted them to move as little as possible. Even so, we strapped them together and tied the tanks down several times over with cargo straps and ropes. And then we filled them with diesel.

Unfortunately, we spilled a fair amount of diesel while filling the tanks. The bungs on top of the tanks were designed to hold water with the tank motionless on dry land. The diesel sloshed against these weak plugs at every wave and soon dislodged the plastic tops. Diesel fuel spilled out the top and puddled on the cabin sole. Troy fashioned new bungs using cloth and plastic, and they held well, although the odor of diesel remained strong.

We were disappointed about the spilled diesel, but all in all, the plastic fuel tanks really seemed a great, financially efficient solution to the fuel issue. It was possible, almost probable, that we could make it to Panama in one shot—a week or so at sea and then the Canal. That one-week jaunt developed into the most challenging slog of my life. Diesel became our maddening lifeblood.

The fuel tanks leaked. The tanks, well anchored, did not move, but the diesel inside sloshed back and forth, especially when we began drawing down their contents to burn in the Detroit. It seemed that for the next few weeks Troy and I were always covered in diesel fuel. Diesel coated the floorboards of the boat and its fumes entered our lungs. Our food pantry was located in the same room as the diesel drums, so diesel eventually soaked all of our food containers. Diesel is a solvent of plastic, and all of our water bottles soon carried the acid taste of hydrocarbons. Our hair and beards smelled so strongly that in the end I grew used to and actually came to like the scent of diesel fuel.

After several days of diesel poisoning, even walking can become an ordeal. For the most part the effects were a vaguely sore throat (not terribly uncomfortable, but unremitting); lost concentration (it became more difficult to fit screwdrivers into slotted screws or to choose the correct wrench for a given nut size); skin that got dry and became blotchy and red; irritability; and just a general tendency to become confused. (I think I actually liked the lightheadedness, but it did slow down our work.)

We blamed these symptoms, at the time, more on the sun and the gentle rolling of the boat than the diesel, but upon returning from the trip, I noticed that virtually all of the symptoms resumed if I worked on a diesel engine and spilled any appreciable amounts of the fuel on my body.

Sometimes, while pumping diesel from one tank to another, a hose clamp would come loose. The diesel, streaming from the hose, sprayed around the room like one of those children's toys attached to a lawn sprinkler. I would look at Troy as if to say "This is the most effed-up thing I have ever done."

Troy would look back at me and say, "Man,

what are you complaining about? This is fresh air compared to a day welding galvanized steel! Now, that stuff is bad for you."

I was so grateful every day to have Troy with me. He could fix anything, and no one can laugh more heartily at folly than Troy.

26. *Ghosts*

*"Intimacy grows quick out there," I said.
"I knew him as well as it is
possible for one man to know another."*
—JOSEPH CONRAD, *MARLOW IN HEART OF
DARKNESS*

Late one afternoon, at no particular impetus, Troy and I decided to head back out to sea and points south. I do things often for no reason, like a cow choosing between which of two bales of hay to begin eating. Many more things needed to be done aboard *Valkyrien*, but she was packed with food and fuel, and Troy was running out of time before he had to return to his job. Whatever still needed to be done could wait for Panama.

We cruised out past the harbor entrance, waving good-bye to Cesar. He told us we should not leave; he had a bad feeling about the boat. I thought to myself, Well, maybe you wouldn't have such a bad feeling if you had done more to repair her. But I kept those thoughts to myself.

When Troy and I finally departed El Salvador, we towed both the Whaler and the hand-carved canoe. Dragging two dinghies created new problems. The boats required a nearly constant watch to ensure that their lines did not foul. Every sailor in every port told me to cast the canoe adrift; it had no value and offered only hassles. But it was designed and built by a true master who had learned the trade from his father, and his father before that, going back to a time before the Spanish came. I wanted badly to bring it home to Cape Cod.

As night fell, we cruised rather serenely along the shores of El Salvador. The sky grew black long before the sun disappeared. Troy and I started to think we heard a screaming. Neither of us said anything. But when the unnerving cry did not let up, Troy turned to me and said, "Do you hear that?"

"Of course I do."

Troy looked at me, alarmed. "Why didn't you say something?"

"What the hell was I going to say? 'Hey, Troy, do you hear that ghost?' "

Troy laughed uncomfortably. "What do you think it is, Max—some sort of animal?"

"Not out here."

Troy was used to me inventing silly stories to create a sense of security on the boat, and I think he found it upsetting that I offered no explanation for the eerie calling.

I saw a tiny light in the distance, barely visible, and dead ahead of us. I stared at the light for a minute or two. Troy looked ahead for the first time and saw the light. He shouted, "Do you see that? What the hell is that?" Troy realized as he spoke that I had been looking at the thing, quietly, for a while. This made him even more concerned. He knew then that I did not know what it was, either—a single unblinking white light, several miles off the shore of a deserted coast.

"I guess it's a fisherman coming in at the end of the day."

"But why is he screaming like that?" Troy asked.

I looked up at the evening sky, which had become astonishingly dark in only a few minutes.

"Maybe about the weather?" I said.

By this time we could make out in the dusk a dark figure, standing over a small canoe and slowly swinging a lantern back and forth. The weather had become suddenly cold. Not merely cooler, but actually cold. The fisherman had pulled some kind of dark shawl over his body against the chill, making him look even more an apparition.

His appalling intonation continued, and it became clear he was sounding an alarm.

Troy said, "Don't you think we should head away from him?"

"No, if he is waving a lantern, either he needs help, or he is offering help to us."

"How could he possibly help us, with his little boat?"

"By giving a warning to people who do not know these waters and their weather."

Troy appeared both demoralized and distressed by my answer. It was unnerving that despite our obvious heeding of his call, the cloaked fisherman continued to howl.

He shouted, long and slow, like a night watchman in a medieval village. His wail was both plaintive and commanding. And it slowly became intelligible. He was repeating the same sounds over and over. "*Tee . . . ray . . . more!*"

He paused for a moment, then stretched the words out a little longer. "*Teeeee raaaaay moooorrrrre.*"

A long pause and then: "*Un teeee raaaay mooorrre.*"

Another pause, followed by: "*Eaar eaar un tee ray moorrre!*"

The sea somehow absorbed the blackness of the sky. There was no wind. It is rare to have absolutely no wind on the ocean. But the sea appeared reflective, like glass, as we approached this lone fisherman with his lantern. He stood at the stern of his little wooden panga, dangling the lantern like a lit skull. He looked like Death as it is portrayed in medieval artwork, continuing to scream his shrill and piercing dirge. "*Ear ear tee ray morrrrrre!*"

What sounded like "ear," spelled *ir* in Spanish, means "Leave!" or "Run away!" Staring at us through huge darkened eyes as though he were driving a raft across the River Styx, the old man shrieked at us to go back. He stood in his boat as we passed within perhaps six feet of his shadowy figure. For a moment, he stopped waving his lantern. It was clear to him, as he looked me in the eye, that I would not heed his warning, and he did not say another word. He simply stood, staring as we moved southward, silent, disappearing several minutes later below our dark horizon. I had no idea what the old man had been shouting, but I that he was warning us against something really bad. And it was headed straight for us.

I turned *Valkyrien* west.

Troy said, "Oh, good, we're turning around. That's a good idea. Good decision, Max. Tough one, going back and all, but I agree with you—it's the right thing to do."

Instead of turning all the way around, though, I just headed west, out to sea, to deeper water. I could see Troy growing agitated.

"Is there something in the water here, Max?" he asked politely. "Is that why you are taking so long to make the turn?"

"No, Troy, we're not going back."

"What do you mean, we're not going back? You heard that guy. Something terrible is about to happen! It sounds like there's going to be an earthquake or something. Maybe a tidal wave! We have to get out of here, quick!"

"Well, the word in Spanish for earthquake is *terremoto*, so that may be what he was saying."

"Well, let's turn this boat around and get back there, quick."

"Troy, you know that if there is an earthquake coming, and the fishermen already know it, then we have very little time to prepare. We would never make it back to port before it hits."

"What if it is something else? A storm or a hurricane?"

"Troy, if we were back in the estero, that would be fine. But by the way he was shouting I don't think we have more than five minutes. We'll never get across those sandbars at night, in a storm, on a falling tide. The safest place for us to be is in the deepest water we can find—and out there is where the deep water is, so that is where we're headed."

Troy knew I did not like to give explanations for my decisions, so he understood how important this issue had become.

"Troy, it's time to start tying down everything you can. Take below anything that cannot get wet. Bring the big pump first, and wrap it in a tarp. Tie it down well so that it can't slide. And then get on the rest of the stuff."

• • •

Midnight. No waves. No wind. About ten miles offshore, I saw another light, and turned the wheel left, changing our angle slightly south to pass close by. An empty boat, illumined by a single 12-volt bulb, came slowly into view—a lone wooden canoe, apparently adrift in the night. I sailed over to this coffin-like bark, which somehow had become, in my mind at least, more menacing than a rocky shore.

As we passed by, a few feet from this dugout, I saw the tiny white light had been taped to the front of the canoe. In the shadow of this light, pinned by his knees into the bottom of the boat, lay a lone fishermen, holding on and braced tight. This man knew that he would never make it to shore in time. Even if it filled with water, though, his little boat, cut from the trunk of a tree, would continue to float. His best chance was to stay with that boat.

I pulled up beside him and he said, flatly, without excitement, as though he were pointing out a wild animal grazing: "*Terremore.*"

I still had no idea what that meant.

"Big wind, rain?" I asked in my awful Spanish.

"Yes! Yes! Much, much wind, much, much rain. *Terremore.*"

I learned later that *terremore* is a unique word, used only by the indigenous people of El Salvador (and sometimes Guatemala and northern Nicaragua), to describe what we would call a white squall, which is a fierce biting storm that can rise out of nowhere, almost without warning, except to those who fish for their lives outside the Gulf of Fonseca.

I stopped *Valkyrien* next to this fisherman and talked with him quietly as the storm built around us. The fisherman made it clear he thought we would die, but conceded that there was now nothing to be done. He refused to come aboard *Valkyrien*. He felt badly that he couldn't at least take one of us in his dugout canoe, knowing I guess that a tender reed can sway in a breeze that will knock down an oak. He figured we would sink while his boat would fill with water, but remain on the surface. He lay back down below the gunwales of his canoe as we motored away. He did not watch us.

The storm hit us hard about fifteen minutes later. It came in and struck us in the face like a straight right from José Torres. Rain smashed us. The biting downpour tore at my eyes. Troy handed me a scuba mask, which I quickly slipped on. I considered using the snorkel too (wearing it upside down), because so much water traveled through the air—a mix of sea foam and rain. It was difficult for me even to breathe. The sea roiled, confused. Lightning crashed all around the boat, and waves struck us from various directions.

Less than half an hour after it had begun, the storm departed. We were left, the two of us, standing together by the wheel, soaking wet and unnerved. But *Valkyrien* had been well prepared for the storm and, aside from taking on a lot of water as she pitched from side to side, *Valkyrien* rode strong. Six hours later, the real storm began. A *Terremore*, it turns out, is a white squall that can last for days.

27. A Bit of a Situation for Troy

There are some things you learn best in calm, and some in storm.
—WILLA CATHER, THEA KRONBERG, *THE SONG OF THE LARK*

The storm that hit us off of the Gulf of Fonseca and drove us to Costa Rica was the worst I have ever been through. The stays came loose, masts shifted back and forth. Mast frames cracked and pulled out of the deck. Without sails, *Valkyrien* dipped violently from side to side and fore and aft. She tipped so much during this storm that her sides dipped into the ocean. Later, as the storm progressed, the entire safety rail would bury beneath the water, first on one side, then the other.

Gradually *Valkyrien's* starboard side would rise out of the sea, lifting water across her deck and pouring it down and off the other side through generous scuttles. Then she would tip below on the port side. As the storm wore on, she began tipping so much that after the bulwarks slipped under, she continued to roll, until finally even the pin rails submerged below the sea. I am not saying that the pin rails were splashed by waves—I mean, they were fully submerged.

I looked at the pin boxes—wooden contraptions attached to the side stays, about three feet above the pin rails, that hold rows of belaying pins in place. Eventually she began tipping so far that these boxes also were going under.

We slogged for thirty-six long hours, tossed and buffeted in the heart of the storm like a bathtub toy. I knew we stood a good chance of tearing out the masts if we tried putting sails up in that wind. It was a challenge just to move about the boat. We tied two lines down the length of her belowdecks and cinched them tight, making a kind of flexible balustrade. She tipped so hard that we walked on the walls as often as we stepped along the floors.

If I were in the galley and needed a tool from the bow, I would begin by crossing along the floor, and then as the boat tipped, I would switch to walking along the wall (which had become the floor), and then as she righted herself, I would walk along the floor again, and then as she continued tipping, walk along the opposite wall.

In the first gusts of the terremore, virtually nothing fell. But during the ensuing thirty-six hours, nearly everything came loose. Though we kept the gas-fired pump and the emergency generator and other "big things" tied down seven ways, the small stuff knocked around everywhere, rolling back and forth, up the walls, along the floor, into the bilge and back again, over and over. Dark, dirty water climbed out of the bilge into our bunks, soaking everything with a putrid foulness. Diesel fuel leaked out of the six gigantic storage tanks in the main saloon. It mixed with the bilge water and the fresh seawater which poured in more and more rapidly as the storm raged and *Valkyrien's* seams continued to open.

The diesel fuel for the most part sat in a thin film on top of the bilge water. As the boat turned over and back, the diesel ran highest up the walls and was first to enter our bunks. It soaked our shoes, and penetrated our exposed skin. My feet swelled so much that they barely fit into my sneakers. But when we walked without shoes, the skin on our feet peeled off. My hands swelled to the point where I had difficulty gripping and handling tools. My eyes grew crazily bloodshot, and I grew nauseous and often vomited up spittle which I spat over the side. Troy and I both experienced these symptoms due to a combination of lack of sleep and seasickness, combined with the diesel poisoning.

I did not want Troy to lose his confidence so throughout the storm I acted not merely as though nothing were wrong, but as if I were thoroughly enjoying the experience. Stalwart Troy reached a point where he refused to step out of the cabin.

I sat up in the companionway, by the cockpit, pushing my head into the galley and singing Neil Diamond songs, trying to lighten the mood. As the gunwales of the boat dipped underwater, I leaned down and said to Troy, "Hey, can you pass me a peanut butter and jelly sandwich and some fresh potato chips?"

"Are you kidding me, Max? Are you really thinking of food right now? We might die, and you want me to make you a peanut butter and jelly sandwich?"

"Troy, come on, man. Don't be lazy. I've been sitting up here for, like, six hours. I'm hungry as hell. I can understand you wanting to go to sleep and all, but seriously, please at least make me a PB-and-J before you go to bed."

At this point, of course, diesel-contaminated bilge water was sloshing over everything—Troy's sleeping bag, his shirts, pants, and socks—coating them in slimy toxic black bilge gunk.

"Sleep? You think I'm going to sleep? You're joking, right? Tell me you aren't scared, Max. I know why you're acting this way—to try and make me feel better. But you are scared, aren't you? Seriously, is this dangerous? Are we going to die?"

"Troy, come on, man, you and I have been out in wind like this so many times. Look, the waves aren't even as high as the spreaders on the smaller mast. The only issue we're facing is that I am hungry and you refuse to make me a PB-and-J, which I think is selfish and, frankly, uncharacteristic of you. So, seriously, there's a fresh bag of chips behind the bookcase by the water bottles. Please bring it up with the sandwiches, because I like to eat them at the same time."

I kept riding him this way and actually succeeded in distracting him at times from the terror around us. Then lightning would crack just a hundred feet or so to starboard, and *Valkyrien* would tremble, and I could smell something burning in the air.

For a moment, on top of a wave, we could see into the distance as the lightning struck and illuminated the cloud-filled sky in a flash of stark white shadow. A moment later, in the trough, we were again enveloped in near-total blackness. The Whaler, tugging behind, sometimes pulled the towline absolutely tight. At other times, the line had completely disappeared, and the Whaler lit up like an apparition only a few feet from the cockpit, having ridden a steep wave and careening toward us.

At these times I would turn to Troy and muster a puzzled look, saying something like: "Do you think I'll be able to find bolts that will match up to that steering linkage?"

Troy would be staring down at the silent motor through floorboards that he had removed in order to keep an eye on things. Quick as a switch, he'd look up, meeting my gaze, trying to figure out whether or not I was putting him on.

"What steering linkage?"

"The Toyota—you know, those last two bolts are weird; they kind of have that cone shape at the end."

Then the lightning would flash again and the thunder would explode and he would jerk his head at me and say, "You're just messing with me, right? You don't really care about those bolts. You're just trying to take my mind off this, right?"

"Troy, why do you think I would give a flying F in a rolling doughnut if you're scared? Have I ever shown any care for your well-being in the history of our relationship? Why would I start right now? You're down here for a limited time. If you were going to quit your job and stay with me, I could deal with all of the other stuff later, but I need to get that Jeep going, so I need to figure out the bolts while you're here. What kind of tool do you think we could use to cut into some number 8s that is strong enough for us to shape as we cut?"

For a moment, Troy would live inside that problem—how to repair a forty-year-old Toyota Jeep. In this way we avoided talking about the storm and the fairly dire situation I had led him into. Sometimes it even took Troy's mind off our predicament entirely. I sang songs and laughed and talked about tools and hardware, and asked Troy about painting the Sperry town water tank green when he graduated from high school. (Troy climbed the tank, the tallest structure by half in his hometown, and painted it all night long.) The tower has never been repainted, and he has that night by which to remember the "Class of 1995."

Sometime after the events in this book took place, safe at home in Los Angeles, I was laughing with my children while relating the story of the terremore and of how terrified I had been. Troy, who happened to be in another room, overheard me. I had forgotten that I'd never owned up to him about it. He was dumbfounded. Troy said he did not think he would have made it through that night if he had known how scared I was—which made me really happy. I actually have come to think of that night as one of my greatest accomplishments. (I do like scaring the heck out of my friends—but not for real.)

The wind and storm lasted for several days. It was at its worst for nearly thirty-six hours, which is the longest time I've ever spent in a boat with the heart of a storm directly overhead.

The storm knocked out the generator, and we lost our auxiliary gas tanks. Our diesel was stored below, but the gas tanks had to be kept on deck for safety; eventually, the storm waves worked them free and overboard. The diesel generator was missing its cooling pump, and our standby gasoline generator had to be run in the open air (not feasible in that storm); running it belowdecks would have poisoned us. Loss of this equipment forced us to rely solely on the standard bilge pump to clear the bilge, and because we had limited battery power, all other electrical equipment aboard the *Valkyrien* had to be turned off.

For two days the storm blew us south, past Honduras, across the Gulf of Fonseca, and down the entire coast of Nicaragua. We never saw Nicaragua. Lightning broke overhead, dramatically illuminating the night sky, yet we never saw another boat. When I say "overhead," I mean, directly overhead. Lightning shook the boat and burned the air around us.

With the need to conserve electricity for the pumps, we couldn't use GPS, and our compass was unreliable at best. Luckily, we were able to make do with a standby compass I had purchased on eBay to use in my truck.

Now and then the storm slackened a bit, leaving only the waves. During those breaks we made what repairs we could to the masts and rigging. The storm finally broke as we stood off the shore of Costa Rica. The sea and our senses mercifully calmed. Troy and I lay down and rested, sleeping well as *Valkyrien* bobbed serenely. Several hours later we woke, rose from our filthy bunks and checked all of the fluids in the engine then, started it up. The diesel ran perfectly.

We motored for most of the following night. Around sunrise, we approached Cabo Blanco and the entrance to the Golfo de Nicoya. We ran headlong into the steep current, pulling out of the Gulf, and just as we reached the tip of the cape, the engine made a terrible sound. A metallic death rattle of finality. Awful, thick white smoke rose heavily from our exhaust.

Troy and I knew we had a big problem.

28. *Puntarenas*

Bullfight critics ranked in rows,
crowd the enormous plaza full.
But only one is there who knows,
and he's the one who fights the bull.
—DOMINGO ORTEGA, SPANISH BULLFIGHTER

We drifted along for much of the morning, with no ability to control our direction. Our efforts to restart the engine produced nothing. Sailing wasn't an option. The masts and stays were too weak to carry sails. And so we were stuck there, on the edge of Costa Rica, with no way to move. We had spent three days battling a terrible storm, and came out of it a couple of hundred miles from where we'd started. Our engine was broken. We found ourselves wholly at the mercy of the wind, tide, and currents. We had very few options.

We drifted along for much of the morning, at the edge of Cabo Blanco. My mind drifted too— often to our last resort—the trusty Boston Whaler still tied to our stern. The wind blew lightly, and eventually the current lifted us into the calm waters of the Gulf of Nicoya.

I walked through our various options in my mind, then called down to waken Troy, asking him come on deck to talk about our situation. I figured we had a few choices, none of them good. I summed up the situation for Troy: Because of the torn bowsprit, ripped stays, and weakened deck, sailing was out of the question. As for the engine, the color of the smoke coming from the exhaust indicated that cooling water had entered the cylinder head, which at a minimum would mean that a seal had broken, and at worst, that the head had warped or cracked. In any event, we would not be able to start the motor.

We were drifting a couple miles off of a vicious coral reef, and the rocky point at Cabo Blanco, at the northern opening of the Gulf of Fonseca in Costa Rica. At any moment, a shift in tide or wind could push us onto the rocks, where the *Valkyrien* would be torn to pieces. Our depth meter no longer functioned, but our charts told us the water was way too deep to anchor.

Our first option was to lay out all of the anchor chain, dangling the old Danforth two hundred feet below us, hoping that the anchor would catch ground in a favorable location. This would buy us time to figure out what to do. Alternatively, we could scuttle the boat right there in the deep waters of the Pacific Ocean and take the Whaler to shore and head home.

The final option was for Troy to drive the Whaler to shore and find a boat that could tow us to Puntarenas. I would remain aboard *Valkyrien*, alone, keeping watch. If we drifted too close to the rocks I would jump in the dugout canoe and paddle to safety ashore.

Troy had an intense desire at that point to get off *Valkyrien*. I don't think he liked the idea at all of letting her sink in international waters, and drifting had no appeal for him. The cost of hiring a tugboat to pull us the fifty or so nautical miles inland to Puntarenas was absolutely prohibitive—in the neighborhood of $10,000. My best hope was that Troy would be able to find a fisherman with a seagoing trawler who would do it for under $1,000—still a huge bummer for me.

The Whaler had worked perfectly for the first eighteen months of our journey, but the engine sounded terrible ever since Cesar had crashed her. We knew that the outboard would quit at some point, but the Whaler is unsinkable, so Troy's trip sounded doable.

I looked at the charts, and climbed up the ratlines with Troy to point him toward the most likely places to find a trawler. Then I said goodbye. I watched Troy race out toward the coast and could hear the engine of the Whaler for a long time before it faded into the other noises of the sea.

I grew up in a family with eleven children. My wife Vicki and I are extraordinarily close. We met when I was twenty-one, and have been together ever since. Unless I am aboard a boat, we rarely go more than half a day without sending at least a brief message to each other. I had essentially spent my entire life without ever being alone. Of course, I sometimes sailed by myself, but always on a day-sailing sloop. I think that the time I spent on *Valkyrien*, drifting at the edge of the territorial waters of Costa Rica, was the first appreciable period of time I had been truly alone in my entire life.

Troy promised that whether or not he found a fisherman to tow us, he would return in two hours. *Valkyrien* barely moved as the current ebbed, and I lay down below for a few minutes on my bunk.

That's when I heard someone on deck.

The boat had been absolutely silent. Then I heard the planks creaking. I knew someone had stepped aboard. I froze in my bunk, and did not make a sound. After a few minutes, I heard men talking on deck. I couldn't make out any words, but it sounded like Spanish, with almost a W. C. Fields accent. I hoped that it was just some old fishermen who had seen the *Valkyrien* drifting, unmanned, and had come aboard to investigate.

I made some loud noises, hoping they would hear me and depart. For a moment they became perfectly still. I waited for the men to paddle away on whatever panga they had arrived on, but then I heard them creeping around and talking again. Their words were unintelligible through the thick deck. But it sounded like three old men. I shouted, in Spanish, "I am here. I am the Captain. Get off my boat!"

The intruders froze. I waited below, with growing concern. Then they started talking again. I guessed they were trying to decide what to do—whether to confront me or just leave. I picked up a knife and a bluefish bat and suddenly, with no warning, I leapt to the deck, screaming.

Just in front of the cabin house, I saw three very large brown pelicans. They looked at me as though I were out of my mind and went back to their conversation. I laughed, and shooed them off the boat.

I walked the deck after that, checking for loose shrouds and stays, and repairing the masts. Troy had been gone a good long time, and I figured that he must have found a fisherman and was negotiating. But I also began to wonder if something could have happened to him. He had only to travel ten or twelve miles on the Whaler, headed toward a harbor that was protected by a reef. Still, I worried.

The breeze came up a bit, to about 5 knots, blowing *Valkyrien* inside the Gulf of Nicoya. I decided to try flying the genoa like a kite, to see if I could steer the *Valkyrien* like a kite-surfer. I tied three lines to the genoa, and stretched it out as far as I could, lifting the puffy triangular sail up into the air slowly until it caught the following wind. Then, with the sheets pulled back through blocks on the deck, I let it out about eighty feet. Remarkably, the kite-sail steadied itself.

I could not sail through the night alone, and I could not anchor in the Gulf of Nicoya (too deep). I had to find some shallow cove to anchor up and spend the night. Fortunately the southern coast of the Nicoya peninsula is dotted with coves, and most have easy entrances. With the precarious kite-sail, I could now turn the *Valkyrien* a few degrees left or right, perhaps just enough to enter one of the coves. The genoa lifted *Valkyrien* along, directly toward a group of two or three coves that each offered a perfect depth to anchor. If the wind held, I would make it to the opening of one of these coves just before dark. Single-handing *Valkyrien* was always tough, but entering a strange cove at night, and anchoring her successfully with no engine and makeshift sails, seemed a long shot. With luck, though I could drift in on mere boat speed, drop the anchor, and hold.

I cruised along the coast for the rest of the afternoon, happily dragged by this huge kite but worried about Troy. I also worried about *Valkyrien*, and, quite frankly, myself.

As the sun set, the wind slipped away, and I wished very much that Troy had not left. I had to edge closer to shore in order to make it into a cove. But the shore was covered with rocks. If the wind fell away, I would lose control and we would be smashed.

Twilight came, and the wind rose once more. I saw the lights of a boat coming toward me. A big boat, running fast. Too fast, I thought, to be a commercial fishing boat. The vessel turned and made a huge loop around *Valkyrien*. She had perhaps thirty men standing along the rails, wearing blue uniforms and flying the flag of the Coast Guard of Costa Rica. At first I thought they had come to rescue me.

I did not want to be rescued. I have had an aversion to rescue my entire life. I knew that if I took the boat out, it was my job to bring her back to harbor. I hoped that, seeing me safely sailing, they would go away. But as I looked more closely at this Coast Guard boat, I saw that all of the men on her side were holding assault rifles, and it dawned on me that this was not a rescue but a boarding party.

The captain called to me in Spanish over his loudspeakers. I could not understand the words, but as he was speaking I saw the entrance to a small cove. I pulled down the kite-sail and turned into the cove, using *Valkyrien's* momentum. The thousands of pounds of lead in her keel drove her forward for nearly a mile with the Coast Guardsmen dogging, close to my side.

As I turned into the wind, *Valkyrien* halted, and I ran to the bow to drop the anchor and show our papers to the Coast Guard. I wondered and worried for Troy; what had happened to him? And how would he find his way back?

But before I could release the heavy anchor, the Coast Guard vessel pulled up just a few feet from my bow. None of the men aboard were smiling, which is unusual in Costa Rica. They brought forward a crewman who shouted to me, in broken English, to shut off all power (which was easy, as I had none) and prepare to be taken under tow.

They had come to arrest me and impound the *Valkyrien*!

29. *Temporary Fixes*

At times, indeed, almost ridiculous.
—T. S. Eliot, THE LOVE SONG OF
J. ALFRED PRUFROCK

The sailors passed me a large rope. Despite my protestations they forced me to tie it off to the bow, and they began towing me out of the cove. The huge rope cut into *Valkyrien's* bow like a forestry cable saw. It was painful to watch, but I could do nothing to stop it.

After an hour or so, we reached another cove, farther into the Gulf of Nicoya, where they released their lines and ordered me to anchor up. At that point, a contingent of ten or twelve armed men approached me in a whaleboat from the CG cutter. The men climbed aboard *Valkyrien*. Three approached me directly and pointed their machine guns at my chest, motioning for me to put my hands in the air, while two others frisked me. They then sat me down cross-legged, my arms held straight up, while their leader (the Capitan) climbed aboard *Valkyrien*.

I realized that this guy would never shoot me. I had no guns, no drugs, nothing that is illegal in Costa Rica. So I knew too, that he would not arrest me. But I figured he would probably detain me for several hours, or more, and I felt frustration at my confinement and a good deal of fear.

He looked at me with a practiced glare of contempt, then shouted: "Where do you keep your guns?"

In an accelerated, emotional series of questions, pronounced roughly, but in a precise and direct manner, like a verdict, he yelled in English: "Why are you entering Costa Rica?"

Then:

"Who is the owner of the boat?"

"Where are the drugs?"

"Where is the money?"

"What is your name?"

"Where is your identification?"

I remained silent, cross-legged, trying to figure out how best to respond in a way that would get me out of this as quickly and with as few repercussions as possible. I do not respond diplomatically when threatened, and it took every ounce of self-control not to lash out at this bully. His men were well armed and in full control, physically and emotionally. I was unarmed, pacific, and remained in the legally required physical position of disadvantage—legs crossed, arms held straight up, and palms facing out toward the armed men. I knew, under those conditions, they would not shoot me. I thought of Prufrock, "Politic, cautious, and meticulous." None of these words describe me.

After a while, the Capitan ordered me to go belowdecks with him. I refused. I wanted to remain in front of as many witnesses as possible. He ordered me again, and had his men thrust their guns at my chest. I also wanted to show that while I would comply with requests for safety, I was unafraid of his weapons.

"There is no way I am going down there with you. No way."

I spoke each syllable clearly, pausing between each word, and never taking my eyes off of him while I spoke (pretending not to look at the guns they had pointed at me, though in reality I was terribly frightened). The Capitan barked an order at his crew and several of his men climbed below.

Two guardsmen returned almost immediately with my leather secretary (from a shelf just below the staircase) filled with our papers—copies of *Valkyrien's* registration, title, the contract selling the boat, Troy's passport as well as mine, and immigration and exit stamps from Mexico, Guatemala, and El Salvador.

I looked through the papers with the Capitan, and had a moment to reflect on the travails of the journey. I did not pay much attention to days and dates on the trip (particularly during the terremore), and when I looked through the official documents I realized that it was Thursday, late in November.

My family at home was celebrating Thanksgiving. I felt the stark contrast of me, sitting alone with my arms in the air on this nearly wrecked boat, while my family sat at the table together, eating sweet potatoes and turkey only a few miles from First Encounter Beach in Eastham. Thanksgiving is the most uniquely American, and in some ways, the most patriotic of all our holidays. I felt so far away from my wife, my children, and my country. They were at home, safe and cared for, but with an empty chair. I wondered how it was for them to celebrate Thanksgiving with me absent. We were in totally different worlds at this point.

I comforted myself with the knowledge that we had less than five hundred miles to Panama—like sailing from New York to Bar Harbor. I knew we could finish the trip before Christmas.

The captain sent a larger search crew below, but their leader returned to *Valkyrien's* deck and reported that they could not see in the dark. The Capitan ordered me to turn on *Valkyrien's* interior lights. None of her interior lights had worked since the day we'd purchased the boat. Everything we did on *Valkyrien* at night was accomplished by flashlight and the little plastic lights you can buy at Pep Boys that stick to the interior roof of your car.

I told the Capitan that the lights did not function, and he became irate, stepping toward me and screaming that he would take me to jail ashore if I did not immediately and fully cooperate. He ordered me to my feet. His men marched me back and forth along the deck, having me sit down, then stand up again, march forward, then march back, always with my hands in the air. I had not eaten a meal nor slept in thirty-six hours.

The Costa Rican Coast Guard search team was absolutely bewildered by the condition of *Valkyrien* belowdecks. Military cases, many of them cracked and broken, had been strewn about during the storm. Miscellaneous equipment lay piled three feet deep from the engine compartment through to the bow. In the center of this pile sat the six huge barrels of diesel fuel. It didn't help that I'd carried nearly every item aboard *Valkyrien* in those military boxes purchased at the government auction (every box seemed to be labeled "Property of US Navy"). The searchers found satellite phones, broken computers, currency from four countries, plus all sorts of fancy (although not-functioning) navigation equipment.

Every single one of my US Army rifle boxes and night-vision binoculars cases had fallen out of their cabinets and shelving during the storm, many colliding together. Nearly every single box had broken, and every bag had torn. The mess was astonishing. I had a ton of stuff in those plastic storage boxes.

A five-gallon bucket of oil had cracked open during the storm. The oil had seeped out of the oil storage area, spilled across the galley, slid down into my bunk, then mixed with the diesel fuel that had sloshed out of the huge plastic tanks. The spilled oil wallowed with all of the clothing and electronic equipment and ropes and first-aid gear and pens and pencils, paper, a Hewlett Packard printer, flashlight batteries, car batteries, bars of soap, folding knives—on and on. Forty-weight engine oil, ninety-weight transmission oil, two-stroke oil for the pump, paper towels, cloth towels, brake cleaner—a seemingly endless mess.

"Why do you have so many computers?" the Capitan asked.

"Why do you have a military computer?"

"Why is everything all over the place?"

"Why did you leave everything all over so we cannot walk?"

"Why don't your lights work?"

"Turn on your lights!"

I told them the lights just didn't work; they hadn't come on since we'd left San Francisco.

That night about an hour after I'd vehemently insisted once more that the lights did not work, all of the lights suddenly blazed on! It should have been funny, but it wasn't. I have no idea what combination of buttons their boarding party hit, or which out-of-place wire bounced back on its circuit and made those lights ignite. They did not merely turn on, they lit up bright as the sun. The inside of *Valkyrien* looked like the grass field at RFK Stadium during Monday Night Football. Every single corner of the boat was completely illuminated.

This really irritated the Coast Guard captain. He came forward and shouted in my face, angry and talking really fast in Spanish, saying something about taking me to jail if I did not cooperate. He stared at me, waiting.

I stared back.

"I don't understand what you just said."

This set him off as though I had lit his feet on fire. He stamped, and shouted: "Yes. You. Do. You-are-a-lying! You speak-a Spanish!"

This was the first time that someone in South America thought that my Spanish was any good. The boarding party spent a lot of time trying to trick me into admitting that I spoke Spanish better than I did. I was pretty good at understanding Spanish—but not when the speaker pronounced the words quickly—and I had never heard such a torrent of language as flowed from the agitated Capitan's mouth. I could pick out some words now and then, and I knew for sure that *cárcel* meant "jail."

Suddenly, without warning or explanation, the

entire CG crew stepped back into their whaleboat and returned to their cutter. They gave me no further instruction. But four men stood duty, watching me through the night from the stern of their vessel. I wanted to ask the guards about Troy, but was afraid that if I told them I had crew, they might arrest him too.

It turned out, they already had.

At about eleven p.m., hungry, and having nothing fit to eat, I dove overboard, intending to buy fish on the beach about four hundred yards away. The watchmen raised a loud alarm. All of the CG crewmen rushed to the deck, staring and pointing at me. They shone their spotlights on me; I ignored them, swimming past their boat, gently making my way to shore, phosphorescence shining off my arms and legs each time I kicked forward.

An old man sat in a chair at the end of a small commercial fishing pier, watching me kick slowly toward him. He stared at me when I climbed out of the water but did not say a word. I walked around onshore for twenty minutes or so, trying to find some food and scared as hell that the CG would send police to pick me up. I did not want to spend the night in a rural Costa Rican jail with no shoes, no shirt, and a wet bathing suit.

Eventually, I gave up on the food and walked back to the piers. A fisherman drove me to

Valkyrien on his panga. The coast guardsmen waved him over though and ordered him never to give me a ride again.

An hour later I saw the blue flashing lights of a police car at the dock. Soon after, the fisherman's panga appeared again, this time carrying Troy and several police officers. The panga brought him across, and moments later we were reunited.

Troy had had a long day. After leaving *Valkyrien*, he reached the reef outside a small natural harbor, home to a rustic fishing village. He ran the boat along the outer edge of the reef to the entrance of the safe harbor. Swells lifted the Whaler four to five feet above the reef, enough for him to see the violence of the waves breaking on the coral. He prayed as he sped toward the narrow opening into the harbor, but the gears in the lower unit seized up, the boat stopped hard, and Troy drifted, pushed by the surging waves toward the reef.

Desperate, Troy waved a life jacket at a wooden panga in the vicinity. The fisherman piloting the panga swung over and took Troy under slow tow. By the time they arrived at the local beach, word had spread that a gringo carrying drugs in a small boat had broken down and was being towed to shore. Police arrested Troy on the beach. Local officials then called the Coast Guard to find the mother ship that carried the drugs, weapons, and cash.

Troy is perhaps the most likable person I have ever met. During an hour of questioning Troy's amiable charm and sincere grace allowed him to make fast friends with the arresting officers. They gave him a ride to the little harbor where I was being held, and that is when he re-joined me. Both of us now stuck in a strange state of non-arrest.

At sunrise the Coast Guard forced me to weigh anchor and took us under tow for about six hours to their main Coast Guard base at Puntarenas (secretly fine with us, because it saved us paying a $10,000 tow fee). Puntarenas is the only port within a hundred miles that had the proper facilities to repair *Valkyrien*.

The route to the Coast Guard base around the little peninsula at Puntarenas took us past all of the residences, nautical supply stores, restaurants, and commercial piers in the ramshackle town. As we passed these enclaves, the CG vessel announced over their loudspeakers that they had caught the American smugglers and would be holding us at the station. We drew large crowds at the end of each dock as we passed by.

At the Coast Guard base, they tied *Valkyrien* alongside a gunship. After towing her, though, the Capitan seemed to grasp the fragile nature of our vessel and realized that we posed no threat to law and order. The base commander concluded that no criminal with any self-respect would use a boat like *Valkyrien* to run guns or money or drugs—and in any case, what American would bring drugs into Costa Rica? After a twenty-four-hour hold, we were free to go once we'd completed the necessary paperwork to enter the country (unfortunately, because of our improper entry, we had a lot of paperwork).

Troy good-naturedly accompanied me during the next four days, waiting for hours in long lines at various bureaucratic offices in Costa Rica: customs, immigration, Coast Guard, captains of the port, federal and local tax offices, and other locations.

All the while, of course, *Valkyrien* continued slowly sinking.

I moved her to a mooring and hired a young man named Gustavo, the nephew of one of the nicer coast guardsmen, to live aboard and keep her pumps running. But when I told him that he would have to scrub the bottom to keep ocean plant life from establishing itself there, he refused.

"Listen, Gustavo," I said, "you simply must do this. The green stuff growing on the side of the boat will destroy the wood, and eventually the boat will sink."

"Well, here in Puntarenas, we pull the boats out of the water at marinas to have the bottom cleaned."

"Gustavo, we cannot spend money to have the boat hauled out merely to clean the bottom. It is easily done with a hard brush. It will take several hours only."

"No, I cannot do that because I would have to swim."

"Gustavo, are you telling me you cannot swim?"

"Well, I can swim, but if I swim here I will be eaten by a crocodile."

I tried to reason with him. "Gustavo, there is no way a crocodile is going to eat you. Watch . . . I will jump in and clean the boat for a while."

"No, no! Please don't!" Gustavo grabbed hold of my arm, pulling me away from the side of the boat.

"Gustavo," I said, "all over the world people are told that they cannot swim because a shark might eat them, or an alligator will kill them, but these things are completely blown out of proportion. You are more likely to be struck by lightning than eaten by a crocodile."

"Not here—here, people get eaten all the time!" he said.

"If you can tell me the name of a single individual you have ever heard of who was eaten by a crocodile, I will never ask you to clean the bottom again."

"Juan Carlos," he said.

"Who is Juan Carlos?"

"The person who was eaten last spring."

"How do you know the story of Juan Carlos is true?" I replied, figuring it was an urban myth. I arrogantly assumed I knew more about this local harbor than Gustavo.

"We went to high school together, and grade school, and we used to clean boats together."

Costa Rica, it turned out, has one of the highest rates of crocodile attacks of any country in the world. Humbled, I apologized and put off the bottom cleaning. I later saw the humongous crocodile that ate Gustavo's friend, sunning himself on the beach, a few hundred yards from our mooring.

30. *Whaler*

Unfinished task . . .
—ABRAHAM LINCOLN,
ADDRESS AT GETTYSBURG

Several days after the Coast Guard released us, Troy returned to Los Angeles while I remained in Puntarenas alone, watching with some dismay as the local mechanic I hired began dismantling *Valkyrien's* engine. Panama was less than five hundred miles out—a distance I could sail at home in four to five days. But as I watched the mechanic take down the busted engine I began to think that I might never make it to the Panama Canal. The boat leaked badly, her batteries had drained, the masts had dangerously loosened, she had no bowsprit. Her boomkin had weakened, our Whaler was missing, and the engine was broken, perhaps beyond reasonable hope of repair in this faraway place.

The mechanic started by removing the broken alternator, then a water pump, both of which seemed reasonable steps, as those parts are really independent systems that can get in the way during a repair. But soon enough his tinkering lost all sense of order. It appeared that he was deciding what to remove based on its proximity to where he was seated.

The engine seemed to slowly disintegrate before my eyes. Everything that the mechanic could reach, without actually standing up, he removed from the engine. He took apart the cylinder head, the injectors and their springs, the valve train. Soon everything sat covered in thick grease combined with a homemade mix of chemicals, mostly from the oil pan.

Meanwhile, the Whaler remained wherever Troy had abandoned her, somewhere on the Nicoya peninsula. He couldn't recall the name of the beach except to say vaguely that the town was "somewhat idyllic." He did, however, remember the name of the fisherman who had promised to look after the Whaler. At least I had that to go on.

I needed to find a truck and a boat trailer; then I would try and locate the fishing village and the fisherman who now had my Whaler so I could haul it back to Puntarenas and get it fixed. Sailors develop special relationships with their boats. We give each a name, and the vessels quickly become anthropomorphized in our heads. I thought of the Whaler as a loyal friend. She had ridden with me across thousands of miles of ocean. She offered protection and salvation in storms. She helped me get supplies, food and fuel, to save sea turtles, and to catch fish for sustenance. She was nearly as old as I was, had survived so much of the same world, and I really felt I could not just abandon her on some beach at the end of an isolated peninsula in Costa Rica. I could not find anyone who would tow the Whaler for me, so I wound up purchasing a nearly completely wrecked Toyota Land Cruiser (also called a "jeep,") to tow the Whaler back. I figured that I would eventually drive the Toyota to Los Angeles.

I called the Toyota Land Cruiser variously "the jeep" "the Toyota" or the "Land Cruiser." It had no side doors, no windows, no roof, no heater. Its rear doors were cut in half. I traded the air conditioner for a PTO winch. The steering column was held together by a piece of a tire. The starter was frozen up and resisted my attempts to fix it with a hammer, so a bit like Fred Flintstone, I had to get out and push to start it (which was fine as long as I remembered to always park it pointed downhill). The jeep had no parking brake (I carried rocks to prop against the wheels to keep it from rolling away). The headlights were out, so I wired off-road lights and screwed them to the front bumper. But it worked, and it had a hitch—which was the main point.

I planned to take a ferry from Puntarenas across the Gulf of Nicoya to one of the villages at the end of the Nicoya Peninsula. I jumped in the Land Cruiser early in the morning, and drove like mad the 800 meters to the ferry dock, sliding on board just as the uniformed deckhands closed the gate.

Nicoya is the largest peninsula in Costa Rica, seventy-five miles long and up to thirty-nine miles wide. Nevertheless, every fisherman had by then, I was certain, had heard the story. Not many Whalers in Nicoya, and not many gringos leaving boats on beaches.

It turned out that the little village that so enamored Troy was probably the most touristy town in all of Costa Rica. It was inhabited mainly by teenaged Americans and those Costa Ricans inclined to profit from the excesses of young Americans on generous travel budgets.

Troy is a trusting soul. Unfortunately, the fisherman who had graciously offered to keep a safe eye on the boat for Troy was a well-known criminal. Late that night, I found the Whaler behind the fisherman's house. This unscrupulous brigand had stolen the keys, all of the lines, the fuel tanks and gas hoses; he did leave the engine, and surprisingly, the propeller was still attached.

The next day, with only a few misadventures, I ended up back in Puntarenas with the Whaler and the Land Cruiser. I lay the Whaler down on a couple of blocks of wood in the driveway that led to the wharf where *Valkyrien* was tied up. The outboard's gears had ground to bits and the engine's lower unit needed to be rebuilt.

I now had a broken truck, a broken Whaler, and a broken *Valkyrien*. I set to work, trying to get everything running, but circumstances impeded me at seemingly every step. Often I could not even get electricity to run my tools. The guy I rented dock space from in Puntarenas promised me electricity, but every time I connected to the wiring, his whole house lost power. I hooked up an extension cord to a "Frankenstein" switch on a pole. This got electricity to the boat, but the precarious setup often caught fire. I needed someone standing at the spot where the extension cord entered *Valkyrien* to tell me whether it lit up at the moment I threw the switch. If the cord didn't catch fire in the first ten seconds, it was usually fine.

The raw-water pump and electronic fuel pump on the generator had both failed, so when shore power from the Frankenstein switch also failed, we had no way to run electric tools or anything else electric on *Valkyrien*. I cut some long clumps of wire from the engine room and used this bonus collection to rewire the genset fuel pump directly to the battery. I also rebuilt the system I had used to wash down the bilge in El Salvador. I ran the discharge from this pump through the genset, which kept it cool. With these two temporary fixes the mechanic could run his tools, and continue—for better or worse—to take apart the main engine.

Friends had continuously asked me to give up the trip, and, finally, I decided that if we needed to buy a new engine, I would agree and come home. But if the mechanic could repair the engine for under $2,000, I would stick it out. With a working engine, I could easily cover the remaining distance to the Panama Canal in under a week.

And once in Panama, the *Valkyrien* could be rebuilt to become the *Spirit of the Pearl*.

I was once again running out of money, and with each passing day, *Valkyrien* seemed to deteriorate more. Like a man floating on a chunk of ice, I was desperate to get south before I had nothing left to float upon. But I had other obligations, too, and so I left the mechanic to work on *Valkyrien's* engine without me. I returned to Los Angeles to spend Christmas and New Year's with Vicki and our children.

I finally returned to Costa Rica near the end of January. The diesel mechanic, who had disassembled *Valkyrien's* engine in such an apparently haphazard way, surprised me by putting it all back together successfully, particularly given the limitations of his tools and the availability of spare parts. He billed me about $1,200, plus the cost of a new starter.

After tedious, seemingly endless days spent in drab government offices (mostly dealing with paperwork regarding my initial manner of entry into Costa Rica), I was finally able to secure permission to leave Costa Rica aboard *Valkyrien*.

My friend, Bryan Tarr, a contractor in Los Angeles, flew to San Jose at the beginning of February and met me at the boat for the final leg to Panama. We planned to leave the morning after Bryan's arrival, but Bryan and I wound up spending ten more days in Puntarenas, finishing repairs. We ended up sailing less than a hundred miles together, to the municipal dock at Quepos, Costa Rica.

By the time Bryan arrived I had become absolutely desperate to leave Puntarenas. Whether it was madness or paranoia or the heat of the tropical sun, I felt as if I were stuck in a hole from which I might never escape. As nice as the people of Puntarenas are, as helpful as they were in assisting me to get back out to sea, it also felt as if each time I got close to departing, they would find a way to keep me there for just one more day. They didn't want to kill me, they did not want to destroy—they just wanted to keep me there with them, to bleed me slowly, keep me hanging on, because they too wanted and needed to get out. It has been said that if Central America ever needs an enema, Puntarenas is where they will insert the tube.

Bryan and I spent the days on *Valkyrien* adjusting the rigging, tuning the engine with the mechanic, and stopping some of the leaks. Bryan rebuilt the mast frames, which helped enormously in stabilizing the rig. Leaks behind the rudder and at the edges of the stuffing box were our greatest challenges after that. We tried covering the box, caulking the sides, hammering tin, forcing rubber. But I never got it to stop leaking. You may have noticed that I have only sparingly used the word "sinking." I will say it here, just this once, because like all New England sailors, I know it is a word that brings no good aboard a boat. But with *Valkyrien*, the reality of sinking was never far from my mind.

31. *Dugout*

A lonely impulse of delight . . .
—W. B. YEATS, *AN IRISH AIRMAN*
FORESEES HIS DEATH

Late one evening, as Bryan and I sat talking after a long day working in the engine room, still with many repairs left undone, we decided to leave Puntarenas that very night. We simply could not bear to spend a single day longer in that awful city.

But my loyal Boston Whaler was still sitting up on blocks with her outboard engine in two pieces, in the driveway in Puntarenas, and the broken-down Toyota Land Cruiser sat parked beside the Whaler. I had a choice: I could stay in Puntarenas and wait God only knew how long until the Whaler was running again, or I could duck out and leave the Whaler and the Land Cruiser behind.

I still had the dugout canoe we had purchased from the indigenes in El Salvador. The canoe moved beautifully through the water, and was unsinkable in the sense that it had almost precisely neutral buoyancy. If it filled with water, it would sink only until the sides sat just at the surface level of the sea. This meant that in a terrible storm, the captain could lie down in the canoe and be safe, as the old fisherman had done during the terremore. I figured it would make a decent substitute as a dingy or a life raft. And we had so little distance left to Panama.

I knew Bryan wanted badly to leave, and I thought that if I didn't take him sailing soon, he would probably abandon the trip and fly back to LA. So we left Puntarenas and my forlorn Boston Whaler and the Land Cruiser behind. I hoped that in the future I would find my way back to retrieve them both.

I had fished often from the stern of *Valkyrien* since leaving San Francisco. When I am messing about in a boat, there is nothing quite so good for me as eating fresh-caught fish. The biggest fishing problem I'd been having was that the line fouled constantly in the Whaler—and then, after El Salvador, in the Whaler and the canoe. I spent hours on the stern untangling the line, knowing it was unlikely that we would find replacement monofilament in any of the small coastal villages where we stopped. In any case, I didn't like to be wasteful with fishing equipment.

After we left the Whaler behind in Puntarenas, I hoped to have better luck not tangling the fishing line. Unfortunately, the rough wood of the dugout canoe caught up the line every bit as often as the Whaler's outboard. Finally, I resolved to lay out about 125 yards of steel wire to drop the lure below the level of the canoe. About six minutes after I trailed the wire back, a sportfishing boat came racing out of some secret anchorage near shore. It sped along, completely unmindful that someone might be fishing off a sailboat.

I jumped up to the transom, picked up the rod and held it over my head, waving it back and forth. Despite my towering vantage on *Valkyrien's* stern, the sportfisherman did not give me even a passing glance. Moments later his propeller caught my wire and began winding it out. The fishing boat was traveling at close to 30 knots. I have no idea how fast their propeller turned, but clearly the line was wrapping around their shaft incredibly fast. I used steel wire and heavy test line because I was not fishing for sport but rather to eat. I did not want to lose a fish to broken line, and I didn't want to lose my line to a fish.

I watched, horrified, as the line spooled out so quickly that the reel literally began smoking. It raced away until there was none left and the rod flew out of my hands. Only a moment later, the line snapped, and I watched the hollow rod, floating just below the surface, slowly drifting aft of *Valkyrien*.

I determined not to jump in after it; I had spent way too much time untangling line. But I kept staring at my old rod. The Lott Brothers had built it for me when I was in college, and I just could not let it go. I jumped into the cockpit, pulled the gearshift back to neutral, and shouted loudly at Bryan to come on deck and take the wheel. Then I dove over the stern, swimming overhand rapidly toward my rod, not realizing that I had pulled the gearshift past neutral, all the way into reverse.

I had tied the canoe about sixty feet behind *Valkyrien*, and I thought that if I swam quickly, I could grab the rod before the canoe passed us. I would then climb into the canoe and pull myself back to *Valkyrien*.

Valkyrien did not stop, nor reverse direction immediately. Her momentum carried her forward. I dove in, swam, sprinting, using up all my energy. But I grabbed the rod with my left hand and at the same time caught the stern of the canoe with my right. *Valkyrien's* momentum jerked me hard, and I lifted up and threw the rod into the canoe, being careful to keep the pressure of my right hand along the centerline. I didn't want the canoe flipping or filling with water while I was being dragged.

As *Valkyrien* slowed I managed to pull myself alongside the canoe and slip in over the gunwale, flat-bellied like a penguin, so I wouldn't tip it. I lay on the bottom for a moment, exhausted from my sprinting swim, looking up at the burning noonday sun and thinking how ridiculous I was to jump in after that old and very broken rod, but happy that I hadn't simply let it float away.

I still had no idea that *Valkyrien* was currently in reverse.

The sun warmed my skin in that wonderful way that only happens when you are soaked with salt water at midafternoon on a scorching tropical day. I sensed a shadow, though, so sat up in the canoe, surprised to see *Valkyrien* towering above me. The reverse gear had pulled her straight back. Her stern had been lifted by the huge wake of the fishing boat and now crashed down, smacking the surface of the sea a couple of feet in front of the canoe, making a sound like a paddle slapping the water—thwack!

I realized that she was motoring in reverse, and as the stern climbed up over the next wave, I knew *Valkyrien* would come slapping down on the canoe with me in it, and I would be crushed. I quickly slid over the side into the water, by reflex lifting my left arm up as high as I could to protect myself. *Valkyrien's* stern smashed down on my hand and pushed me deep under the water. I was grateful she had not cracked my head but it occurred to me that I had broken my very basic rule of not swimming near the prop.

The suction of a boat propeller is much exaggerated in movies; most seaweed will float within a few inches of a propeller without being sucked in. But a boat driving backwards is a completely different situation—the propeller will tear your body to pieces. I looked down along my chest and legs and saw *Valkyrien's* huge, 46-inch-wide propeller spinning horribly toward my feet. I took one hard stroke backward and up with both arms, desperately hoping that would lift me up and away from the prop. My paddling arms had no effect. *Valkyrien* bore down on me, her propeller getting closer and closer.

The canoe surfaced a few feet above me, upside down. I reached my left arm up, just able to wrap my hand around the narrow keel along the bottom of the canoe, barely gripping it. The propeller churned hard, only a couple of feet away, like a chain saw in a horror movie. I pulled myself up beside the canoe, and, desperately pushed the front end of the canoe downward and jerked my legs up to my chest. The propeller violently struck the bow of the canoe—bang, bang, bang! It snapped a chunk off the front end and knocked the canoe hull violently aside. The canoe, now tipped sideways, acted as a funnel. I slid along its slimy bottom toward the murderous spinning propeller.

Just in front of me, the prop sucked in the canoe's thick towrope. I kept my knees bent up to my chest as *Valkyrien's* spinning prop wrapped the heavy line around itself and jammed. The blades stopped just before they cut me to pieces.

The canoe popped up from the severed line upside down, and I climbed up on its bottom and lay there for a moment, thinking how completely ridiculous it was to have almost died like that, and how weird to be clinging, like Ishmael, to something almost precisely the size and shape of a coffin.

Bryan looked down at me and smiled. I don't think he understood how close he had come to sailing *Valkyrien* alone.

32. *Days in Quepos*

Restless nights in one-night cheap hotels.
—T. S. Eliot, *THE LOVE SONG OF J. ALFRED PRUFROCK*

Bryan and I sailed for a couple of beautiful, uneventful days down the coast of Costa Rica, anchoring up in small coves and swimming ashore for breakfast at little bodegas on the beach. But Brian had to get back to LA, so we pulled into Quepos to drop him off.

Quepos was the perfect antidote to the sinking, sweltering misery of Puntarenas. The small town sits about halfway between Puntarenas and Golfito in southern Costa Rica—less than 150 miles from Panama. Quepos is the gateway to the meandering Manuel Antonio National Park, protecting miles of white-sand beaches, coral reefs, and rain forest. It is truly a tropical paradise.

When we reached Quepos, I rented a small room at a little hotel in Manuel Antonio, where the trees overflowed with blue monkeys. Bryan flew back to Los Angeles and I lay on the bed, grateful to be on land, and stared at the ceiling fan, thinking about Martin Sheen in *Apocalypse Now*, and wondering if I would ever get *Valkyrien* to Washington, DC.

Alone again. I had less than 350 miles left to the Canal, and couldn't stand the thought of giving up—but I needed to find crew.

Valkyrien leaked badly. I could not remain at the hotel for more than two or three hours, or seawater would begin to fill her cabins. I lay on that hotel bed, lonesome and exhausted, wondering what the hell I was doing with my life. I had not seen my family for weeks. I called Vicki. She tried to buoy me up by sharing news about our children: Summer and Maxey had won their last three flag-football games, and Summer, the only girl in the league, had been elected team captain. Vicki reported that the boys had taught Summer how to spit farther, and she'd taught them how to use their left hand in the huddle (because it is closer to your heart). Noah had gotten a role in the school musical, and the house was filled with song.

Vicki told me that Maxey had been home sick for a few days with a bad cold, but that he was happy to have all six dogs in bed with him. Vicki then signed off to go pick up some soup for Maxey. They felt very far away.

Lying atop that hotel bed, I thought about an old friend, Dennis Daniels, who had passed away. Dennis grew up in Dorchester, Massachusetts, abandoned by his father. He had never graduated high school and had done his share of jail time. Undaunted, Dennis had fought and clawed his way up to become city editor of the *Boston Herald*.

We played paintball once and I caught Dennis by the shoulder. He had no ammo left. I had a full clip, and stood eighteen inches from him. I told Dennis to give up (so I would not have to shoot him), and Dennis replied, "Fuck you—I ain't surrenderin'."

So I shot him from eighteen inches away, on the bare skin of his chest. The pellet left a welt the size of a 50-cent piece. Dennis didn't care. He would have done it again—"in a haht-beat," he told me in his heavy Dorchester accent.

I admired Dennis's single-mindedness, his sense of his own direction and the fact that once he'd committed to a course of action, he stuck with it no matter what. Even if it led straight down.

My own single-mindedness had spun into unrelenting obsession. I was losing my perspective. For a time, without knowing it, I would have given up everything I loved to stay aboard *Valkyrien*. I had long since stopped sailing for the *Pearl*. My chaotic being found a home on *Valkyrien*—like a storm making landfall. I told my friends and family that I was doing all of this for the *Pearl*, but it made no sense. I had set sail out of charity, but by the time I reached Quepos, I skippered *Valkyrien* only to sail. I had surrendered to this odyssey. I would have sailed her all the way across the world to keep from giving her back. I could not stop.

But God, how I loathed that boat!

I moved into that monkey-house hotel in Quepos with some relief, but keenly aware that, like an unruly child, I could not leave *Valkyrien* untended for more than a few hours. Rain fell in torrents for the next several days, and I left the hotel only to go back and forth to *Valkyrien* to run the bilge pumps and keep her from sinking.

I had moored *Valkyrien* in a quiet, protected bay outside of the small harbor at Quepos. She sat, without the vibration of the engine, and bathed in pouring rain for a couple of weeks while I searched for teak and crew and retrieved the old Land Cruiser. Her sides swelled up, tightening the gaps, and many of the more serious leaks slowed. I could leave her for several hours before the bilges overflowed the floorboards. Sitting still, and with her boards full, *Valkyrien* healed herself nicely.

I hitchhiked from the hotel or rode in tiny taxis to the municipal docks every few hours to charge the batteries, run the engine, check for new leaks, and, above all, pump out the water. I needed to put fresh gasoline into the powerful trash pump each day. At first I siphoned the fuel by sucking on the small gasoline line. Gasoline tastes much worse than diesel, and coats your mouth and throat in a way that keeps you tasting it for hours.

After getting a couple of mouthfuls of gasoline, I rigged up the ball pump from the Boston Whaler, which worked slowly but made for a great culinary improvement.

The genset had to remain on deck while running and yet had to be completely protected from the heavy rains. I strung various tarps from the mast and over the boom and tied them down along the railings. *Valkyrien* began to look more like a squatter's camp than a schooner.

I was exhausted. But I had less than 350 miles to the canal, and I was sure the *Valkyrien* could make it, if I could find some crew and a decent shade-tree mechanic who would keep the diesel running.

33. *Bad Medicine*

I should have been a pair of ragged claws
Scuttling across the floors of silent seas.
—T. S. Eliot, THE LOVE SONG OF
J. ALFRED PRUFROCK

Some years ago I found myself in a predicament eight miles south of the 10 Freeway in the Mojave Desert. I had torn the knuckle and spindle out from the front right axle of my Ford Bronco; after a night in the desert and a day spent towing, I searched through Craigslist for people who were selling trucks with Dana 60 front axles, and I finally found a guy out in the desert named Trent who did all of his own work. We pulled my truck back to his place, and he toiled on that axle day after day. We searched through hundreds of advertisements on Craigslist finding difficult-to-source parts—gears of the same ratio, and spindles with the same number of splines. I became convinced Trent could get any diesel engine to run.

I knew that if I could convince Trent to come down to Costa Rica, he could keep the engine on *Valkyrien* working long enough to get us through the Canal and I would be able to get some much-needed rest. Fortunately, I succeeded. For the first time I would be able to leave *Valkyrien* for a full day, knowing that Trent would run the pumps, and she would be afloat when I returned.

I picked Trent up at the airport in San Jose, and instead of driving to Quepos, I had the taxi drop us off in Puntarenas to rescue the Whaler. A couple of local mechanics, using mostly a hammer, had taken apart the lower unit of the outboard and, though it was not fixed, they did get it running.

Trent and I filled all the fuel tanks and drove a wild 60 miles down the coast to Quepos, where we tied her up behind *Valkyrien*. I did not realize at the time how terrifying this ocean run aboard the Whaler had been for Trent. He immediately regretted his rash decision to join me, but said nothing. We spent the next several days getting *Valkyrien's* various electrical systems, motors, and engines running.

I also persuaded a young Costa Rican named Elias to come with us, but when he first saw *Valkyrien* he refused to climb aboard. Elias said he had a bad feeling about the boat. Eventually I convinced him that it would be okay. I don't think he regretted any decision in his life more than agreeing to sail with me.

The day after both men arrived I hired the two women who cleaned my room at the little monkey-festooned hotel in Quepos to come out and scrub down *Valkyrien*. They had grown up beside the sea but had never been on a boat. They had heard many frightening stories about the ocean from local fishermen, and it took me some time to convince them they would be safe aboard *Valkyrien*, even at the mooring.

I gave them a little tour after they nervously stepped aboard, and eventually they began cleaning. When I returned that evening, *Valkyrien* had never looked better inside. I noticed they had left a bunch of bananas on the galley table. I immediately threw the bananas overboard and washed my hands. As every New England sailor and fisherman knows, bananas on a boat are bad luck. The women came back the following day to finish up. I had Trent and Elias sleep in the little hotel that night while I slept alone aboard *Valkyrien*, doing bilge duty.

I awoke in the morning with a tropical thirst and, still groggy from a sweltering night of waking every hour or so to look at the bilge, I climbed out of my bunk and up the companion-way. A half-empty bottle of water sat on the galley table at almost precisely the spot where I had found the bananas.

In Costa Rica many of the water bottles are tinted blue, which is kind of nice. I had brought several cases of water aboard *Valkyrien*, owing to my disquiet over dehydration. As I raised the blue-tinted bottle to my lips, I thought for the briefest moment about the bananas before tipping the bottle back and taking a huge glug.

Almost immediately I fell down to the cabin sole, dropping the bottle, which landed near my head. For a moment I could not remember what had happened. I lay there, utterly confused. The powerful scent of chlorine burned my nose. My mouth and throat felt as though they were on fire. I began vomiting violently. Later, it would occur to me that the cleaning women, who, like most Costa Ricans, were mindful of wasting things, had poured their leftover bleach into an empty water bottle and left it on the galley table for me. Unfortunately, they had failed to mention it.

I stood up and climbed the ladder to the cockpit, then fell down again, this time with my head over the side, a white spume foaming out of my mouth and forming bubbles in the blue ocean below me.

I remember watching the bubbles and thinking that my wife, who knows more than anyone, said she didn't worry about me when I sailed because she knew that I would never be killed by the ocean. I followed that thought immediately with the realization that dying from drinking bleach while on the ocean would not count. I could feel myself becoming not merely dizzy but also confused, and then I thought, "You will not have long before you will no longer know how to deal with this issue, so you'd better figure out a solution now."

I stood up on the deck. I could see a small boat coming in to land at the pier and I shouted to them as loudly as I could. To my horror, no sound came from my lips. I fell to my knees on the deck and looked up at the boat. I thought if I went below for the horn I might not make it back up. Near me a shirt had been tied to dry on the rail, and somehow I was able to untie it and raise it over my head, waving it back and forth— the international sign that emergency aid is needed.

The boatman looked at me, staring for an interminable period, and then somewhat reluctantly turned his boat toward *Valkyrien*. He arrived at our side and I sort of fell in and onto his small deck. I looked up at him and asked him to take me to the dock. Again, though, no sound came from my mouth. I pointed to the dock with all of the energy I could muster and he turned his little boat and brought me to the float.

I climbed, befuddled, to the top of the ladder, trying to figure out how to get myself to the landward end of the pier and then to the hospital. The wharf was used exclusively by fishermen. Foreigners were not allowed on the pier except by special permission. In the days I had been there I had seen an American only once.

But as I climbed the ladder I saw two men and a young American woman. They had hired a local captain to take them on a half-day snorkeling trip.

I walked, nearly stumbling, toward them. They thought I was drunk or high, but I leaned forward and whispered, "I need to go to the hospital immediately, please help me. I drank bleach."

"I am a doctor," the woman said. "My name is Mary. You are going to survive."

I thought to myself "You're damn right I am," but I mumbled only, "Thank you," as I walked them toward my old Toyota. Given my horrendous condition—foul clothing covered in spittle and vomit—the two men were reluctant to get involved. They worried, I suppose, that the Jeep did not belong to me. But the doctor wasn't fazed, and they drove me in my Toyota to the local hospital.

The nurses refused, at first, to treat me as an emergency case. Mary, the American doctor who had brought me to the hospital, insisted they call the emergency physician immediately. Mary explained that I had accidentally swallowed bleach. She said that my symptoms would not become fully emergent until the burning in my stomach was irreversible. I would die if not treated immediately.

The Costa Rican doctor told us that he knew a good deal about medicine and I would be fine for now. And with that the doctor walked back inside the closed area of the Emergency Room. I stood alone then with Mary.

I looked at Mary, my savior, and asked quietly,

"Are you sure I will die without immediate treatment?"

Mary looked at me straight and nodded grimly.

I pushed past the two nurses and into the closed emergency ward. Then I stumbled up to the doctor and gripped him hard on his shoulder.

I still could barely speak, and so I leaned my lips straight up against his ear. I said to him, "My name is Maxwell Taylor Kennedy. My uncle was President of the United States. You may be right. I may not need any treatment. But if you are wrong and I die, you will never receive your *pension.*"

The doctor lifted his head when I said the word *pension* and looked me straight in the eye for a few moments. Then he began speaking very quickly in Spanish. The two nurses, now quite confused, rushed in and half carried me to a table. They gave me an injection, put sensors on my chest, and inserted a tiny tube through my nose.

Mary assured me I would recover. It would take a few days before I could move well, probably only one night in the hospital. I fell into a restless sleep, my half-conscious thoughts revolving around whether or not Elias and Trent would go out to pump *Valkyrien* on their own without me coming up to the hotel to wake them.

Three hours later I sat up on the cot and told the nurses I had to go. They called the doctor, who told me that I absolutely could not leave the hospital. Worried for *Valkyrien's* bilge, I pulled the sensors from my chest and stomach and, wearing the odd hospital clothing, made my way outside and climbed into a taxi. I felt bad about threatening the doctor's pension, but figured it had been necessary.

By the time I made it back to the boat, Trent had already bailed her out. Even so, the watermark was well above the floorboards in my cabin. I felt stronger by that evening, albeit with a very sore throat.

Soon after that misadventure we completed most of our repairs. With the leaks stopped as best we could, and the generator functioning decently, the backup generator perfect, the gas pump and all three electric bilge pumps working well, and the engine running smoothly, we headed south toward Panama. I was very excited. We had only 130 miles to the Panamanian border.

Valkyrien caught a gentle wind and we put up a couple of the sails. She moved southward, beautifully, for two days.

34. *Pirates!*

It is not down on any map; true places never are.
—HERMAN MELVILLE, *MOBY-DICK*

On the third day, evening fell clear, without wind, and we crossed the border. The water became like glass, and I motored four or five miles offshore of the swamps and islands around Bahia de los Muertos—one of the most isolated areas of Panama's Pacific coast. Many times since we had crossed south of the U.S. border we had seen fishermen working in pangas near shore, often diving for lobster in among the rocks, or catching dorado on hand lines. We would cruise alongside and buy three or four lobsters or a filet of fish, handing over a few pesos as the boatmen tossed their catch to us. These pangas never had more than three men aboard, always with only a small outboard motor.

I saw in the distance of the evening light, racing out of a narrow cove, five boats arcing out toward us.

This doesn't look like fishermen, I thought.

As the boats grew near, I observed that each vessel carried five or six men aboard. The boats cruised in formation, each perfectly aligned in the wake of the boat in front.

The first boat headed directly at our stern, coming fast. Elias looked at me with real concern and said, "Pirates?"

I nodded.

We had no weapons. Nothing we could use to defend ourselves, save the sword Jasper had generously left aboard. I figured our best chance was to bluff. If they thought us well armed and willing to fight, they might wait for easier prey.

I turned *Valkyrien* hard around, 180 degrees, headed directly toward them and accelerated, on a crash course toward their lead boat. I told Elias to go below, wait for one minute, then walk back up, pretending to carry guns and ammunition. I told Trent to grab a three-foot section of iron pipe from the army case on deck and hand it to me as though it were a shotgun.

The intruders headed straight at us, bow to bow. Their boats were expensive American-made center-consoles, with quiet, 4-stroke 200-horse-power outboard engines. None carried fishing equipment.

I looked directly at the lead helmsman, unmoving and unblinking as he zoomed in. At the last moment he swerved slightly to port, passing us starboard to starboard. As the other aggressors cleared close by our starboard side I swung *Valkyrien* hard around again, now following the bandits back onto our old course south. They increased throttle in unison, then turned around and passed us like sharks about 150 yards off our port side, headed back toward their cove.

I took a deep breath, hoping they would leave us alone. But once again they turned toward us. This time they spread out, running their boats hard in circles around *Valkyrien*, over and over. All the while they watched us, assessing, looking for weakness and points of attack. I told Elias to crouch over the steering wheel with one hand held below the captain's chair, out of sight.

Trent bent down and passed me the iron pipe low along the deck. I pushed my right foot on top of it. The pirates could see only what appeared to be a long-barreled weapon, hidden just below the gunwale. I stood over the pipe, looking down at the brigands.

The first boat slowed and drove up alongside *Valkyrien*. Their helmsman steered just a foot or so off our side, and the four other men aboard eyed me coldly, ready to leap. Our faces were only about two feet from each other. The outlaws closed on each other's crafts, less than a boat length apart.

The first vessel rode up, going only about half a knot faster than *Valkyrien*. Each crewman stared eye to eye with me, unflinching. The second boat, with six men aboard, did the same. Then the third boat sidled up menacingly, carrying their leader, a huge man standing at the center of the boat. He too looked at me with the cold eyes of a killer. Four of the five boats had lined up close enough to *Valkyrien* for all of their crews to step aboard at once.

The three of us on *Valkyrien* met the stares of the twenty or so men without flinching, trying to look as though we dared them to step aboard and be slaughtered.

Amid this standoff I spoke, finally, in Spanish: "Sufficiente. We are not in need of fish."

Their leader turned his head and shouted a single word, unintelligible to me, toward his helmsman. Their boat turned hard outside, at full throttle. Only a second later each of the other boats copied him, peeling out in unison and falling in behind. They headed back, arcing toward their nameless darkening cove, disappearing as night fell.

We never saw them again.

That night, we relied upon the engine, fighting a steep current on our final leg to the Canal. I took the *Valkyrien* further offshore to avoid entanglements, and to give us time to deal with things if the engine conked out, so we would not be pushed immediately against the rocky beach.

I asked Trent to drive a minimum of fifteen miles offshore and slept for a couple of hours. When I returned to the cockpit, we were only two miles offshore. I spoke again to Trent, more sharply, saying we must stay at least fifteen miles offshore.

The pirate incident had deeply disturbed Trent and Elias, and the leaking *Valkyrien* gave them little confidence. I explained that the farther offshore we sailed, the safer we would be—no rocks to run into, no shore to be smashed upon. But once again, after I returned to my cabin, Trent turned *Valkyrien* in close to shore.

I exploded, but Trent replied impassively, "Fifteen is just a number."

I said, "Well, yes, it is just a number, but it is the number of nautical miles that I ordered you to remain offshore."

I climbed below and fell asleep again in my bunk. A couple of hours later, Trent, afraid of being so far off the coast, steered *Valkyrien* back toward the beaches. This time I woke up when the engine conked out. Trent had driven *Valkyrien* into a fish trap only a mile off a rocky point. The current pushed us in toward the rocks, with the trapline hopelessly tangled in the propeller.

I dread the deep ocean; recalling especially the first chapter of the novel *Jaws*, I am filled with fear when I swim at night. Both Elias and Trent refused to jump in the water to help clear the prop. Slicing out the line, holding a flashlight, a knife, the propeller, and my breath was a difficult job. I spent an hour alone cutting the rope from the propeller and the driveshaft as we drifted closer to the rocks.

Eventually, I cleared the shaft and climbed back aboard. The atmosphere on the boat had become tensely clouded with resentment, shame, fear, and doubt. We made our way along the shore, trading shifts through that night, running the generator, charging the batteries and pumping out *Valkyrien*.

By late the next evening, we slid around Punta Mariato, the southernmost point of land in North America.

Long ago on a rafting trip, a German aristocrat had whispered earnestly to me as I faced a disorderly crew, saying, "There are places where a hierarchy is needed." This sounded completely crazy and against all of my values as an American. However, while sailing off a foreign shore at night, in a leaking boat, order must be kept.

Trent had become quite terrified of the water. In the desert, independence is prized perhaps above all other qualities. He had never known the need to follow the orders of another man.

Although Elias understood the importance of chain of command, his fear had taken him long past the place where he could do as he was told. He had signed up for a sunny trip south in a beautiful wooden boat. The shore was home to him: He spoke the language; he understood the risks. After the pirate incident I figured Elias would abandon *Valkyrien* the first chance he got.

I was not sure whether Trent would stay or go. He had been told horror stories about Mexico and the world south of the United States his whole life. When he first came aboard the *Valkyrien* he was grateful to be away from a land that he thought was populated by robbers, thieves, drug dealers, corrupt police officers, and communists. But that night I realized that Trent had come to fear the sea even more than the people onshore.

I anchored *Valkyrien* in a small cove near Tonosí. I suspected the crew of treachery but slept anyway, too tired to chastise or inspire them. I wondered as I fell asleep whether they would both desert in the morning.

35. *Considering an Ending*

Can't go on,
everything I had is gone—
stormy weather.
—BILLIE HOLIDAY, *STORMY WEATHER*[6]

When I woke the following morning, I was alone on *Valkyrien*. Trent and Elias had taken the canoe ashore and made a run for it. Elias was Costa Rican. He could cross the border back to his own country with only his national ID.

Trent, on the other hand, would face great difficulty. He had no entry papers for Panama, and without entry papers they would not let him fly home. He would first have to explain how he came to be in their country. Panamanians frown on sailors who abandon ship. They certainly did not want merchant captains plying the Canal to worry about whether their crews could simply walk off the job midway through an ocean crossing.

I looked out at the cove. The clear blue water extended a few hundred yards to shore and a small fishing village. The lower unit on the

---

6. The song "Stormy Weather" was written by Harold Arlen and Ted Koehler, and sung by many great artists.

whaler's engine had by then completely frozen up. So I dove overboard, swam slowly to the beach, and retrieved the canoe from where the mutineers had abandoned it. The paddle was missing, so I swam the canoe back out to *Valkyrien*, pushing it through the surf at first, then pulling from the bow, and finally climbing in and paddling with my hands.

I made myself a bit of food and put *Valkyrien* in order. Alone, I began thinking hard about whether to give up the voyage. I had sailed her over eight thousand miles through all sorts of storms, those in my head, sowing doubt and obsession, always being the most challenging.

We were told that *Valkyrien* was ready for this journey when we purchased her. It turned out the deck leaked badly, so we sealed the deck. Then the rigging had to be replaced. With help we installed new stays. Then we had to replace the bulletproof engine—and the propeller, too. The bowsprit and boomkin were rebuilt by hand, but then we lost the new bowsprit in a blow off Guatemala. Most of the sails tore on the way south. The steering wheel clanked off. The GPS and the VHF radio stopped working, along with the depth sounder, the radar, and the stove. The head and holding tank leaked. The masts came loose and worked the hull. The stuffing box leaked, and the major frames around the stuffing box rotted out. Wood frames on the "house" rotted completely away, leaving a gaping hole in the corner six feet long. The winches failed, as did the blocks. Many of the systems were at the breaking point or had been driven to failure. Most of the pumps had broken, and both motors for the anchor windlass broke. The freshwater system, the other head, the auxiliary battery charger, the alternator, and the generator—all of them broke. The desalinator did not work. The starter broke, then failed again, then broke a third time. The Whaler engine was broken by negligent joyriding.

But we persevered. Through it all, *Valkyrien* remained afloat.

I have met an astonishing number of people in my life who believe that they know God's will for them and seek only to carry it out. As I agonized over the prospect of whether or not to abandon *Valkyrien*, so close to the Canal, I thought to myself how much easier life would be if one could actually receive a sign from God about what to do next.

I stepped across the jib that lay on the deck of *Valkyrien*, and within seconds of wishing for a sign, a huge, completely random wind struck the boat, literally out of nowhere. I have never before or since experienced a wind like this. The wind caught the huge jib, lifting it up and carrying me with it, tumbling over the side of the boat. I struck the water headfirst, with almost no air in my lungs. The sail covered the water above my head.

Of course I have come up for air below sails and tarps many times in my life, so although my lungs felt as though on fire for need of air, I did not panic. I kicked until my body was tight up against the sail, then pushed as hard as I could with my hand open against it. But the sail did not lift off of the sea. It remained in place as though glued to the surface.

I swam up again, kicking hard, and hit it with both hands, but still the sail did not move. It occurred to me then that I might well drown. The sail darkened the sea, and with no air in my lungs, it became difficult for me to see, and I felt disoriented.

I swam like hell in one straight line, hoping for the best, only to swim straight into the keel of *Valkyrien*. I knew I would not be able to make it under the boat and up on the other side, so I darted out once more, taking several strokes before I got past the sail and sunlight penetrated the water. I lit to the surface, gasping for breath.

I swam over to *Valkyrien* and climbed up the side using the portholes as a ladder. I looked down at the sail that had almost drowned me and thought to myself, That was weird. These words encompassed a range and train of thought about God, the existence of God, how we make things happen in our lives, free will, and also about people who think God has given them a specific message. I held doubt in my heart. I looked across the calm blue water at the rough-hewn huts and hardscrabble roadway at the edge of this fishing village, then lay down on the deck of *Valkyrien*, staring at the whisps of white cloud, turning red as the sun set. I began reflecting upon where I was, who I was, and what I was doing. I had set out on a fool's errand that has come to nothing.

36. *The Waves at Punta Mala*

Lord, help me . . .
My boat is so small,
and your sea is so immense.
—FRENCH MEDIEVAL PRAYER

Punta Mala sits at the far corner of the Azuero Peninsula and separates the Gulf of Panama from the Pacific Ocean. It is known for vicious, unpredictable weather, and a powerful current that pushes hard against any boat sailing toward the Canal. Punta Mala and Punta Mariato are the southernmost points of the voyage from San Francisco to Washington, DC. I had made it south of the Panama Canal. Once I rounded Punta Mala, I would be traveling north all the way to Washington.

The waves at Punta Mala resemble those of the Great Lakes more than the Pacific. They run high and sharp with a short period that rattles boats—especially wooden boats. Thunderstorms, heavy weather, lightning, and squalls may come from any direction without warning. One of the other tough things about Punta Mala is that there is no safe anchorage within any reasonable distance on either side of the point. People wait for days and even weeks for a window to make the crossing.

But waiting was not an option for me.

I set off, sailing solo the next morning, trying to reach Punta Mala before the tide turned. As I sailed closer to the point I got absolutely hammered by the changing tide and wind. *Valkyrien* was moving at 6 knots through the water, but because of the opposing currents, we made almost no progress toward the landmass ahead. *Valkyrien* literally sailed backwards at times, and I did not get near Punta Mala until evening.

I knew that once I rounded Punta Mala I would make it to the Canal. Rounding that point would mean clearing a huge psychological, geographical, and seafaring hurdle. I slogged for four more hours that evening against the current with the wind in my teeth and made only one mile of forward progress—one mile in four hours. Long after sunset, I gave up. With no safe spot to land anywhere near Punta Mala, I turned *Valkyrien* and motored back to the small fishing village where my crew had deserted.

I slept that night, exhausted, with *Valkyrien* anchored and nearly out of fuel. Most of the Pacific Coast of the United States is dotted with marinas where you can pull up to a pier just like an ordinary gas station. But Panama has no facilities before the Canal. The only way I could get fuel would be to fill up jerry cans at a local gas station and then carry the fuel to *Valkyrien's* tanks. But there are also no stores where you can buy jerry cans. And I had no car. And no dinghy. The local fishermen share gas jugs with each other, but no one ever buys more than a couple of gallons at a time. I needed two hundred.

In the morning I rode the canoe ashore, using a 2 X 4 as a paddle. Two fishermen looked on as a wave washed me onto the beach. They ran into the spray to help me pull the dugout up the sand beyond the high-tide mark. They introduced themselves as Pedro and Fernando, and offered to help. We drove from village to village, borrowing variously shaped bottles and jugs and filling them up with diesel. After several hours, we had nearly fifty gallons of fuel, in fifteen differently sized containers. We headed back to the village and the canoe.

Pedro, Fernando, and I carried the fuel jugs to their small panga. Waves broke more fiercely on the beach, and a group of men helped us to push the panga down the beach and into the breaking waves. *Valkyrien* was the most interesting thing that had happened in this village in communal memory, and everyone wanted to take part.

A huge wave lifted the panga over our heads and tossed it sideways on top of Pedro and me. We dove quickly under. The bottom of the boat scraped our backs as we pressed our chests against the hard sand bottom. When we popped up on the other side, the little panga had completely flooded. Our diesel jugs floated about, bobbing away. Pedro jumped aboard and to my astonishment, started the small outboard and floored it into the next breaking wave. That wave lifted the panga almost vertical and emptied her flooded cockpit over the stern. Pedro bounced over the wave in a now-dry panga. (Apparently these boats flip all the time in the surf, and villagers commonly use the steep waves to bail them out.) I grabbed the free-floating diesel bottles and swam out to the calm beyond the breaking waves, where Pedro and Fernando picked me up. Then the three of us motored out to *Valkyrien*.

We made four more trips for fuel. I showed Pedro and Fernando how to start the generator and use the trash pump, and I hired them to sleep on the boat, mostly to keep pumping the bilge every few hours. Then I hitched a ride to a hotel and slept for two days.

I returned the evening of the fourth day, paddling out to *Valkyrien* in the canoe. When I climbed aboard, wielding a small flashlight, I was horrified to see bilge water filling the cabin a foot over the floorboards. Pedro and Fernando had abandoned their posts—not out of malice or lethargy; they were fishermen and they had become too superstitious to sleep aboard *Valkyrien*. They told me there was something unlucky about the boat.

Pedro told me that he knew a route close to shore where we would not be caught in the current. Despite their misgivings I convinced the two fishermen to guide me beyond Punta Mala. We left an hour before dawn.

I have traveled extensively in Latin America, and early on I learned that many of the people on land are so friendly and anxious to be helpful, they cannot stand to turn away a traveler in need. They will good-naturedly offer directions even if they have no idea where something is. Unfortunately, the same turned out to be true of fishermen in Panama.

We sailed far offshore at first, and then motored in tight along the coast. But we never escaped the fierce southwest current. Far from being able to competently pilot *Valkyrien* around the point, Pedro and Fernando seemed terrified by the waves that gathered sharply off Punta Mala. They finally admitted, under some rather severe questioning, that this was the farthest they had ever been from their village in their entire lives.

Around sundown, still a mile from Punta Mala, and unable to make headway against the brutal current, I was again forced to give up. Tired, sore and dejected, we sailed—forlorn—back to the village.

I decided to try one more time the following morning. But no one from the village would go with me; they all had a bad feeling about the boat.

I slept for a few hours, then late that night I pulled up the anchor and, sailing *Valkyrien* alone, drove once again toward Punta Mala. Two or three hours later the engine conked out. I changed the filters and restarted it, but after another two hours or so, it again stopped running. I opened up the fuel filters and found they were packed with rust and dirt and probably a dozen other types of particles. I had purchased contaminated diesel.

I had no more filters, so I washed out the old ones several times, then reinstalled them. I poured the cleanest diesel I had into the old plastic holding tank I had cleaned back in the estero in El Salvador. With the tank half-full, most of the diesel remained inside, below the crack on top.

I began cannibalizing *Valkyrien*. First, I cut out a section of her fuel lines and looped them into the broken holding tank. Then, I cut the return hose and looped that into the holding tank as well. The jury-rigged auxiliary fuel supply system worked.

I ran up and down the stairs every forty-five minutes to add fuel to the holding tank. *Valkyrien* chugged her way up the coast, now and then finding little eddies and places where the current was not overwhelming. As evening fell, I turned her just enough to round the last point of land at

Punta Mala. But the wind beat us down hard for the next hour, and I made no progress. I still felt it was possible I would make it, but only if I held very tight—dangerously tight—to the shore. I cruised her to just a few hundred yards from the tip of the point when the engine quit. I had no time to deal with re-cleaning the filters.

I rushed to raise the repaired mainsail and the storm sail. *Valkyrien* pointed high enough to make it just around Punta Mala. I had an hour of falling light, and I figured with some good luck I could round the point before dark, then sail the calmer waters of the bay through the night. It would be easier to have the engine repaired the closer I got to the Canal. I sailed straight, but the powerful current pushed back against me. Again, I made no forward progress.

The wind built until the waves stood sharply up against *Valkyrien's* bow. She leaned hard over and spray blew off the top of the waves, creating whitecaps and mist all around me.

As I approached shore I could see the individual rocks on the tip of Punta Mala, but a storm was building around me. I was not sure whether I would make it around the rocks if I kept going, but I knew that if I tacked I would be pushed back to the village. This was my last chance. So I sailed on, closer and closer to the rocks. And then, bang!

The boom exploded. I have been on boats

several times when masts or booms cracked. But I have heard that explosion only once. The break sounded sharp, like the crack of a traditional high-power rifle. The sail began snapping back and forth immediately, crashing pieces of the boom across the cockpit.

Valkyrien was pushed hard over to port by the waves breaking against her bow. I jumped up and tied the boom as best I could, wrapping the mainsail and putting tie after tie around it. Once again pulled only by her jibs, *Valkyrien* sailed within a couple of hundred yards from the rocks. She could not make it around the point, and with no mainsail she could not turn up into the wind. The only way to miss the rocks would be to make a jibe. But *Valkyrien* required a wide radius to jibe, and it looked like we would be crashed against the rocks before she could complete the turn.

I ran below and moved the jury-rigged fuel tank so that it sat on the floorboards above the engine, hoping gravity would push enough fuel to the injection pump. Then I cranked on the engine. It started and ran hard, coughing and clanking, as the foul fuel jammed through the tired injectors. I knew I would have the motor for only a few minutes at best. And I had no way of sailing at night, or of anchoring along that coast. A small cove lay nearly dead ahead of me, just a few hundred yards below Punta Mala.

I have heard so many times (in various contexts) "any port in a storm." This cove was the most dangerous harbor I have ever tried to enter. Gigantic, sharp rocks, all smashed by waves, ringed the cove. The entrance was formed by rock cliffs. Nonetheless, the cove was my only chance. I quickly created a plan to get inside and anchor up.

A rocky promontory jutted out from shore, into the center of the cove, splitting it in half. The lower half of the cove was filled with rocks on shallow ground—entirely unusable. The upper half offered the most dangerous anchorage I have ever used. Fifteen-foot swells rolled into the narrow entrance of the cove, then crested in the shallower water, two hundred yards off the beach, becoming breakers that would lift *Valkyrien* and crash her to pieces. But a powerful wind blew straight out from that beach, so if I timed it right I could turn up into the wind and drop anchor at the edge of the break. The wind might be strong enough to hold me off the beach; if it became too strong, it would push me onto the promontory.

I had almost no time to prepare the anchor and steer her into the cove. I needed to drop the anchor in the shallowest possible water right up close to shore at the beginning of the break. I ran to the bow, locked the windlass, and pushed the anchor over the side to dangle from about ten feet of chain. It swayed back and forth, smashing into *Valkyrien's* bow, shaking the entire boat. I ran back to the helm, but I was too late. *Valkyrien* rattled into the cove, headed straight back onto the rocks.

But the cliff walls blocked the wind, and I was nursed the spluttering motor, edging *Valkyrien* just above the rocks. A moment later *Valkyrien's* engine cut out again, for the last time. My relief turned to horror.

I quickly weighed my options: The Whaler was broken. I could not possibly paddle the canoe. My best chance would be to jump overboard and try to swim out of the cove then tread water through the night in the currents off Punta Mala. This was the worst contingency plan I've ever had.

Fortunately, I was given another reprieve. Beyond the cliff walls the wind inside the cove gusted up so strong that *Valkyrien's* masts and sides acted as sails. She picked up speed "sailing on bare poles," and I steered hcr again just above the rocks. I swung *Valkyrien* hard to starboard, into the wind and directly toward the little beach. I thought for a moment that she would be lifted too far, and like a lost surfboard we would be caught in the breaking waves and tossed ashore. Miraculously, though, the wind halted *Valkyrien's* forward motion just before the break.

I scrambled to her bow and struck the windlass with a hammer, dropping the anchor and chain straight down. *Valkyrien* hovered there, frozen in place for two or three of the longest minutes of my life. Powerful wind pushed her back toward the rocks, and strong waves lifted her in the opposite direction—toward the beach. Slowly the wind won out and pushed *Valkyrien* backwards above the swell.

I ran to the bow and stood beside the windlass, working the chain. Every sixty feet I locked the windlass, jerking the anchor to catch the bottom. *Valkyrien* pulled and pulled. About halfway to the promontory the anchor caught, and she snapped into the wind. The anchor held her in place, perfectly equidistant from the beach and the promontory.

The return waves (coming from the beach) grew so tall that they buried *Valkyrien*'s bow, flooding her decks. While the ordinary waves, around fifteen foot swells, lifted her stern, the two sets coming from opposite directions twisted her wildly. Spray hit so hard into my eyes that even at anchor it was difficult to look toward the bow. Daylight faded just minutes after the anchor grabbed, and with the loss of light came the start of a long dark night.

The anchor chain pulled at the capstan, which pulled at *Valkyrien*'s critical bow timbers—and these began to loosen. She was coming apart, leaking at her bow for the first time, beginning to die.

37. *End of the Line*

And in short, I was afraid.
—T. S. Eliot, THE LOVE SONG OF
J. ALFRED PRUFROCK

The waves and chain and wind pulled at *Valkyrien's* bones. Either her bow would split and she would sink, or her capstan would be ripped out and she would be smashed to pieces. I did not think she would make it through the night. I began to feel increasingly afraid. Anxiety dominated my thoughts. For a time I could think only of the many ways I might die here, losing sight of the possible ways out.

For the longest time, I had been trying to figure out whether I was being vain and hardheaded in forcing the voyage to go on, no matter how much it seemcd a sane person would stop. My mother had raised me with the powerful belief that I should never quit. Failure seemed a terrible option. But despite this core tenet, I whispered a silent prayer, promising that if I got through this night, I would give up the trip and admit failure. I would abandon the *Valkyrien* to her fate and go home.

I had a tiny bit of signal on the Panamanian cell phone I had purchased at a Chinese hardware store, but only a couple of minutes left on the plan. The phone would stop working when my minutes ran out. I called my friend Jonah, who is a computer genius, extraordinarily loyal, and a person I knew I could always count on. I spoke with him very briefly, and told him the name of the Panamanian cell carrier, my Panamanian cell number, that I was in a bad position, and needed more minutes.

I have no idea how he did it, but Jonah, late at night, somehow convinced the carrier to add minutes to my plan. Around midnight I called Vicki, waking her. We spoke for half an hour.

ME: "Baby, this boat is really rocking. I think she may not make it through the night. You know how I never seem to get scared? Well, I'm actually scared this time."

VICKI: "Well . . . [long pause] . . . I don't understand. Everything will be okay. [pause] What's happening there? Where exactly are you?"

ME: "I'm sorry, Vicki—so completely sorry. [pause] I had no choice. This effing cove was the best of a really bad set of options. Basically, the engine quit, for good. The wind was against me. The waves were really against me. The current was completely against me. I could barely sail—I mean, just barely. The current is so tough here. Anyway, it's fairly tough to sail this boat without a crew, and then, I'm out here in this horrendous area where there is not a single effing safe harbor for literally, like, a hundred miles of the coast. The masts are effed up, and then the boom snapped. I was incredibly lucky to make it into this place; the whole rest of the area would have smashed *Valkyrien*. But this place is awful—just ridiculously bad. The Whaler is toast—at least for now. Anyway . . . I am so, so sorry. [long pause] I actually really don't know what to do. I am so effed, completely scared as hell. You cannot even believe how effing scared I am. This boat and I are completely effed."

Vicki, hearing the fear in my voice responded with complete calm. "Everything will be okay, [pause]. . . Max, you have always been fine on a boat. You will work this out, I'm sure of it."

It sounded to me as though she had not understood a word I'd just said. I thought to myself, "Vicki really does not understand much about boats." But her tone also calmed me. I knew that I didn't want to scare Vicki, but I really wanted her to understand the level of danger here. I was angry as hell at myself. A phrase from Hamlet kept running through my head—"that it should come to this."

Vicki continued to talk to me, her voice reassuring me all the way from our house in Los Angeles, across to that miserable, rock-filled cove.

VICKI: "Max, you know how to do this. Remember when we were first dating and we'd go to the Cape for the weekend? Whenever a big storm blew in, we would paddle out in the sea kayak to the end of the break wall, and when we got to the really broken part of it, you would jump out and swim right up next to the wall through giant waves. The waves would be smashing against the rocks, but you were always comfortable. You are at home in waves like this. [long pause] Max, you have been testing yourself for so long. You can definitely handle this."

ME: "Baby, I think this may be different. I could always find some place on the break wall that offered a chance, but here, there is nothing—just sharp rocks and huge waves and so much wind. *Valkyrien* is coming apart."

VICKI: "If you have to swim, you will make it. You can definitely do this."

ME: "I truly am effed here." [long pause] I love you so much. I am so sorry to have put myself in this position."

Vicki suggested that I pretend a video camera was mounted to the mast and that she and our children were there, watching and cheering me on. This thought gave me an immediate measure of calm. She was right: I had been in bad situations before. I knew what to do. I knew how to behave. The right thing to do was to stay calm, and to go through the boat all night long, fixing things as they broke, checking on systems, making sure the bilge was working, figuring out the best spots to swim ashore. Watching how the boat moved and trying to figure out what would happen if she came apart. Would she sink? Would she break the chain and be pushed backward? Would the masts break through the deck?

If my wife and children or friends or crew members were here with me, I would certainly do the right thing. So I decided to just pretend that others were with me, seeing me, and I'd do the right thing.

VICKI: "Max, you will be completely fine. Sleep if you can. If the boat doesn't make it through the night, you will swim ashore. Then the trip is over. That is all."

ME: "Vicki, I don't think I can stand to quit. I don't know how I would tell everyone that I gave up."

VICKI: "Max, look. So the trip did not work out? It doesn't matter. You tried hard and had a great adventure. None of your friends will judge you because you did not make the trip. They know you. They know that no one else could have made it this far."

ME: "Baby, it does not matter how far I made it; if I don't make it all the way, I failed. No one cares what storms I hit along the way; the question is: Did I bring the boat home? And I have not."

VICKI: "Your friends do not care. Your children do not care. They love you. They don't love you because you're a good sailor or because you weathered a wild storm. It is not the sailing or the rafting or the trips into the desert. It is you that they love. You need to really know this, Max, deep down. Once you do, you will be ready to get off that boat."

• • •

Vicki had done her best not to sound worried. Her words warmed my heart and gave me the courage to make it through that night, doing what needed to be done aboard the boat—despite my fear. I spent the night methodically going through *Valkyrien*, until dawn broke and I watched a beautiful red sunrise as the waves and wind continued to pound us.

Everything on a boat seems safer in daylight, but the wind blew just as hard. And the waves stayed just as big. The engine was broken, the boom was gone. The Whaler did not have enough fuel to get me to safe harbor. The sun had been setting when I'd entered the cove. With the dawn I was able to look around for the first time with real light, searching for a way out. I could see huge amounts of water entering the cove, as waves, and knew that all of this water must also be going out somewhere. It appeared that when the ocean water crowded against the promontory in the center of the cove, it was pushed out to sea.

I knew from having worked as a rafting guide that when a current hits the steep wall of a gorge, the river often acts like a pillow. Even when a raft is thrown hard in the direction of the gorge wall, the piled-up water holds it off from actually hitting the wall. I couldn't sail out of the cove, and I had no chance of motoring out; but it occurred to me that it might be possible to float out along that line of exiting current.

I watched the lines of wind and waves. I thought that I might just make it. The only way to be sure was to try. This meant cutting *Valkyrien* loose from her anchor and floating in toward the waves breaking against the promontory. By this point, I had little to lose. My only hesitation was the thought that I might have a greater chance of survival if I jumped into the ocean and swam to the shore across the bay. The waves striking the beach there seemed smaller, and the rocks, not quite as sharp.

To help me figure out my best move, I decided to cut loose the Whaler, letting it ride the current through the cove so I could see whether it smashed against the rocks. If the Whaler made it out of the cove, I would make a run with *Valkyrien*. If the Whaler were obliterated on the rocks, I would swim for the beach. It was one or the other.

I would not get a fair idea of what might happen to *Valkyrien* after I cut her loose unless I first lowered the engine on the Whaler. With the engine up, the Whaler would be subject to wind more than current, but with the engine down, the lower unit would hold the Whaler a bit like *Valkyrien's* rudder and keel.

The Whaler bounced terribly in the wind and waves tethered to the *Valkyrien* like an angry bluefish. I thought of jumping into the ocean, swimming to the Whaler, and climbing in. But I doubted I could actually climb aboard. Not reaching the Whaler would be a terrible way to end this adventure, so I decided to try to pull her in close enough to *Valkyrien* and then jump from one boat to the other. Pushed by wind and waves and heavy with fuel, I could not pull the Whaler standing up. I pinned myself into the cockpit and, using my legs against the bulwarks, I gradually hauled the Whaler toward *Valkyrien's* stern.

The waves bouncing back from the beach struck us only a few seconds apart. First the wave would break over *Valkyrien's* bow, then, running along her hull, it would lift *Valkyrien* out of the water, dipping the bow down and raising her stern up. When *Valkyrien's* stern came up, the Whaler's bow, just a few feet aft of *Valkyrien*, dove into the trough created by the leading edge of the wave— as though both boats were on opposite ends of a seesaw. At the same time, other swells rolling into the cove from the Pacific collided with the waves sent back from the beach, rendering the position of each boat unpredictable.

With the Whaler as close as I could get her, I leaned over and picked up the knife I always kept in the cockpit; then, as the waves pushed the Whaler away from *Valkyrien*, I threw the knife into the Whaler. It bounced but stopped short of falling off the stern. Then I danced out to the end of the boomkin and made a sudden leap, landing and rolling bruised aboard the Whaler.

I reached around and quickly flipped the metal locking bolt, pivoting the engine into the sea. I picked up the knife, crawled to the bow of the wildly bouncing Whaler, and pulled her in as close as I could to *Valkyrien's* stern. With one clean swipe I sliced through the heavy towline, threw the knife back aboard *Valkyrien*, and leapt off the bow into the sea, barely grabbing hold of *Valkyrien's* boomkin stay as I hit the water.

As *Valkyrien* slid down off a wave, the stay dipped deep underwater, giving me a chance to firm my grip. The next wave lifted up *Valkyrien's* stern—and me with it—and using that momentum I rolled myself back up onto the stay and then climbed atop the boomkin and slid quickly aboard, snapping to my feet to watch the Whaler.

Pushed by the wind, the Whaler drifted quickly down to the rock promontory. Then, to my glad astonishment, it hovered a few feet from the rocks and eventually caught the river of water exiting the cove. The Whaler, lifted up and down by entering swells but pushed relentlessly into and over them, made its way to the entrance of the cove. I stared with all of my energy, as a tennis player leans in to help a ball fall inbounds, and watched with glad relief as the Whaler moved along. The little boat disappeared into the waves off the tiny point of land, safely in the ocean.

I could not pull in the anchor chain, so I tied two fenders to it, with fifty feet of line, and got ready to release the chain. The fenders would float at the surface, marking the spot where the anchor and chain lay on the bottom. I figured that if I made it out I would try to come back sometime for the anchor and chain. If I did not, some curious and lucky fisherman would come across a windfall.

I pulled the lock, and *Valkyrien* tore backwards like a kicking horse, freed. Chain, fenders, and line tore across the deck. The speed at which *Valkyrien* came loose surprised me. I watched, horrified, as we raced toward the rocks on the promontory. But just as the Whaler slowed when it neared the rocks, so did *Valkyrien*. Gradually we were lifted around the promontory, past the rocks at the edge of the cove, and finally, into the current that had been my enemy for so long.

I tied makeshift sails to take advantage of the wind and rode the current at more than 5 knots back toward the fishing village. A few hours later a larger diesel-powered boat steamed by and towed me to the village, where a crowd gathered as we approached the beach. I had a smaller anchor for emergencies, and in the calm of the protected water off the village, I dropped it down, then dove in after it, to make sure it held, and swam ashore.

When I walked up the beach the crowd approached me, asking if I were truly the American from the wooden boat. When I said yes, they wanted to know if it were true that I had killed my two crewmen? And did I plan to kill Pedro?

Shortly after that, the police arrived. They had heard that a drug smuggler was signaling to his coconspirators onshore during the night, and that he had unloaded cash and illegal drugs in a small Boston Whaler, which he later abandoned. It took a while in my poor Spanish to convince them that I was not a killer or a drug dealer or a smuggler.

I was merely an American who had lost his way.

Epilogue

Vicki flew down to Panama the next day and we spent a week unpacking *Valkyrien* and setting her up to be towed to the Canal. I hired local fishermen to tow her to a harbor of refuge, and on the highest tide pulled her up to the beach and carried the small anchor ashore, setting it hard in the sand beside some trees.

Valkyrien settled into the mud just off the beach over the days that followed. I made friends with a remarkable hotelier, and Vicki and I spent our nights at his place. He hired men to watch over the *Valkyrien* and protect her from looters. Eventually, I sold her to an American who had crewed on her as a child.

Vicki and I returned home.

Socrates said that the unexamined life is not worth living. It is my understanding that he spent a hell of a lot of time reflecting on his life, and then killed himself.

I have met many people who quote Thoreau's contention that "Most men live lives of quiet desperation." I find this to be one of the most irritating quotations in American literature. It strikes me as insufferably condescending. The words of someone entitled, snobbish, and self-satisfied. I suppose I feel this way because it is so easy for me to slip into a snide and selfish place myself. But this doesn't mean that I like that side of myself. I struggle against it with all my being. Still, some days I'm sure I don't struggle hard enough.

I read Sterling Hayden's memoir in which he ridicules the yachtsmen (like me) who ply along the coasts, claiming to be sailors. Hayden sailed around the world with a misfit crew on a gigantic old schooner with no engine and no electronics. He is 100 percent right about the courage it takes to set out across open ocean. It is far beyond anything I attempted on this trip. Every risk I took was mitigated by the fact that during almost every leg of the voyage I could have simply swum ashore if things got really bad. I make no claims for extraordinary bravery. Doggedness and determination, maybe. Foolishness, for sure, and a good measure of self-sabotage.

A friend told me that those nearest and dearest to me all agree: I am the person they would most want to be with in a life-threatening situation at sea—or frankly, anywhere. But my friends and family are also quick to point out that I am the one most likely to bring them into a life-threatening situation.

Meanwhile, The *Pearl* Coalition is thriving— working with playwrights, authors, and student groups in the District of Columbia, spreading the word about the heroes of that extraordinary episode in American history. Soon, they will have a true *Pearl* sailing the waters along the Anacostia and Potomac Rivers. *Valkyrien* sits in a boatyard in Panama; her new owners have repaired the keel broken in the mud, and are painstakingly restoring her for sailing.

I hope by now that it's clear this book is not so much about the attempted salvage of a decrepit schooner as it is one man's attempt to come to terms with personal demons through the challenges of an ocean voyage. It is clear to me that abandoning the *Valkyrien* and accepting "failure" was a choice of life over death, the love of my family over the kind of love that can only be felt—and even then, only ethereally—in the rare exhibition of some kind of legendary, world-saving courage. Those are awful, cruel terms for love. They're impossible to live up to. My life was and is more important than sailing a noble wreck against terrible odds to prove myself. The fact that I chose to end this voyage, in the end, was, perhaps, a victory.

So many people have asked me why I sail. I cannot come up with a satisfactory answer. The truth is, I do not know. But no sailor has ever asked this question—they all understand. Sailing, I think, connects us in some way to our most basic selves. We know, when sailing in that great sea, that we are only dust, but we sense that when the wind fills our sails and we are surrounded by our nearest and dearest, there remains within us a fire that is lighted by wind and carries us all along.

My children have grown remarkably used to the craziness that so often flows out of me. When I interrupt our family with some new idea, completely out of sync with what is going on in all our lives, they look at me and tell me how much they love me.

Vicki has taught them how to save my life. Quiet smiles, sincere attempts to understand, an empathy that goes well beyond sympathetic nods, are gifts given to me freely and lovingly by my wife, my children, and my friends.

My children are growing up, moving toward adulthood. Vicki and I remain in love, fully dedicated to each other. And they all still sail with me.

Risk and danger heighten my sense of living. But I am no longer so attracted to a life of risk. The great thing for me about sailing is that when all of the other trappings of civilization are left behind, even for a night, the real reasons for choosing to live another day are revealed starkly amid the struggle and fear and pain. We are all in this together, and as long as we share the load, we will endure.

Acknowledgments

I wish to thank my editor, Genevieve Morgan; Genevieve believed in the book from the beginning and stuck with me throughout the process, with helpful thoughts, ideas, and observations that helped me so much.

I also wish to thank Richard Abate. Richard worked well beyond what anyone could ask of a friend or agent. His generosity, advice, and kindness were great encouragements on this endeavor. Thank you so much Richard. I want to thank, too, Nick Frenkel at 3Arts. Nick's enthusiasm and goodness led me through the project; he gave freely of his time and insight, and inspired me. Kimberly Carver gave me encouragement and guidance throughout the process of writing. The three together—Richard, Nick, and Kimberly— carried me along.

I also want to give a special thanks to Dean Lunt, my publisher at Islandport Press, and to the whole Islandport crew, including publicist Jennifer Hazard; Melissa Hayes, for copy editing; and the wonderful designer, Teresa Lagrange.

Several people read early drafts of the book. Peter Alson worked very hard and was extremely effective; Matt Rigney went out of his way to make truly helpful suggestions; and

Michael Morgan gave generously of his time.

David Michaelis and Ted Widmer taught me to be a better writer, and I am so grateful to them.

My greatest thanks, though, go out to the people of New England, and around this country, who love wooden boats. When I was a child, fiberglass threatened to take over a way of life, and a way of sailing that is completely unique and wholly different from sailing on any other material. The library of knowledge from the great carpenters, shipwrights, and sailmakers was quickly disappearing when I was a teenager. This group of dedicated women and men, including many in the Northwest, dedicated themselves to the preservation of this knowledge and this way of life; without their love of wooden boats, this book would never have been possible.

So I thank the WoodenBoat School and the wooden boat yards up and down the coasts, but especially Crosby Yacht, the Brooklin Boat Yard, Gannon and Benjamin, Karl Anderson, and Roy Downs. The men and women at Crosby Yacht deserve special mention: Dick Egan, Greg Egan, Malcolm Crosby, Betsey Crosby Thompson, Brian Thompson, Cheryl Niemi, Mike Bigelow, Brian Varney, Bill Pasik, Liam Henry, Glen Barton, Heidi Leonard, Dave McCarthy, Margaret Defrancisco, and Matt McAulliffe. Steve White and Brian Larkin have taught me so much about sailing. And Barry Clifford stoked my imagination of storms at sea so many years ago. A most special thanks goes out to my old friend, Dirk Ziff, who came to love wooden boats in his twenties, and has been at very important times my most trusted friend and guide.

My admiration and thanks go out to the boat boys who have sailed with me: Ethan Brown, Randy Bell, Bryan Idler, Peter Stobierski, Nathan Graf, Adam Hootnick, Paul Janka, Zach Bassett, Jade Bennett, Reed Horton, Peter Meyerdirk, Mike Belzer, and Jay Senter.

I also thank the following: Sabrina Padwa, Sarah Nixon, Mlezko, Peter McLaughlin, Bob Pavone, Momo Suguwara, Doug Spooner, Marc Shmuger, Louise Hamagami, Fernando Mezquita, Gustavo Mesquita, Clara Bingham, Carol Ann and Moise Emquies, Jill Goldman and Jon Reiss, Wendy Riva, Charlie Lord, Avi Garbow, Natasha Ziff, Susan and Chris Graves, Jayma Cardosa, Chris Bartle, Kent Correll, Eddie Bureau, Henry Bloomstein, Mike Bindcr, Michael Stevens, and Bolla Semans.

I also want to thank my friends who have sailed with me in wind, rain, and storm, and under starry nights: Evan Strauss, Joe Driscoll, Paul Ryan, Brando Quilici, Vio Barco, Michael Mailer, Pedro Mezquita, Amir Farman-Farmaian, Marsha Cohen, Zaab Sethna, Bobby Nixon, Michael Karnow, Lance Khazei, Max Loeb, Trevor Mullen, Karen Tenkhoff, Anthony Shriver,

Richard Farley, Charlie Shaw, Josh Berger, Frank Smith, Rahul Sonnad, Jimmy and Monica Shay, Mike Wilcox, Mark Hyman, Peter Cazas, Jimmy and Wendy Abrams, Frank Gehry, John Gregg, Heather Gregg Earl, Scotty Dickson, and Richard Farley.

I also wish to thank Andrew Sullivan, Liz Young, Brian Strange, Carla Sullivan, Keith Butler, Peter Kaplan, Doris and Ian La Frenais, Brad Blank, Joe Hakim, Richard Zuckerwar, Jeff Esther, George Molsbarger, and Ron Karlsberg. And thanks to Maria Popova and Walter Lippman for their inspiration and insight. I owe a debt to David Smith, Matthew Cutts, Dan Tangherlini, and all of the people at The *Pearl* Coalition for their hard work, dedication, and support for the *Spirit of the Pearl*.

My brothers Joe and Chris Kennedy, John Fallon, Kevin Gaughan, and Jack Fallon taught me the fundamentals of sailing and the thrill of racing.

The *Glide* has been sailed by a special crew for more than the past twenty years. These indispensable young people are more fun to sail with than any group of individuals in the world, and I am grateful to each of them for our many days on Nantucket Sound, including Grace Allen, Kiley Kennedy, Carly Hayden, Allie Kenny and Gracie Tenney, Doug Cruikshank, Kathleen Shriver, Conor Kennedy, Chrissy Kennedy, Sarah

Kennedy, Clare Kennedy, and my warmhearted goddaughter, Kate Kennedy. Of course, my children Maxey, Summer, and Noah lead the lot of them.

I would not be able to sail as I do without the loyal friends with whom I have sailed since I was a child, including Shannon Hayden, Courtney Clark, Margot Mehm, and Lauren Clark.

The most special thanks go out to my close friend, David Lande, who has slogged through many journeys with me, and is the finest attorney I know.

The people who sailed with me aboard *Valkyrien* deserve special praise. They demonstrated courage and a sense of fun that made the trip so much easier: Troy Campbell, Roger Freeman, Kevin Ward, Daniel Voll, Brian Tarr, Cris and Jonah Goodhart, Wes Hill, and, of course, Bob Nixon and Vicki.

I will never be able to sufficiently thank Chelsea Gottfurcht, whose clear sense of the world helped me to understand how to see these things.

I have a huge family, and want to thank in particular some who have shared many days on the water with me. The entire Shriver family brings so much laughter aboard with them, and Steve Smith, Spencer Strauss, Iliana Strauss, Patrick and Amy Kennedy, and Joe and Lauren Kennedy make every sail better. Matt and Kate

Kennedy are my particularly loyal crew. I owe special gratitude to Ted Kennedy Jr. and Kiki Kennedy, for transferring the *Glide* to me.

I am grateful for the love and support of my brothers and sisters, and especially for the time they spend sailing with me; I have a lot of them, and love them all: Courtney, Kerry, Joe, and Beth, Kathleen, Bobby and Cheryl, Vicki G., Chris and Sheila, and Douglas and Molly and Rory and Mark. No one could ask for a better family.

Bonnie Strauss and Roger Gould and Ben Strauss gave me the greatest gift of my life, and I am forever grateful to them.

I owe an endless debt of gratitude to my mother, who took me sailing every day of summer and taught me how to read the wind and the waves, and the special privilege it is to sail a wooden boat.

Maxey, Summer, and Noah are the loves of my life. They bring me more joy than any person could ever hope for, and there is nothing I would rather do than spend an afternoon sailing with them. They are my best guides.

My greatest thanks by far go to my wife Vicki. Vicki's cool head and clear mind, her overarching calm and intuitive reasoning, and her astonishing capacity for compassion have given me the chance for a life fully lived. Sometimes Vicki's laughter pours out of her like a fountain and her playful love of adventure overflows; all of us, Maxey, Summer, Noah, and I, are caught up, sharing her delight and her knowing the joy that is in all of us. Thank you, My Love.

About the Author

Maxwell Taylor Kennedy is a sailor, attorney, historian, and teacher. He is the author of *Danger's Hour: The Story of the USS Bunker Hill and the Kamikaze Pilot Who Crippled Her*, and the best-selling compilation, *Make Gentle the Life of this World: the Vision of Robert F. Kennedy and the Words that Inspired Him.* He lives with his family in California and Cape Cod.

Center Point Large Print
600 Brooks Road / PO Box 1
Thorndike, ME 04986-0001 USA

(207) 568-3717

US & Canada:
1 800 929-9108
www.centerpointlargeprint.com